The French Alps

The French Alps made-to-measure

The French Alps à la carte

Contents

ARCHITECTURAL HERITAGE 88

FAMILY OUTINGS 96

SAVOIE 132

The French Alps in detail

Contents...98

HAUTE-SAVOIE 102

ISÈRE 156

INDEX 185

A weekend in
Samoëns

The little village of Samoëns is absolutely charming and makes the perfect base for touring the picturesque scenery of the Giffre valley.

Samoëns' Gros-Tilleul square takes its name from the old lime tree, which was planted in 1453. It also boasts an attractive fountain carved by local stonemasons, long renowned for their skills (p.109). The village's other treasure is the colourful Alpine garden of Jaÿsinia (p.108), created by Marie-Louise Cognacq-Jaÿ, founder of Parisian department store *La Samaritaine*, who used to play there as a child. Designed at the beginning of the 20thC. by the famous landscape gardener Louis-Jules Allemand, it appears totally naturalised; a 3-km/2-mile trail takes visitors on a wide-ranging tour of the botanical world. The *Fer à Cheval cirque* ('horseshoe amphitheatre', p.109), to the east of the village, is at its most spectacular in June, when its waterfalls are swollen by melted snow.

A weekend at
Aix-les-Bains

'Ladies and gentlemen, place your bets!' The casino is a jewel, but the spa town of Aix-les-Bains has plenty of other charms to attract the visitor, such as the panoramic viewpoints near by, reached via pretty footpaths, and the famous spa itself.

The spa town of Aix (p.132) acquired its Grand Cercle casino in 1849 (p.133). Apart from the gambling, the building itself has several points of interest. The main gaming hall has a mosaic ceiling created by Antonio Salviati (1883), a Venetian who worked on the basilica of St Mark, and the casino's opulent theatre, where many of the concerts take place during the town's festival (p.135), has seen many great and celebrated performances. After an evening at the roulette tables, take a morning walk in the forest of Corsuet (p.135), then treat yourself to an afternoon tea fit for a queen at La Chambotte (p.136). If you have the energy, and don't suffer from vertigo, climb up to the cross at Nivolet from Saint Jean d'Arvey (p.146) (but take care, as the ground is often slippery).

GETTING USED TO THE EURO
On the 1 January 2002 the euro replaced the official currency of 12 European nations, including France. The franc ceased to be legal tender on 17 February 2002, although banks will still exchange notes and coins for some time. The euro, which is divided into 100 cents, has a fixed exchange rate of 6.55957 francs.

A weekend in the
Beaufortain region

The Beaufortain region, known as the 'country of a thousand chalets', offers great mountain biking and heady scenic hiking paths. Gourmets and amateur historians will enjoy this weekend, too.

Stay at Beaufort or Arèches (p.142) and make an early-morning start aiming in the direction of Boudin. The road, one of the most beautiful in the region, winds through a landscape of forest and mountain pastures. There's a breathtaking view from the Col du Pré, which overlooks the man-made lake of Roselend. You can either take it easy and watch the sailing boats or, if you're feeling a little more energetic, follow the mountain bike trail around the lake (p.143). Be warned – it's pretty steep in places. For further spectacular views, head off on the vertigo-inducing iron walkway, Roc du Vent *via ferrata* (p.142), suitable only for the fittest and bravest walkers! Leave time to explore the Baroque chapels at Hauteluce (p.143) and the medieval city of Conflans (p.148), near Albertville. For gourmets, there's the celebrated Beaufort cheese, known as the 'prince of Gruyères'.

A weekend in an
Alpine fortress

It's not often you get the opportunity to sleep in an authentic fortress. Now you can stay in the former mountain stronghold of the King of Piedmont-Sardinia – and at a surprisingly reasonable price, as well!

Near Aussois, at the 'gateway to the Vanoise', one of the forts of the Esseillon (p.153) has been converted into a charming gîte. The rooms at Fort Marie-Christine have breathtaking views, from the narrow arrow-slit windows, originally constructed as a defensive measure. There is also an excellent restaurant that specialises in Savoyard cuisine. Using this as a base, you can explore the whole area, where five fortifications, built between 1817 and 1830, stretch along the banks of the River Arc, connected by a network of pathways that can be followed on a mountain bike or on foot. Visiting all five fortresses on foot takes a full day. The village of Aussois itself is charming and unspoilt, while the nearby village of Bessans (p.155) is famous for its colourful carved wooden figures of the devil.

A weekend in
Chambéry

Capital of the *département*, Chambéry still recalls the splendour of the House of Savoy, and retains some fine vestiges of its aristocratic past. With its narrow lanes and arched passageways, it's a pleasant place to visit.

Follow in the footsteps of the Dukes of Savoy to discover the real Chambéry. Start with a visit to the château (p.145) and to the *Tour de la Trésorerie* (treasury tower), where a family tree traces the history of the House of Savoy. Walk down into the old town

(p.144), Chambéry's historic centre, and wander through picturesque alleyways and squares that have been restored to their original glory.

Many of the townhouses retain beautiful Renaissance façades, and balconies and windows are decorated with ornate ironwork. At lunchtime, you can sample a delicious Apremont or Abymes wine, produced from grapes ripened in local vineyards. In the afternoon, visit the local museum (Musée Savoisien, p.144), where colourful medieval murals have been restored, then head for the Musée des Charmettes, housed in a beautiful country house on the outskirts of the town (p.146). Philosopher Jean-Jacques Rousseau lived here, in this romantic setting, with his mistress Madame de Warens. The following day, visit Chambéry's modern quarter. In the Jean-Jacques Rousseau multimedia library, the Galerie Eurêka (p.146) has an interactive exhibition that explains everything you need to know about mountains. Visit

historic Montmélian, with its old and typically Savoyard square (p.147), and the

impregnable stronghold of Miolans (p.147), perched on a rocky outcrop. If the sun is too hot, head for Lake Aiguebelette (p.146), where the emerald-green waters are ideal for swimming, or you can hire a 'surfbike', a pedalo-bike that rides on the surface of the water. Alternatively, you might prefer to end the day by doing some sailing at Lake Bourget (p.134) or by taking a cruise to the magnificent abbey of Hautecombe (p.137).

A weekend in
Sud-Dauphiné

Lying between the northern and southern Alps, the Sud-Dauphiné region offers a variety of contrasting landscapes. Whether you choose to visit on foot, by train, by boat or by car, this area is perfect for a weekend away from it all.

Set aside a morning to visit the Château de Vizille, and find out about the time of the *sans culotte*. The Musée de la Révolution (museum of the French Revolution, p.170) is housed in some of the château's beautiful rooms, while animals roam freely in the immense surrounding parkland. At Saint-Georges-de-Commiers you can catch the little La Mure train (p.170), originally used by miners, which follows the Drac river through some magnificent scenery, dominated by the Vercors cliffs and the mountain tops of Oisans. The Mine Image de La Motte-d'Aveillans (p.171), a museum that informs visitors about the working conditions of local miners, has an underground gallery lit by torchlight, as in days gone by.

Later you can soak up the atmosphere at Mens, the capital of Trièves. With its roofs dressed with flaking tiles, its little squares lined with plane trees, and its fountains, the town has a distinctly southern feel (p.171).
The following day, visit the European ecological centre of Terre Vivante, which puts organic theory into practice over an area of 50 ha/123 acres, and demonstrates many tricks of the trade for getting the most from plants and vegetables – a real gardener's paradise. Spend the rest of the day at Lake Monteynard (p.171), where you can take to the water on the *Mira*, and enjoy a peaceful cruise along the gorges of the Drac and Elron rivers. If you have time, stop

at Grenoble (p.168), gateway to the Sud-Dauphiné, and explore its various quarters. Its architecture testifies to a long history – from Gallo-Roman ramparts and late medieval houses, to a proud *bastille* with 19th-C. fortifications, and a museum of contemporary fine arts.

A week in
Reblochon
country

You'll need at least a week to explore the winding roads of the region at the foot of the Aravis mountains, where the local speciality is Reblochon cheese. This will give you the chance to do some 'valley-hopping', visit some farms and go walking in the Alpine pastures.

As with anything that has achieved fame, Reblochon cheese, noted throughout France, has its own legends (p.74). It is believed to have first been made in the Annes pass, in Alpine pastures belonging to Carthusian monks (p.123), but there are many different versions of its origins. To get an idea of what the cheese is like, start by visiting the markets at Thônes, La Clusaz and Grand Bornand, where trading is done in the traditional way, without any paperwork. In the early morning, crates of cheese pass without much ceremony from producer to wholesaler. To find out how the cheese is produced, visit a local farm, many of which offer guided tours, followed by a tasting of their own cheese, accompanied by a glass of white Savoyard wine. If the farm visit gives you an appetite, rest assured that you'll find Reblochon featured on menus throughout the region, mainly used in *tartiflette* (a filling dish of potato, bacon and onion, topped with melted cheese) and varieties of fondue.

Other local specialities include *parmentier*, a type of cottage pie, and a substantial stuffing for meat. The region also has typical architectural features, which are easily discovered on foot. Look out for the roofed chalets of Ancelles or Tavaillons and the little chapels dedicated to St Anne or St Guérin, tucked away in the high mountain pastures. Stop at the plateau of Glières (p.120), the scene of one of the greatest tragedies in the history of the French Resistance in March 1944. Finally, take time to wander down the narrow lanes of La Roche-sur-Foron (p.121), the ancient capital of the Dukes of Geneva, which has retained its authentic medieval character.

A week in the
Vanoise

With over 500 km/310 miles of marked footpaths, from little tracks to long-distance trails, the Vanoise is ideal for walking and hiking. On all the walks between the high Isère and Arc valleys, there are plenty of opportunities to spot wildlife, including ibex, chamois and marmots.

More than 100 of the peaks in this area rise to over 3,000 m/ 9,842 ft high, so stamina and fitness are essential for some of the routes. Depending on your own personal preferences, your level of fitness, and whether or not you're accompanied by children, you should be able to work out a programme of activities, from a day's excursion led by a guide to a three-day walking tour around the glaciers. (Note: you should never embark on such a trip without first reserving a place at a *refuge*, or mountain shelter, for the night.)

Keep a careful look-out for wildlife while you're walking. The Parc de la Vanoise, for example (p.149), is home to some 2,000 ibex – they are less shy than chamois and relatively easy to spot, with a distinctive silhouette. The males are impressive in stature and can weigh around 100 kg/ 220 lb. Ibex like to laze in the sunshine and are often seen perched on a grassy rise. The best time to observe them is May-June, before they have climbed up to their

summer pastures on the flanks of the Grand Casse (3,852 m/ 12,638 ft). You may also learn to recognise the strident whistling of marmots. For something different, you can follow the *Chemins de la Baroque* (Baroque trails), which will take you on a tour of the little churches, chapels and wayside shrines dotted around the Tarentaise (p.148) and the Maurienne (p.152) regions. The contrast between the rough and ready exteriors of the buildings and their luxurious interiors, with colourful paintings and magnificent altarpieces, is quite striking.

A week in the
Vercors

The Vercors region, with its rugged limestone crags, is the ideal place for those who want to take part in sporting activities, or simply for lovers of good food and breathtaking scenery.

Begin your tour in the north of the massif, the Pays des Quatre Montagnes ('land of the four mountains'), where Villard-de-Lans (p.164) makes a good base for exploration. Visit Villard's Maison du Patrimoine (heritage museum) and the museum of *santons* (traditional crib figures), or find out about the bears that once roamed the Vercors region by visiting the Tanière Enchantée (wildlife discovery centre, p.164). Continue your trip by following part of the magnificent and impressive road that winds through the Gorges de la Bourne (D531), which is cut right into the cliffs in places (p.166). Stop off at La Chapelle-en-Vercors (D103), where the Maison de l'Aventure (p.165) organises potholing tours in the Vercors limestone caves for beginners and experienced potholers alike. Further on, at Vassieux-en-Vercors (D178), a poignant memorial bears witness to its strong associations with the French Resistance (p.165). In the fascinating museum of prehistory, 4 km/2.5 miles from Vassieux (p.165), a flint-carving workshop, thought to be at least 4,500 years old, has been preserved intact. The climb towards the Diois is made via an attractive route that runs through the Lachau pass, the forest of Lente, the Machine pass and the forest of Cote-Belle (D76, then D2). At Saint-Laurent-en-Royans, stop off at Bérard (p.167), where you'll find typical Royans wood-carvings. Gourmets should

visit Saint-Jean-de-Royan, where Jean-Luc Odeyer (p.166) sells a delicious wine made from nuts, and Ravioles à l'Ancienne (p.163) is the home of traditional ravioli stuffed with cheese or herbs (a speciality of Diois). Travel as far as Pont-en-Royans (D54) to take a look at the picturesque old houses perched above the Bourne river (p.167) and end your journey in the caves at Choranche (p.167). In the half-light, the lake and the giant stalactites make a magnificent spectacle.

A week in the
Chartreuse region

Spend a week discovering this beautiful wooded mountain range. Go walking in the spectacular countryside or visit the region's many places of cultural interest.

The *Route des Savoir-faire* tourist trail is the best way to explore the heritage of the Chartreuse region (p.179). There are 23 stops, at farmhouses and workshops, where local artisans and craftspeople demonstrate many skills. Visitors can discover the secrets of cheese making, knitting with mohair, carving walking sticks or making paper by hand. Alternatively, you can put together your own itinerary and visit the churches, châteaux and monasteries of the area. At Saint-Pierre de Chartreuse, stop at Grand-Chartreuse (p.179), where the monks still keep secret the recipe for their famous liqueur. Within the confines of the monastery, a museum reveals some of the mysteries of monastic life (p.179). At the end of July, the village plays host to the Rencontres Brel music festival, and a wood-carving competition (p.179). At Saint-Hugues, you can admire the murals of the contemporary painter Arcabas on the church walls (p.179), then recharge your batteries with lunch at the Brévardière farm *auberge* (p.180). At the eastern end of the mountain range, the château of Touvet is worth a visit; its French-style gardens have been so intricately sculpted that they look like green lacework (p.180).

Don't leave the Chartreuse region without going on one or two of the beautiful walks in the mountain range, which was declared a regional nature reserve in 1995. You can climb to the natural rock amphitheatre known as the Cirque de Saint-Même and enjoy nature at its purest (p.181), travel the 700 km/435 miles of pathways on a donkey (p.181), or take the funicular railway at Saint-Hilaire, which climbs an impressive route up the mountainside, with a view of

the majestic Belledonne mountain range opposite (p.180). Once at the top, if you're brave enough, you can try the unforgettable experience of paragliding for the best views of all (p.180).

Ten days around
Mont-Blanc

I n this area, the star of the show is of course Mont Blanc, which at 4,877 m/16,001 ft, is western Europe's highest peak. Ten days are barely enough to explore the ever-changing character of the mountain.

The village of Chamonix-Mont-Blanc (p.126) is an ideal place to serve as a base camp from which to explore the entire valley. To arrange a guided tour in the mountains, pay a visit to the Maison de la Montagne, previously the old presbytery of the church of St-Michel. In the mean time, explore 'Cham' at your leisure, preferably on foot.

The Alpine museum (p.127) is packed with mountain memorabilia, while the

Aiguille du Midi cable-car (p.128) offers thrill-seekers an unforgettable experience. Travelling close to the vertical face of the mountain, this heady ride offers extraordinary views of the forests, glaciers and crevasses below. At the top, 3,842 m/ 12,605 ft above sea level, where rock meets sky and snow meets clouds, you can see novice climbers roped together taking their first steps on the Arête (ridge) des Cosmiques. Sometimes, harsh winds of up to 250 km per hour (155 miles per hour) sweep across the mountain, and the summits seem to 'smoke', as the snow is whipped around and blown into the sky. For a different adventure, climb aboard the

little Montenvers train and travel up to the Mer de Glace (sea of ice, p.128), discovered in 1741 by William Wyndham and Richard Pocock. These two explorers were amazed when they first saw it, and claimed: 'It was as if a breeze had ruffled the sea and the waters had instantly frozen.' If you're fascinated by this world of ice, you can also take a trip to the glacier of Argentière or Bossons (p.129), the biggest fall of ice in Europe, some 3,500m/11,375 ft long. But this isn't the only way to discover the Mont-Blanc region: you can take a ride in a hot-air balloon (p.125), go hiking from Combloux along the Sentier du Baroque (Baroque footpath, p.131), or rummage around the summer flea markets at Saint-Gervais (p.130).

A fortnight by the great
Alpine lakes

This is the most romantic of regions, where the beauty of nature and the elegance of sophisticated resorts go hand in hand. There are five great lakes in the northern Alps, with Lake Geneva the largest and Lake Paladru the smallest, and they make an excellent location to try out a variety of watersports.

The tour of the great lakes starts with Lake Geneva (known as 'Lac Léman' to the French). Évian (p.112) is a charming place, with Art

Nouveau architecture and lovely gardens, a picturesque footpath along the lake shore and pleasure cruises on the water in a flat-bottomed boat. Just 10 km/6 miles away, at the port town of Thonon-les-Bains (p.110), is the Écomusée de la Pêche et du Lac (fishing and lake museum), which explains all about fishing Lake Geneva. From here, you can make a tour of the lake in a steamboat (p.111). Afterwards, head for appealing Annecy and its silvery lake (p.114). There are many temptations in the lovely arcaded streets of the old town, not least the sweet treats at the Meyer chocolate shop (p.115). Annecy's best spots include the Palais de l'Île (island palace), Jean-Jacques Rousseau's 'golden balustrade', the banks of the River Thiou and the Pont des Amours (lovers' bridge). On Lake Bourget (p.136), follow in the footsteps of the Romantic poet Lamartine by taking a cruise (p.136) and getting one of the best views of the abbey of Hautecombe (p.137). The lovely town of Aix-les-Bains (p.132) is an excellent place for sailing (p.134) or for fishing (p.135) enthusiasts. The spa building may be quite new, but the town's 'palaces' testify to a far older history. On Lake Aiguebelette (p.146), at the gates of Chambéry, visitors can enjoy all kinds of water sports, including the 'surfbike', a sort of pedalo in the form of a bike. Near Lake Paladru, visit the museum in Charavines (p.158) and find out how the historic gentlemen farmers of 1,000 years ago, and their Neolithic ancestors, lived. Finish your tour of the lakes with a mountain bike ride on one of the designated cycle paths at Lake Paladru, and enjoy an uninterrupted view of the mingling of the blues of lake and sky.

The French Alps à la carte

Nature

Nature lovers will find much to enjoy in this region. Discover the local flora and fauna, find out how glaciers and mountain lakes are formed, and investigate how people living in the mountains are able to use their natural resources. For hikes and beautiful vantage points, see also the map on pp.32-33.

Parks and gardens

1. Aix-les-Bains:
   Municipal greenhouses
   p.134
2. Chatte: Model railway
   p.161
3. Évian-les-Bains
   p.113
4. Col du Lautaret:
   Alpine garden
   p.175
5. Mens: Cottage garden
   at Terre Vivante
   p.171
6. Col du Petit-Saint-Bernard:
   Chanousia Alpine garden
   p.151
7. Samoëns: Jaÿsinia
   Alpine botanical garden
   p.108
8. La Sône: Park and
   'petrified' fountains
   p.161
9. Le Touvet:
   Château gardens
   p.180
10. Vaulx: Secret gardens
    p.119

Botanical walks

11. Aillon-le-Jeune
    p.138
12. Col des Montets
    p.129

Wildlife

13. Aix-les-Bains: Aquarium
    p.134
14. Le Bourg-d'Oisans:
    Museum of Alpine
    minerals and fauna
    p.173
15. Les Houches: Merlet
    animal reserve
    p.134

16. Megève: Black grouse
    habitat
    p.125
17. Morzine: Ornithological
    discovery trail
    p.105
18. Saint-Pierre-de-Bressieux:
    Chambaran nature and
    animal reserve
    p.159
19. Valsenestre: On the
    chamois trail
    p.174

RHÔNE-ALPES

Ain

Lyon

Vienne

Isère

Drôme

Valence

La Tour-du-Pin

Chambéry

Lac du Bourget

Grenoble

Mont Aiguille 2,086 m (6,842 ft)

SWITZERLAND

Lake Geneva
(Lac Léman)

㉓ ㉛ ③

Thonon-
les-Bains

㉗ ㉝   Grand Mont
Ruan
3,047 m
(9,994 ft)

Haute-
Savoie

Bonneville

⑦

Geneva

⑫

㉕

Annecy

⑳   ㉟   ⑯   ⑮ ㉖

㉒
Lac
Annecy   Mont
Blanc
4,807 m
(15,766 ft)

Albertville   ⑥

Savoie

Pointe de
la Grande Casse
3,852 m (12,634 ft)

Saint-Jean-
de-Maurienne

Tunnel
du Fréjus

㉘ ④   ITALY

La Meije
3,983 m
(13,064 ft)

Hautes-
Alpes

PROVENCE-ALPES-
CÔTE D'AZUR

● Gap

0 10 20 30 40 50 Km

0   10   20   30
miles

Discovering the natural world

⑳ Annecy: Regional observatory of Alpine lakes **p.115**

㉑ Prémol: Luitel nature reserve **p.176**

㉒ Talloires: Roc de Chère nature reserve **p.117**

㉓ Thonon-les-Bains: Dranse nature reserve **p.111**

㉔ Tupin-et-Semons: Île du Beurre nature observation centre **p.183**

Glaciers

㉕ Argentière: Discovering glaciers **p.129**

㉖ Les Bossons: Open-air exhibition on glaciers **p.129**

Caves

㉗ La Balme-les-Grottes p.156

㉘ La Grave: Meije ice cave **p.175**

Natural resources

㉙ Allemont: Hydroelectric power museum **p.172**

㉚ Allevard: 'Iron Trail' **p.177**

㉛ Amphion-les-Bains: Évian mineral water bottling factory **p.113**

㉜ Lancey: Hydroelectric power museum **p. 177**

㉝ Morzine: Slate quarry **p.105**

㉞ La Motte-d'Aveillans: Mining museum **p.171**

㉟ Thônes: Wood and forest museum **p. 122**

Peaks and summits,
at the heart of the alps

There are two sides to the northern Alps. The first and most striking impression is one of stark magnificence – a range of massive icy peaks dominated by Mont Blanc at the very heart of the Alps. The other face – the impassive limestone walls of the pre-Alps – is more easily accessible, but still to be wondered at.

Age is relative

Born of the remains of ancient Hercynian mountains, the Alps were formed during a time of great upheaval in the Tertiary Era, which began 65 million years ago. This is the most significant European mountain range, extending over an area of more than 1,000 sq km/385 sq miles from France to Yugoslavia. The undulating terrain, high peaks and steep valleys are typical of younger mountain formations. The western section in France is roughly 350 km/215 miles long and covers an area of 33,000 sq km/ 12,741 sq miles from north to south.

The great Alps

The crystalline central massifs – Mont Blanc, Vanoise, Beaufortain, Belledonne, Grandes Rousses and Écrins – form the heart of the Alps, and are nearly all over 3,000 m/ 9,845 ft high. In all, there are ten Alpine peaks over 4,000 m/ 13,125 ft high and around 60 over 3,000 m/9,845 ft. Mont Blanc, the highest mountain in western Europe at 4,807 m/ 15,772 ft, dominates the range, but other peaks are almost as legendary – Grandes Jorasses (4,206 m/ 13,800 ft), Aiguille Verte (4,127 m/13,541 ft) and the Aiguille du Midi (3,842 m/ 12,606 ft, p.128). From the Brévent summit at Chamonix, the magnificent view will make you feel really quite insignificant.

The pre-Alps

These are chiefly limestone ranges at the edge of the central Alps. They are generally lower, with an average height of around 2,000 m/656 ft, with a variety of features that

The Blanche valley and the Grandes Jorasses

COMPAGNIE DES GUIDES

In 1820, three guides died while climbing Mont Blanc, leaving their families destitute. The *Compagnie des Guides de Chamonix* (guides' association) was created a year later with the aim of giving financial support to sick or injured guides and their families. Louis Lachenal, Gaston Rebuffat and Lionel Terray, members of the expedition that first conquered Annapurna's 8,000-m/26,248-ft summit on 3 June 1950 (p. 42), are just a few of the association's famous names. Today, over 150 members of the Compagnie lead expeditions and tours in the Alps and the world over. A celebration of the service they provide has been held every 15 August in Chamonix since 1924 (p.126).

include high limestone façades at Vercors (p.162) and Chartreuse (p.178), steep cliffs and huge glacial lakes at Bornes (p.120) and Bauges (p.138), and the compact mountain range of Chablais (p.102). As the pre-Alps have

Landscape of the Bauges

more rain than the Alps, this is verdant countryside, with beautiful forest walks.

The glaciers

Over many thousands of years, successive snowfalls have packed together to form the glaciers. Because of its huge mass, the dazzling bluish-white crust is not stationary, but constantly moving, sliding and melting. As the glaciers have moved, they have shaped the landscape, and the valley of Grésivaudan and the Cirque du Fer-à-Cheval (p.109) are breathtaking examples of this. With the sliding movements, faults were formed,

creating sinister crevasses, much feared by climbers. As the snow melted, beautiful lakes such as Lake Geneva (Lac Léman, p.110), Lake Bourget (p.136) and Lake Annecy (p.114) were left behind. High-altitude Alpine lakes were also formed (p.176). Visit the Mer de Glace (sea of ice) at Chamonix (p.128) and admire the frozen beauty of the glacier. A two-day hike with a guide will help you to appreciate the majesty of this unique landscape.

Myth and legend

For centuries, the mountains have had a sinister reputation, and many Savoyard villages have their own legends of demons and werewolves. Each mountain had a nickname; Mont Blanc was the 'mountain of horrors' or the 'cursed mountain', while Mont Aiguille was the 'impregnable mountain'. Today, the greatest fear is of avalanches. In summer, it's easy to spot avalanche corridors, where the mass of snow has collapsed.

Tenneverge dominates the Cirque du Fer-à-Cheval

Nature parks and reserves,
nature at its best

The Vanoise park

Two national parks, three regional parks, a variety of nature reserves and numerous natural open spaces make this area ideal for all lovers of mountain flora and fauna.

National parks

The regulations set down for France's national parks aim to protect the environment and the biological diversity of a region, while at the same time attracting members of the public in ever-increasing numbers. Before visiting the park of La Vanoise (p.149) or Les Écrins (p.173), be aware that pets, even under control, mountain bikes, picking or uprooting plants, camping, weapons, dropping litter and lighting fires are all strictly forbidden. There are 500 km/ 310 miles of marked footpaths in the park of La Vanoise and 740 km/460 miles in the park of Les Écrins.

Regional parks

The parks of Bauges (p.139), Vercors (p.162) and Chartreuse (p.181) are the three regional parks of the northern Alps. They were created and part-financed by the regions themselves, and are administrated by a syndicate formed of representatives from the local communities. There are no strict regulations, but all the local communities have signed up to a charter that defines the parks' objectives: protection of the natural environment, management of the landscape, and economic development.

The Bauges park

The River Arc in Vanoise park, near the hamlet of Écot

Nature reserves

There are over 20 nature reserves in Isère, Savoie and Haute-Savoie. They were created by government decree in order to protect the delicate ecosystems supporting particular species of plants or animals, or those of special scientific interest, and have the same status and regulations as the national parks. Follow the hiker's code of good conduct when in a nature reserve. The largest French nature reserve is located at Vercors, on the high plateaux (p.165). For information, contact the Comité Départemental du Tourisme de l'Isère (CDT: ☎ 04 76 54 34 36), the Association Touristique Départemental de Savoie (ATD: ☎ 04 79 85 12 45) or the ATD de Haute-Savoie (☎ 04 50 51 32 31).

The flora and fauna of the parks and reserves

These protected areas are a natural paradise, and each park or reserve has its own particular attractions. Orchids, especially the lady's slipper, thrive in the Hauts de Chartreuse reserve.

Beavers have made their home on the Île de la Platière (Isère) and in the nature reserve at the far end of Lake Annecy. As many as five thousand chamois live in the Écrins park, and more than 2,000 ibex are estimated to inhabit the park of La Vanoise. The Vercors is one of the rare sites in France to be home to all six types of wild hoofed species – chamois, ibex, moufflon (wild mountain sheep), hart, deer and boar. Bauges park is specially noted for the European cyclamen, but also has numerous varieties of orchid (p.138).

Natural open spaces

After decentralisation regulations, each *département* was allowed to raise taxes to finance the protection of its vulnerable areas. These natural open spaces are usually very well run and can be extremely interesting and informative. In Isère, six sites have been established as natural open spaces, with information points and signposts, brochures and discovery trails. One of these, the pool at Lemps (near Crémieu) is a conservation

THE BAUGES BY BICYCLE

Information: ATD de Savoie (brochure: *Cyclotourisme et VTT*) ☎ 04 79 85 12 45 This route at the heart of the Bauges regional park is suited to those who like steep climbs. Set out from Chambéry on the Av. Verte Nord (motor vehicles prohibited) to Aix-les-Bains, following the Sierroz as far as the L'Abîme bridge. The descent towards Montmélian is very steep, and the route continues along the D911 and the Frêne pass, before returning to Chambéry on the Av. Verte Sud. The route climbs through a number of mountain passes, such as the Prés (D206), the Plainpalais (D62) and the Revard (D913). This difficult route is 100 km/60 miles long, with a total change in altitude of 1,000 m/3,280 ft.

area for the cistude turtle, a small variety with a flat shell. If you're lucky you might also spot kingfishers, frogs, stoats and the speckled salamander. Information from Avenir (agency for the protection of Isère's natural open spaces, ☎ 04 76 48 24 49).

Delicate environmental balance at the Lemps pool

Alpine wildlife, horned, furred, and feathered

Each year, successive management programmes ensure the reintroduction and preservation of various species in the mountains, from ibex and marmots to bearded vultures, royal eagles and wild vultures. With a little luck and a bit of patience, you may spot one of these species while out walking. Rare lynx and wolves have also crossed the Swiss and Italian borders into the French Alps, but they are very fearful of humans and usually remain well out of sight.

Symbol of the Vanoise

The Vanoise national park was created especially to protect the ibex (p.149), but today the creature also inhabits the Belledonne mountain range, the Vercors and the Écrins national park. To catch a glimpse of an ibex on a rocky outcrop, you'll need to make a very early start and climb to 2,500-3,500m/ 8,200-11,485 ft; at the first sign of heat, the animals lie down and are no longer visible against the rocks. Even at a distance the male is easily

distinguishable from the female – the horns of the female are small, whereas those of the male can grow to a magnificent 1 m/3 ft in length.

Chamois

Smaller than ibex, chamois, or wild goats, are constantly on the move. The females and young roam in groups, jumping fearlessly from rock to rock.

If you focus on a patch of snow, you may be able to spot them, as their red coats stand out very clearly against the white background. Otherwise, you'll have to climb up to the Alpine pastures, at 2,000-2,500 m/6,560-8,200 ft, where the chamois graze early in the morning. Chamois can be found all over the Alps but they exist in particularly large numbers in the Écrins national park, where over 5,000 have been counted. A hike from Valsenestre (p.174) crosses their habitat and comes close to many of their favourite hideouts.

King of the peaks

It's very rare to see the royal eagle in flight, but the best observation points are the Alpine pastures, which are its hunting grounds. This big predator generally flies only above 1,500 m/4,920 ft but can nest as low as 1,200 m/3,940 ft and up to 2,000 m/6,560 ft. Its wingspan is relatively modest,

never exceeding 1 m/3 ft. A dozen pairs of royal eagles are currently known to be resident in the Vercors, but they can also be found in the parks at Écrins, Bauges and in the Haut de Chartreuse nature reserve.

Black grouse

The black grouse, a small heathland bird with black feathers in the male and red feathers in the female, is the symbol of the Vercors national park. It can be found all over the Alpine mountain ranges, in forests and Alpine pastures at an altitude of around 1,400-2,300 m/4,595-7,545 ft. Take care not to disturb it in the mating season, as the numbers of black grouse are in decline, and the species is in urgent need of restocking. To get to know the black grouse a little better, you can follow the discovery trail at Megève (p.125).

Tanned in summer, pale in winter

The hare is a favourite prey of the royal eagle, but has developed its own camouflage – a coat that's white in winter, to blend with the snow, and brown in the summer. Its only weakness is its tail, which stays white all year round. The hare lives at an altitude of 1,000-3,000 m/3,280-9,845 ft.

The whistling marmot

Stretched out in the sun, or standing up on its back feet ready to make its distinctive whistle in the event of danger, the lovable marmot is relatively easy to spot. It digs its burrows in the meadows between 1,500 and 3,000 m/4,920 and 9,845 ft and never ventures far from home. At the end of summer it is plump, having accumulated the necessary fat for its six-month winter hibernation.

Alpine plants,
a magical garden

More than 2,000 species come into flower each spring in the Alps. All over this region, there's an explosion of form and colour that's at its best in May and June. There are many botanical trails marked in the national and regional parks and nature reserves, which you can follow either alone or accompanied by a specialist guide. Look out for lilies, clematis, columbines, orchids, gentians and rhododendrons, among many others, and remember that almost all mountain flowers are protected species and must not be picked.

Lady's slipper

This beautiful, large variety of orchid (botanical name *Cypripedium calceolus*) gets its common name from the unusual shape of its lemon-yellow lip, which resembles a shoe, and is set off by three or four flat brown petals.

It favours limestone terrain, undergrowth or shady pine forest. Those who are familiar with its habitat prefer to keep their knowledge secret, so it's a very difficult flower to find. According to local legend, those who search for the lady's slipper will never find it, while any man who finds the flower will marry a pretty young girl.

Yellow gentian

The gentian family is huge, with 800 different species found throughout the world. In the Alps,

the yellow gentian is the most abundant. Gentian root is renowned for its stimulatory and tonic properties, and is believed to reduce fever and

The botanical garden at Mount Cenis

STAR OF THE MOUNTAINS

Immortalised in the *Sound of Music*, the tiny edelweiss plant is known by many names: Lion's Foot, Silver Star, Queen of the Glaciers, Immortal Flower of the Snows. Its most common appellation comes from the German edel, or 'noble', and weiss, or 'white'. The flower has a downy surface, resembling cotton wool.

Minute, pale yellow petals form a pretty centre encircled by a crown of white leaves, on a stem just 10-15 cm/ 4-6 inches long. The edelweiss can only be found high in the mountains, from 1,400-3,000 m/4,595-9,845 ft, often on steep slopes or in little rocky outcrops. It flowers from July to September.

assist digestion. When distilled, it can be drunk before or after a meal, and is also one of the 130 different plants that go to make up the famous Chartreuse liqueur (p.178). You can find gentian blooming in July and August, up to around 2,500 m/8,200 ft, on limestone terrain.

The Alpine columbine

Belonging to the Ranunculus family, this pretty blue flower grows only in the Alpine massif and in forest clearings, between 1,000 and 2,000 m/ 3,280 and 6,560 ft. Its large flowers, standing proudly on their stems, bloom in the middle of summer, from June to August. Note: avoid touching this plant, as the flowers contain poisonous substances.

Lilies

The Latin name of St Bruno's lily, or lily of the Alps – *Paradisa liliastrum* – perfectly

describes this graceful plant with its pure white flowers. From June to July, it flowers in the meadows up to 2,500 m/ 8,200 ft. Its cousin the Martagon lily has a more

unusual shape, resembling the shape of a Turkish turban, and grows at the same altitude and at the same time of year, on limestone terrain, in the meadows, or in woodland and undergrowth.

Ferruginous rhododendron

This shrub, which thrives on slopes exposed to the north, develops its buds at the end of summer, and comes into flower with the first snows. It owes the term 'ferruginous' (rust-coloured) to its pinkish colour, but it is also known by the more poetic name of Rose of the Alps. The ferruginous rhododendron prefers acid soil and grows well up to an altitude of 2,500 m/8,200 ft on the slopes of the Vanoise and Vercors national parks. It has a strong, peppery aroma, which you'll be able to detect long before you actually see the flower.

Nature's own gardens
a riot of colour

I n the Alps you usually have a long trek to reach the best 'gardens', but the explosion of colours on the high slopes makes the effort worthwhile. June is the ideal month to climb to the Alpine pastures and enjoy this immense natural garden at its most spectacular.

The Alpine garden at Lautaret

Natural flora

Alpine gardens teem with a variety of botanical plants and flowers that flourish at high altitude. Tucked into rocky outcrops and pastureland, hundreds of different varieties – rhododendrons, orchids, cyclamens, columbines and lilies – grow wild. A discovery trail makes an ideal

walk with children, introducing them to mountain flora and teaching them to respect it when they come across a specimen. To discover a high-altitude Garden of Eden, head for the Petit-Saint-Bernard pass (La Chanousia, p.151) and the Lautaret pass (Alpine garden, p.175), Samoëns (La Jaÿsinia, p.108), and many other Alpine hamlets.

French style or exotic

If you like French-style gardens, don't miss the magnificent grounds of the Le Touvet château (p.180) in Isère. The upkeep of the garden is enormously time-consuming – weeding is done by hand, the eight pools and the superb stepped water feature need to be cleaned on a continuous basis, and miles of tree-lined walks and box hedges are comprehensively pruned twice a year. If you prefer exotic gardens, take a trip to Sud-Grésivaudan, to the limestone fountains at La Sône (p.161) and the Chatte railway garden (p.161), which children will love.

Kitchen gardens

There are 50 working farms in Megève, and 50 kitchen gardens that supply them with food. You'll find these attractive little gardens, neatly laid out in squares of flowers and vegetables, in the heart of the village, near the public washing-place, in the Cinq-Rues quarter and near the church. Onions, leeks and potatoes are the hardiest vegetables and can be grown at up to 1,100 m/3,610 ft. But you'll also see lettuce, sorrel,

The 'garden of the five senses' at Yssoire

rhubarb and cabbage, as well as strawberries and blackcurrants perfuming the summer air, and an abundance of colourful flowers – clematis and marigolds in the flowerbeds, and geraniums on the balconies.

The secret gardens at Lagnat-Vault

Living earth

If you fancy yourself as a vegetable gardener, head for Sud-Dauphiné and visit the 50 ha/123 acre gardens of Terre Vivante, or 'living earth', at Mens (p.171). Every day in the middle of the afternoon, the resident gardener shares his tips for growing fruit, flowers and vegetables, and combating parasites and disease in an environmentally friendly way. He can introduce you to companion planting and show you mutually beneficial varieties – how carrots and leeks, for example, protect each other against carrot fly and leek worm, and how nettles are deadly to blackfly but enhance vegetable fertilisation. All the staff here are passionate about organic gardening.

Green Chambéry

The historic capital of Savoy has more than 140 ha/345 acres of green spaces, making it one of the 'greenest' towns in France. However, in the Buisson-Rond park, the colour pink predominates. The first Alpine rose garden has 6,000 plants, comprising 87 different varieties. At the Charmettes park, medicinal, culinary and kitchen garden plants are cultivated, and ancient varieties of apples abound in the orchard.

THERMAL BATHS
The officials of the Alpine spa towns are masters of the art of landscape gardening. In between treatments, visitors are encouraged to walk in the town gardens, where precisely-managed flower beds, ornate statues and sparkling fountains make a charming and peaceful haven. In Belledonne, the perfect green lawns of the shady Uriage-les-Bains gardens are reminiscent of London's Hyde Park. In summer, there are free open-air film screenings (p.176). In Haute-Savoie, Évian has many gardens, each one more romantic than the last (p.113), and in Savoie, the flowers at Aix-les-Bains are the epitome of refinement (p.134).

The lakes,
mirrors of the Alps

Lake Besson

I n the northern Alps, there are as many lakes as there are mountains. Great stretches of turquoise and emerald, the lakes of Geneva (Léman), Bourget, Annecy, Aiguebelette and Paladru are the perfect spot for a romantic break. The high-altitude lakes are small stretches of deepest blue, straight from the glaciers, and a true fisherman's paradise.

Little mountain seas

Formed from melting glaciers, the five large natural lakes of the northern Alps soften the harsh mountain landscape. Lake Geneva is the largest, stretching from Switzerland into France over 582 sq km/ 225 sq miles, of which 239 sq km/92 sq miles lie in France.

This is a real inland sea, with waves and its own tides and currents (p.110). The next largest is Lake Bourget (4,400 ha/10,870 acres), which is also the deepest (145 m/475 ft) of the French lakes (p.136). Lake Annecy may be smaller (2,700 ha/6,670 acres) but is very picturesque.

Nicknamed the 'silver lake', it is renowned for its purity and the water quality is meticulously monitored (p.114). In Savoie, Lake Aiguebelette (545 ha/1,345 acres) is a beautiful shade of emerald green (p.146). The smallest of the five lakes is Lake Paladru in Isère (nearly

Lake Annecy

400 ha/980 acres), with neolithic and medieval sites close by (p.158).

A breath of fresh air

The majority of the small high-altitude lakes lie at an average altitude of 1,400-2,500 m/4,595-8,200 ft, chiefly in Savoie and Haute-Savoie. They are frozen for several months of the year, and only thaw in the spring. It generally takes an hour or two's steep climb to reach these lakes, but the effort is rewarded by panoramic views, with snowy peaks reflected in the depths of the clear blue waters. To explore this paradise on foot, take the Chamrousse cable-car for the Achard and Robert

Lac Vert ('green lake', 1,368 m/ 4,488 ft) at Plaine-Joux

lakes (p.176), or you can take a tour around the shores of Lake Roselend on a mountain bike (p.143). Take a rod with you for a fishing trip above Les Menuires, on Lake Lou (p.151).

Pleasure cruises and boating

Take a trip on a river boat on Lake Bourget (p.136) or try out the very latest in pleasure cruising on Alain Prud'homme's new catamaran-yacht (p.134). You can also go out in a flat-bottomed boat on Lake Geneva (p.112) or catch a water bus at Annecy (p.114). The Alpine lakes are an ideal location for cruising but there are other charming trips on the waters, such as taking a rowing boat out on the Isère (p.161), or going for a trip on the Blue Dolphin on the Haut-Rhône (p.157) or

the Mira, which travels down the Drac and the Ebron gorges (p.171).

Natural or man-made lakes

There are many lakes in Sud-Dauphiné, both natural and man-made. Around 25 km/ 15 miles from Grenoble, on the Route Napoléon (Matheysine), the natural lakes at Laffrey are popular with vessels of every kind. Hemmed in by dams, the Sautet (Beaumont) and Monteynard (Trièves, p.171) lakes are ideal for bathing and water sports. At the foot of the Taillefer mountain range (between Matheysine and Valbonnais) you can go for pleasant walks between Lake Poursollet and Lake Fourchu, with a wonderful view of the Taillefer and Belledonne ranges.

FRESH FISH

There are 34 different species of fish in Lake Bourget alone, which gives an indication of the abundance of life in the Alpine lakes. The arctic char fish, inhabitant of the deep, favours the waters of Lake Bourget and can be caught by dragnet. The pollan is another Alpine fish found in Lake Bourget, and also in Lake Aiguebelette; in other Alpine lakes it is known as the ferra. It tastes delicious and is a favourite with local chefs.

Expect perch and pike, zander and trout, roach, salmon, tench and carp in most lakes, and freshwater salmon, Canadian char fish and rainbow trout in those at a higher altitude.

Alpine waters,
the purity of the mountains

T he reputation of the Alps as Europe's most significant water reservoir dates right back to Roman times, when rich families would come to take the waters at Uriage or Thonon-les-Bains. Today, hot tubs and 'aqua gyms' continue the traditions of the appealing 19th-C. spa towns.

Rouget waterfall near Sixt-Fer-à-Cheval

Fresh mountain waters

When the snows thaw, waterfalls gush from the rocks in foaming white streams. Their characters are reflected in colourful local nicknames such as *Pissette* and *Pissevache* (two waterfalls at the site of the Cirque du Fer à Cheval, p.109)! Mountain streams and rivers are fed by the waters of the mountain ranges and then swollen by the melting snows. In Haute-Savoie, the Dranses, Arve and Giffre rivers come straight from the glaciers of Mont Blanc, and the Borne, Nom and Fier descend from the Aravis mountain range. These waters are a paradise for fishermen, but they are also popular for rafting and kayaking, as are the Dorn and the Haut-Isère in Savoie, or the Vénéon in Isère, habitat of the fario trout.

Cheers!

In Haute-Savoie the water comes straight from the springs. At Évian, the water gushes from the ground close to the spa building, after a 15-year journey through the rocks of the Chablais. Évian's mineral water has been

WATER FESTIVAL
Information: Notre-Dame-de-Bellecombe Tourist office ☎ 04 79 31 61 40
Last Sun. in July and last Sun. in Aug.
The pretty little Savoyard village of Notre-Dame-de-Bellecombe, perched high above the gorges of the Arly river, organises a water festival twice a year at the Plan Dessert lake. The festival starts in the morning with a fishing competition, after which everyone gathers together for an open-air meal. In the afternoon, sailing boats are taken out on to the lake and their crews 'joust' with poles, attempting to topple their opponents into the water. On land, other competitors try to fill an ancient water pump, lent by the fire brigade, as fast as they possibly can.

famous for more than 200 years, and is now sold all over the world. A visit to the bottling plant makes an interesting and instructive excursion (p.113). A few kilometres away, the Thonon springs emerge on to the Versoie plateau at a constant temperature of 13°C/55°F. Thonon water has been endorsed by France's Academy of Medicine since 1859. Like the water of its neighbour, Évian, its mineral content – bicarbonate, calcium and magnesium – is excellent.

Good health!

Spa towns have been a feature of the northern Alps for over a century. There are nine spas

Challes-les-Eaux

in all: Aix-les-Bains (national spa and Aix-Marlioz spa, p.132), Brides-les-Bains, Challes-les-Eaux and La Léchère in Savoie; Évian (p.132), Thonon (p.110) and Saint-Gervais (p.130) in Haute-Savoie; and Allevard and Uriage-les-Bains (p.176) in Isère. The centres treat skin disorders, rheumatism, disorders of the respiratory tract and central nervous system, as well as digestive and gynaecological disorders. The distinctive 19th-C. architecture of spa towns such as Aix-les-Bains, Évian, Saint-Gervais, Uriage or Allevard is an added attraction.

Feeling on top of the world

A visit to a spa town also offers the chance to tackle some of the stresses and strains of modern life – working too hard, unhealthy weight gain and smoking. Today, most spas offer health and fitness programmes with sports included as part of the package. For example, the Rando-Altiforme programme at Saint-Gervais (p.130) combines hiking and a variety of health treatments, guaranteed to ease your aches and pains. At Uriage-les-Bains (p.177) the hydrotherapy institute has a varied programme which includes hydro-massage, solarium, beauty treatments, and exercise in the heated swimming pool, all of which will leave you feeling toned, refreshed and like a completely new person.

Saint-Gervais-les-Bains

Walking and hiking

Whether you're an experienced hiker or prefer family walks, the landscape of the French Alps is spectacular and the air is wonderfully clean. On gentle walks or full hiking excursions, the passes, summits and mountain pastures boast panoramic views that will simply take your breath away.

Hikes

1. **Aillon-le-Jeune:** Margériaz plateau **p.139**
2. **Méaudre:** Hiking across the Vercors **p.164**
3. **Mer de Glace:** Hiking across the glaciers **p.128**
4. **Saint-Jean-d'Arvey:** Nivolet cross **p.146**

Nature trails

5. **Aix-les-Bains:** Corsuet forest **p.135**
6. **Argentière:** Hiking across the glaciers **p.129**
7. **Bellecombe-en-Bauges:** Donkey trekking **p.141**
8. **Chamrousse:** Lake Achard **p.176**
9. **Cirque du Fer-à-Cheval** **p.109**
10. **Corrençon-en-Vercors:** Hauts-Plateaux nature reserve **pp.164-165**
11. **Entremont-le-Vieux:** Donkey ride **p.181**
12. **Lans-en-Vercors:** Bruyant gorges **p.163**
13. **Modane: 'Happy walk'** **p.152**
14. **Pont-en-Royans:** Choranche grotto **p.167**
15. **Saint-Pierre-d'Entremont:** Cirque of Saint-Même **p.181**
16. **Samoëns** **p.109**
17. **Valsenestre:** Spotting the chamois **p.174**

RHÔNE-ALPES

Ain

Lyon

Rhône

Vienne

Isère

Grenoble

Valence

Drôme

La Tour-du-Pin

Chambéry

Lac du Bourget

Mont Aiguille 2,086 m (6,842 ft)

SWITZERLAND

Lake Geneva
(Lac Léman)

Thonon-
les-Bains

Haute-
Savoie

Grand Mont
Ruan
3,047 m
(9,994 ft)

Geneva

Bonneville

16   9

29

26   6   3

Annecy   33

35

Lac
d'Annecy   Mont
Blanc
4,807 m
(15,766 ft)

7

Albertville

1   27

Savoie

Pointe de
la Grande Casse
3,852 m (12,634 ft)

Saint-Jean-
de-Maurienne

31

30   13   Tunnel
du Fréjus

La Meije
3,983 m
(13,064 ft)

17

Hautes-
Alpes

PROVENCE-ALPES-
CÔTE D'AZUR

Gap

0   10   20   30   40   50 Km

0   10   20   30
miles

ITALY

Cruises

⑱ **Aix-les-Bains:**
Lake Bourget
p.134

⑲ **Annecy: The lake**
p.116

⑳ **Chanaz:**
Savières canal
p.136

㉑ **Évian-les-Bains:**
Lake Geneva (Lac Léman)
p.113

㉒ **Montalieu-Vercieu:**
The Haut-Rhône
p.157

㉓ **Lake Monteynard:**
The Drac and Ebron
gorges
p.171

㉔ **The Sône: Isère**
p.161

㉕ **Thonon-les-Bains:**
Lake Geneva (Lac Léman)
p.111

Panoramic views

㉖ **Chamonix-Mont-Blanc:**
Montenvers train and sea
of ice
p.128

㉗ **Combe de Savoie**
valley
p.147

㉘ **Nivolet Cross**
p.146

㉙ **Flaine: Platé desert**
p.107

㉚ **The summit of Lake Blanc**
p.174

㉛ **Mont Cenis pass**
p.154

㉜ **Saint-Georges-de-**
Commiers: La Mure tourist
train
p.170

㉝ **Saint-Gervais-les-Bains:**
Mont Blanc tramway
p.130

㉞ **Saint-Hilaire: Funicular**
p.180

㉟ **Talloires: The belvedere**
route
p.117

㊱ **The Vercors routes**
p.166

Discovering the mountains,
on foot or on horseback

L eave your car behind and take time to explore the mountains. Whether you choose the legendary Mont Blanc tour, stride out in the massifs, or set off on a gentle family walk, making your way on foot or on horseback is the best way to enjoy the pure air and impressive scenery of the Alps.

high sugar content foods, such as dry fruit, chocolate or cereal bars. Wear suitable, comfortable footwear and light clothing and carry additional clothing in case of bad weather.
The scenery is particularly spectacular in the mountains, so take your binoculars with you – indispensable to any walker. Lastly, always make sure someone knows where you're going, especially if you plan a long excursion.

Where to go

There are three types of marked footpaths in the region. The GR long-distance routes (red and white markings) include the Mont Blanc tour, which covers more than 200 km/125 miles and crosses over into Switzerland and Italy. The GRP routes (red and yellow markings) are confined to a single region, and include the tours of the Chartreuse or the Beaufortain. The PR footpaths (yellow markings) are local circuits which criss-cross the country-side; the Dents Blanches PR, for example, comprises eight panoramic walks.

How fast?

In an hour, an average walker covers 3 km/2 miles, climbs 300 m/985 ft and descends 500 m/1,640 ft. Find your own pace and adapt accordingly. Take enough water and make sure you drink regularly. Avoid fatigue by taking along some

SADDLE UP

Association 'Isère Cheval Vert'
☎ 04 76 42 85 88
This association includes companies at Belledonne, Chartreuse, Matheysine, Nord Dauphiné, Oisans, Trièves and Vercors, all of which offer trekking on horseback for one or more days. If you don't have much riding experience, try the Platary tour at Trièves, a 5-hour trip that is suitable for beginners. For more experienced riders, the Carrières Romaines track, setting off from the Rousset pass (Vercors) is a 6-hour long hike, where participants have the chance for a good gallop.

Topoguides

The topoguide is the Bible of the French hiker, and indispensable for planning any walk. For the Isère, Savoie and Haute-Savoie there are 13 topoguides published by the Fédération Française de la Randonnée Pédestre (FFRP), or French hiking federation, ☎ 01 44 89 93 93: *Tour de l'Oisans* (GR 54, 541), *Massifs et Lacs en Dauphiné* (lakes and mountains in Dauphiné) (GR 549, 54, 50, GRP), *Tour et Traversée du Vercors* (GR 9, 91, 93, 95, GRP), and

Tour et Traversée de la Chartreuse (GR 9, GRP) (tours of Vercors and Chartreuse), *Parc National de la Vanoise* (Vanoise national park) (GR 5, 55), *Tour du Beaufortain* (GRP), *Tour et Traversée des Bauges* (GR 96), *Tour du Mont Blanc* (GR TMB), *Tour Pédestre du Pays du Mont Blanc* (GRP), *Du Léman au Mont Blanc* (GR 5, GRP), *Préalpes de Haute-*

Savoie (GR 96, GRP), *Tour et Massif des Dents Blanches* (GRP, PR) and *Les Glières* (PR). Look out for them in bookshops.

Where to stay

If you venture up into the mountains, you may need to spend the night at a mountain refuge. There are many of these in the high mountain ranges and on the GR trails (42 in Écrins, about 60 in Vanoise), and they can only be reached on foot. They supply a communal meal in the evening prepared by the warden, and dormitory accommodation. Make sure

you book a place in advance in the more popular refuges, such as those located on the tour of Mont Blanc, as they can get very crowded. There are a number of gîtes located close to the PR footpaths, which can be reached by car. Families and small groups can stay in a gîte overnight or for a few days.

For information

The CRT Rhône-Alps (☎ 04 72 59 21 59) publishes a comprehensive guide every year, free of charge, called *Balades et Randonnées* (walks and hikes). This will help you plan your itinerary and accommodation and will tell you where to go for information, as well as providing suggestions for themed hikes and details of who organises them.

The Isère CDT (☎ 04 76 54 34 36) and the ATD for Savoie (☎ 04 79 85 12 45) and Haute-Savoie (☎ 04 50 51 56 48) also publish a selection of itineraries (Balades). Haute-Savoie has also published around 40 itineraries online at www.hautesavoie-tourisme.com.

Sporting activities

There are many different types of leisure sports to enjoy in Savoie, Haute-Savoie and Isère, from skiing and paragliding, to canyoning and rock climbing. This is a golden opportunity to try out something new. For demanding hikes, see also the map on pp.32-33; for ski resorts, see pp.38-41.

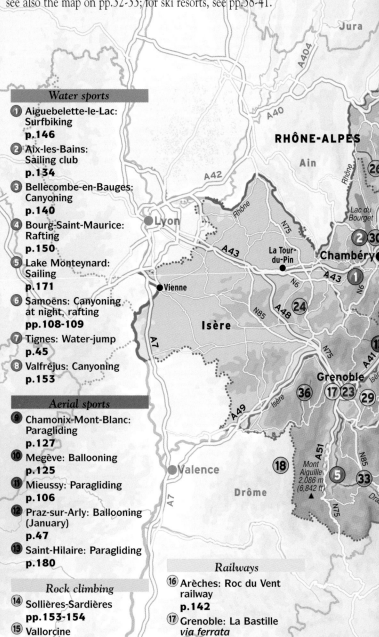

Water sports

1. Aiguebelette-le-Lac: Surfbiking **p.146**
2. Aix-les-Bains: Sailing club **p.134**
3. Bellecombe-en-Bauges: Canyoning **p.140**
4. Bourg-Saint-Maurice: Rafting **p.150**
5. Lake Monteynard: Sailing **p.171**
6. Samoëns: Canyoning at night, rafting **pp.108-109**
7. Tignes: Water-jump **p.45**
8. Valfréjus: Canyoning **p.153**

Aerial sports

9. Chamonix-Mont-Blanc: Paragliding **p.127**
10. Megève: Ballooning **p.125**
11. Mieussy: Paragliding **p.106**
12. Praz-sur-Arly: Ballooning (January) **p.47**
13. Saint-Hilaire: Paragliding **p.180**

Rock climbing

14. Sollières-Sardières **pp.153-154**
15. Vallorcine **p.129**

Railways

16. Arèches: Roc du Vent railway **p.142**
17. Grenoble: La Bastille *via ferrata* **p.169**

RHÔNE-ALPES

Jura

Ain

Rhône

Lac du Bourget

Lyon

La Tour-du-Pin

Chambéry

Vienne

Isère

Grenoble

Valence

Drôme

Mont Aiguille 2,086 m (6,842 ft)

Potholing
18 La-Chapelle-en-Vercors
p.165
19 La Diau cave
p.121

Biking, rollerblading
20 L'Alpe-d'Huez: Cycling
p.174
21 Annecy: Cycling, rollerblades
p.116
22 Combloux: Mtn. biking
p.131
23 Grenoble: Cycling
p.169
24 Lake Paladru: Mtn. biking
p.158
25 Lake Roselend: Mtn. biking
p.143
26 Rumilly: Mtn. biking
p.119
27 La Toussuire: Mtn. biking
p.155

Horse riding
28 Megève: Les Coudrettes
p.125
29 Saint-Martin-d'Uriage:
Le Mas de Loutas
p.176

Fishing
30 Aix-les-Bains
p.135
31 Châtel
p.103
32 Les Menuires
p.151

Other sports
33 Ponsonnas:
Bungee jumping
p.171
34 Saint-Gervais-les-Bains:
Ice skating
p.130
35 Talloires : Lake Annecy Golf
Club
p.117
36 Autrans: 'La Foulée
Blanche' cross-country
skiing
p.163
37 Les-Deux-Alpes: Summer
skiing
p.174

Map labels: SWITZERLAND, Lake Geneva (Lac Léman), Thonon-les-Bains, Grand Mont Ruan 3,047 m (9,994 ft), Bonneville, Haute-Savoie, Annecy, Mont Blanc 4,807 m (15,766 ft), Albertville, Savoie, Pointe de la Grande Casse 3,852 m (12,634 ft), Saint-Jean-de-Maurienne, La Meije 3,983 m (13,064 ft), Hautes-Alpes, ITALY, PROVENCE-ALPES-CÔTE D'AZUR, Gap

Scale: 0 10 20 30 40 50 Km / 0 10 20 30 miles

Winter sports

This is a paradise for winter sport lovers, with 6,000 km/3,730 miles of ski runs on the slopes of Isère, Savoie and Haute-Savoie. On Alpine or cross-country skis; on a snowboard; in walking boots or snowshoes; towed by a horse or even riding in a piste basher, you can explore almost every corner of the Alps. There are around 200 ski resorts to choose from, at varying altitudes, from 800 m/2,625 ft to 3,600 m/1,810 ft.

A vast area for skiing

There are 600 km/375 miles of linked ski runs in Savoie. The Trois Vallées (three valleys) in the Tarentaise make up the largest ski area in the world, with its seven resorts amongst the most prestigious – Courchevel, Méribel, Les Menuires, Val-Thorens, Saint-Martin-de-Belleville, La Tania and Brides-les-Bains. With the Trois Vallées pass (from €30 per

day) you can ski from resort to resort and cover a vast area. And if that's not enough for you, a special 6-day pass allows for a day's skiing in the Espace Killy, too – a further 300 km/185 miles of ski slopes at Tignes and Val d'Isère. In Haute-Savoie, the Portes du Soleil ('gateway to the sun') ski area links 12 separate resorts – eight in France, including Morzine and Avoriaz, and four in Switzerland. Together they cover a total of 650 km/405 miles of ski runs. Elsewhere in Haute-Savoie, Savoie and Isère, there are around 20 significant ski areas. For further information

contact the Comité Régional du Tourisme de Rhône-Alpes (☎ 04 72 59 21 59) or local Tourist offices.

A fantastic journey

Experienced skiers should not miss the chance to see the majestic Vallée Blanche (white valley), taking the Aiguille du Midi cable-car up to 3,842 m/12,606 ft, and then skiing down 25 km/15 miles on the glacier. The trip passes through the impressive landscape of the Grandes Jurasses and Mont Blanc, finishing at the foot of the Drus and the Aiguille Verte.

This is high-mountain terrain, and there are deep crevasses, so the services of a mountain guide are essential.

Something for everyone

Les Arcs, Avoriaz, Le Corbier, Valmeinier and Valmorel are ideal family resorts. Cars are not permitted in the villages, and you can get around on skis all day long in complete safety. If you prefer pretty villages with snow-laden wooden chalets, consider a trip to Megève, Samoëns, Abondance or La Clusaz in Haute-Savoie; Arèches, Pralognan-la-Vanoise or Bonneval-sur-Arc in Savoie; or the villages of Chartreuse or the Vercors in Isère. For

THE SYBELLES PROJECT

After lengthy discussions, the draft agreement for this enormous project has now been drawn up and signed by the respective mayors and the Prefect of Savoie. The Sybelles project will be one of the last major developments in the Alps, connecting six ski resorts – Saint-Sorlin-d'Arves, Saint-Jean-d'Arves, Le Corbier, La Toussuire, Les Bottières and Saint-Colomban-des-Villards – in the mountain range of Arvan-Villards, in the Maurienne. It will create the fifth-largest ski area in France, with 300 km/185 miles of runs. To date, €19 million have been invested in the construction of new ski lifts; the project should reach completion in 2002.

maintained, and an area reserved for beginners. An annual pass, valid in all resorts in France, costs €66; depending on the resort, a day pass is €4-8 and a week's pass €15-30. For further information contact the Comité Régional du Tourisme Rhône-Alpes (☎ 04 72 59 21 59) or local Tourist offices.

Crossing the mountains trapper-style

Invented several thousand years ago, the wood and leather snowshoes of the native Americans have been replaced by a modern version in moulded plastic. All the Tourist offices and guide associations in the Alpine resorts offer whole- or half-day snowshoe outings (around €15 per half-day). on your trip you may come across fox or chamois tracks. The more energetic might like to try crossing the mountains in the Bauges, Chartreuse, Vercors, Aravis, Chablais or Beaufortain, staying in a gîte or hotel along the way.

plenty of nightlife and partying into the small hours, try Flaine, Les Deux-Alpes or Val-Thorens, where there's a great atmosphere 24 hours a day.

An industry that's on the up and up!

Ski-lift companies in France have an annual turnover of three-quarters of a million Euros, of which over €600,000 is raked in by the three *départements* of the northern Alps. However, since the skiing industry is essentially seasonal, most inhabitants of the Alpine regions have two jobs, and many ski instructors or ski-lift attendants make their living as farmers or stockbreeders in the summer months.

Cross-country skiing

Whatever their level of ability, cross-country skiers will find plenty of opportunities to practise in the Alps. Autrans is the undisputed Mecca of cross-country skiing, but the resorts of the Vercors (Corrençon, Méaudre, Gresse-en-Vercors, Villard-de-Lans) have marked trails on the plateaux and through pine forests, at 1,100-1,800 m/ 3,610-5,900 ft. There are also good places for cross-country skiing in the Chartreuse mountains (Le Sappey, Col de Porte, Saint-Hugues-en-

Chartreuse), on the Revard plateau in Savoie, in Grand-Bornand, at Praz-de-Lys and at Sommant in Haute-Savoie. In the three *départements* of the northern Alps, around 50 resorts have *France ski de*

fond (French cross-country skiing) status, which guarantees at least 15 km/ 9 miles of safe slopes, suitable for any level of ability, all signposted and properly

Board games in the snow park

Snow parks reserved for snowboarders are appearing all over the Alps and more than 60 resorts now have facilities for this increasingly popular sport. You'll generally find a *half-pipe* is provided,

so that snowboarders can practise spectacular jumps, flips and turns, as well as a series of moguls and space for carving. If you aren't a freestyler yourself, you can still visit a snow park and enjoy the show.

Ski Joëring

If you want to conserve some energy in your ski resort, simply strap on a pair of skis and get a horse to tow you along. Originating in Finland, *ski Joëring* has long been practised in Scandinavia, and as soon as the first snows settle on roads and footpaths people come out and enjoy this unusual way of getting around. In the Alps it's a sport for all skiers to enjoy, whatever their level of ability. All you need to be able to do is stand up straight and know how to make a turn. Attached to the horse by a harness, you simply glide over level ground. Once you are confident on your skis, the horse can go faster and you can slalom behind it at speed. Further information from the French Association for Ski Joëring (☎ 04 79 07 24 97).

Snow-grooming machines

Riding the piste bashers is the very latest popular after-dark attraction in many ski resorts. At night, after the ski runs have closed, or very

early in the morning, you can climb into one of these impressive machines and glide majestically down the slopes. During the journey, the driver will tell you all about the

WORLD SNOWBOARDING FESTIVAL
Les Deux-Alpes
Information from the Tourist office
☎ 04 76 79 22 00
End Oct.-beginning Nov.
Each year, just before the ski runs open, the resort of Les Deux-Alpes hosts the *Mondial du Snowboard* (world snowboarding festival), where devotees of this relatively new sport gather together to exchange new ideas and show off their skills. Board technology and techniques are ever-changing, and on the resort's glacier, at an altitude of 3,200 m/10,500 ft, the experts test the latest equipment, loaned by manufacturers and distributors. The event also attracts keen snowboarders who are not particularly interested in the demonstrations, but who come instead to party into the early hours.

mountains and explain his job – smoothing the snow and preparing the slopes for the skiers who are all tucked up in bed. Further information from Tourist offices.

Climbing in the mountains

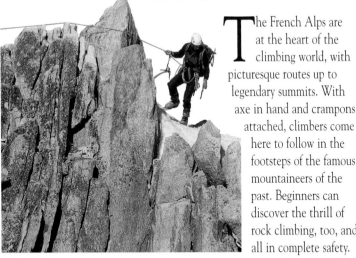

The French Alps are at the heart of the climbing world, with picturesque routes up to legendary summits. With axe in hand and crampons attached, climbers come here to follow in the footsteps of the famous mountaineers of the past. Beginners can discover the thrill of rock climbing, too, and all in complete safety.

A history of mountaineering

Mountaineering as we know it began at Chamonix on 8 April 1786, when Balmat and Paccard first scaled Mont Blanc (p.126). Their achievement opened the door to further successes over the course of the 19th.C, chiefly by English climbers.

Once several Alpine peaks had been conquered and techniques had improved, a new level was reached with the conquest of the Cervin, which had been considered unsurmountable, by Edward Whymper on 14 July 1865. The Himalayas, with summits over 8,000 m/ 26,250 ft, were the next target. The conquest of Annapurna, by Lachenal and Herzog's French-led expedition, paved the way for 13 more of the highest peaks to be assailed, including the legendary Mount Everest, which was eventually conquered by a team led by the New Zealand climber Sir Edmund Hillary.

Climbing techniques

All kinds of techniques have been used in an attempt to reach the top. By using the strength in their arms and legs, Balmat's successors developed rock climbing, a technical sport derived from mountaineering. Ice-picks and mountain boots were replaced by carabiners and climbing shoes. Whether

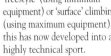

'freestyle' (using minimum equipment) or 'surface' climbing (using maximum equipment), this has now developed into a highly technical sport.

Lessons

Beginners should always employ a guide. Climbing in the mountains requires geological and meteorological know-how as well as technical expertise and experience on

rock and ice. Don't bother with Mont Blanc – although the route is technically undemanding, it's far too popular, and the beds at the Goûter mountain refuge are often completely full. The less well-known ranges, such as the Maurienne, Haute-Maurienne or Belledonne, are

the Vercors (information from the Maison de l'Aventure at La Chapelle-en-Vercors, p.165). This is a major climbing area which has at least seven rock faces and around 80 routes.

Walking in the air

Originally conceived in the Italian Dolomites, the *via ferrata* allow climbers to reach

excellent training grounds to acquire the basics. Once you have the necessary skills, head for the Oisans, which is less crowded than the Mont Blanc massif but just as vast, with a choice of beautiful routes. For a guide, enquire at the Fédération Française de la Montagne et de l'Escalade (French federation of mountain climbing) (FFME ☎ 04 76 40 63 26), the Club Alpin Français (French Alpine club, ☎ 01 53 72 87 00) or at Tourist offices.

almost every corner of the Alps. Equipped with handrails and ladders, these metal walkways offer fantastic views.

You don't need ropes and crampons to reach the high spots – but a fear of heights would be a major drawback on these thrilling excursions. Every year, more and more sites are developed, suitable for varying levels of ability. You can walk with children on the *Diablotins via ferrata* at Assois (p.153), or hire a guide for the extremely impressive *Bastille via ferrata* at Grenoble (p.168), or the *via ferrata* at Roc du Vent at Arèches, where there are wonderful panoramic views (p.142).

Routes to choose

There are numerous climbing locations in the Alps to choose from (information from Tourist offices). Climbers start on rocks no higher than 25-30 m/80-100 ft, then move on to the routes at Presles in

WALKING ON A GLACIER

Walking across glaciers is possible only in summer, at the Vanoise, Oisans or Mont Blanc sites. Walkers are roped together, with crampons on their feet and ice-axe in hand, and led by a mountain guide. The climb is a gentle one, and no particular technical skills are required, just good walking ability. At least one night in a refuge is nearly always included in the trip so that you can see the sun rise in the mountains. The landscape at dawn is simply magical. To find a mountain guide, contact the local tourist offices.

Water sports
taking to the Alpine waters

There may be no sea in the Alps, but there is a tremendous amount of water, from vast lakes lying at the foot of the mountains, to rivers and torrents gushing through rocky gorges. Here you can do almost every type of water sport, as well as going sailing and swimming.

Rafting

The exhilarating sport of white-water rafting involves a large inflatable raft, with a crew of seven plus a river guide, covering a relatively short distance. A 'hot dog' is a small inflatable canoe with rigid edges, with a maximum crew of two. Bourg-Saint-Maurice is a white-water paradise (p.150), where rafters can choose between the lively waters of the Vénéon at Saint-Christophe-en-Oisans, the Giffre between Sixt-Fer-à-Cheval and Samoëns (p.108), the Dranse at Morzine and Abondance, and the Chéran in the Bauges. Information from the Fédération Française du Canoë-Kayak (French federation for canoeing and kayaking) (☎ 01 45 11 08 50) or the Comité Régional de Rhône-Alpes (☎ 04 78 23 90 55).

Hydrospeeding

This is a real treat for good swimmers – clinging to a streamlined plastic float and being swept along the foaming waters of the rivers and the torrents. Wearing flippers and a helmet, and protected by a wetsuit, you can swim like a fish until you reach your destination. Further

information from the local guide associations and Tourist offices.

Canyoning

This relatively new sport is a combination of climbing and potholing, following the flow of the water into the steepest, narrowest gorges. It involves abseiling down waterfalls, swimming along river beds or travelling on a water toboggan, and should only be undertaken with a qualified instructor. Further information

from the Fédération Française de la Montagne et de l'Escalade (French federation of mountain sports and climbing ☎ 04 76 40 63 26). There are many canyoning routes in the Alps, but the Pont du Diable (devil's

bridge) gorge (p.140) is particularly good, and for a truly amazing experience, try night-time canyoning at Samoëns (p.109).

Setting sail

There are opportunities all over the region for sailing dinghies and catamarans. Sailing organisations cater for would-be sailors, whatever their ability, including the Centre Nautique de Voile d'Aix-les Bains (p.132) on Lake Bourget; the Société des Régates à Voile d'Annecy (☎ 04 50 45 48 39) and the Cercle Nautique de Talloires (☎ 04 50 60 70 64) on Lake Annecy; the Société Nautique du Léman at Thonon-les-Bains (☎ 04 50 71 07 29); the Cercle de Voile d'Évian (☎ 04 50 75 06 46) at Lake Geneva; and the sailing school at Charavines (☎ 04 76 06 61 21) on Lake Paladru. Lake Monteynard (p.171) specialises in wind-surfing, which is also available on Lake Laffrey and some of the larger Alpine lakes.

Information from the Fédération Française de Voile (French sailing federation, ☎ 01 44 05 81 00).

Taking the plunge

The temperature of the water at the Annecy, Paladru, Aiguebelette, Bourget and Geneva lakes is a pleasant 20-26°C/68-79°F in summer, ideal for bathing. Lifeguards patrol many of the lakeside beaches, some of which are also equipped with games, toboggans or small boats and pedaloes. Try out a surfbike, a cross between a pedalo and a bicycle, at Aiguebelette (p.146). There are other beaches along the riverbanks and lake shores in Isère, Savoie and Haute-Savoie.

Information from the ADT at Savoie (☎ 04 79 85 12 45), at Haute-Savoie (☎ 04 50 51 32 31), and the CDT at Isère (☎ 04 76 54 34 36).

THE WATER-JUMP
**Espace Acro-Land
Tignes
☎ 04 79 06 36 38
for details of opening hours.
Around €15 per afternoon, all activities included.
This activity centre at Tignes has artificial ski slopes with built-in diving boards. You can slide down the slope on skis, on a surfbike, on rollerblades and even on a BMX bike, take flight, then plunge into the refreshing waters of the lake, protected by a wetsuit and a helmet. Some people visit Acro-Land to train for various acrobatic sports, others just for the fun of it. Henri Authier, who won the silver world medal for acrobatic jumping in 1975, and acts as instructor, is there for advice and training. If you don't feel like taking part, you can also watch the impressive sight from the ground while you sunbathe.**

In the air and under the ground

I n the soft rock of the pre-Alps you can stare into the abyss and explore the underground world of caves. In the sky above the Alps, paragliding has really taken off at Mieussy, in Haute-Savoie (p.106). Buckle up and get ready for take-off.

Hangliding and paragliding

Free flying involves many different techniques, which can often be rather confusing. The oldest, hangliding, was invented in the USA and first arrived in France in the 1970s. The technique somewhat resembles a bird in flight. The pilot lies face down, harnessed to a triangular sail, and uses his body weight to control the speed and steer his craft. Paragliding was perfected 10 years later, with the pilot seated around 6 m/20 ft below the sail, using a braking system to control steering. ULMs (ultra-light motorised craft or microlights), parachutes, sky diving, ballooning, paragliding and rigid gliding (which lies somewhere between paragliding and deltagliding) are among the many options available today, and even kite-flying has its own place in the Fédération Française de Vol Libre (French free flying association).

Where to take flight

Free flight in all its forms is popular throughout the Alps, from Chablais to the Maurienne, from the Vercors to the Aravis (p.152, p.162, p.122). There are a number of training centres which offer a variety of courses, including beginners' flights and introductory courses (information from Tourist offices). The minimum age requirement is 14 (15 for ULMs). Training takes place in a two-seater craft, with an instructor (€45-75 per flight). An introductory course takes around 5 days, after which you can fly solo (€305-455 for paragliding and hangliding, €915-1,830 for ULMs).

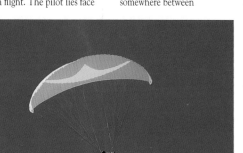

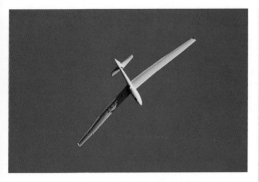

Hot-air ballooning

Skimming the mountain tops in a hot-air balloon is an unforgettable experience. In January each year, the resort of Praz-sur-Arly organises a series of balloon trips that teach pilots how to fly a hot-air balloon in the mountains, as well as a balloon festival with dozens of colourful hot-air balloons taking to the sky, and a longer trip of a few days (information from the Tourist office, ☎ 04 50 21 90 57). Praz-sur-Arly, the first resort in the French Alps to specialise in aerial sports, is also the only place to have two ballooning companies, offering flights over Mont Blanc and across the Alps into Italy: Aérovision (☎ 06 09 78 51 16) and Ballons du Mont Blanc (☎ 04 50 21 03 07, p.125). Other resorts in the Alps offer flights for around €150 per trip. Further

information available from the Fédération Française d'Aérostation (FFA ☎ 01 47 23 56 20) or the Commission Sportive de la FFA at Lyons (☎ 04 72 32 10 61).

Caving and potholing

The mysterious landscapes and rock formations of the subterranean world have been sculpted millimetre by millimetre over many thousands of years. In Isère and Haute-Savoie, there are spectacular caves throughout all the limestone terrain of the pre-Alps. The Jean-Bernard caves, the deepest in the world (1,602 m/5,256 ft), were discovered at Samoëns, in the Giffre valley. There are some 60 km/35 miles of underground passages in the Chartreuse, and the Berger d'Engins cave in the Vercors is the fourth-deepest in the world (1,278 m/4,193 ft). Whether beginner or expert, you'll be in safe hands with the instructors at La Maison

THE ICARUS CUP
Sainte-Hilaire
Rens Tourist office
☎ 04 76 08 33 99
Third weekend in Sept.
It may sound strange, but a kayak, a giraffe, Tintin and a rickshaw have all been spotted in the skies above the Chartreuse. Every year in September a group of crazy pilots meets up at Sainte-Hilaire to compete for the Icarus cup (p.180). At least 200 participants join in the 'fancy dress' competition, with their magnificent flying machines specially decorated for the spectacular occasion. Added attractions include a festival of relevant films, a display of aerial sports and various street entertainments.

de l'Aventure at La Chapelle-en-Vercors (p.165), in the Chartreuse or in the Arve or Giffre valleys and you can discover this magnificent landscape for yourself. Further information from the Fédération Française de Spéléologie (French caving federation) ☎ 01 43 57 56 54.

History and culture of the region

Discover the history of the northern Alps, its famous artists and the traditional Alpine way of life. For historic buildings, mountain strongholds and châteaux, some of which house museums, also see the map on pp.88-89.

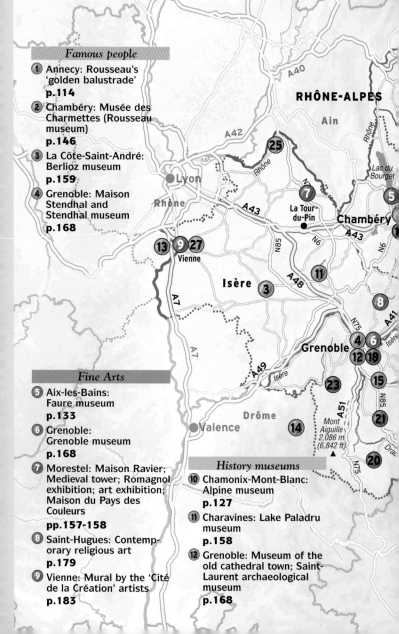

Famous people

① Annecy: Rousseau's 'golden balustrade' **p.114**

② Chambéry: Musée des Charmettes (Rousseau museum) **p.146**

③ La Côte-Saint-André: Berlioz museum **p.159**

④ Grenoble: Maison Stendhal and Stendhal museum **p.168**

Fine Arts

⑤ Aix-les-Bains: Faure museum **p.133**

⑥ Grenoble: Grenoble museum **p.168**

⑦ Morestel: Maison Ravier; Medieval tower; Romagnol exhibition; art exhibition; Maison du Pays des Couleurs **pp.157-158**

⑧ Saint-Hugues: Contemporary religious art **p.179**

⑨ Vienne: Mural by the 'Cité de la Création' artists **p.183**

History museums

⑩ Chamonix-Mont-Blanc: Alpine museum **p.127**

⑪ Charavines: Lake Paladru museum **p.158**

⑫ Grenoble: Museum of the old cathedral town; Saint-Laurent archaeological museum **p.168**

Local history

16 Chambéry:
Museum of Savoy
p.144

17 Le Grand-Bornant:
Heritage museum
p.123

18 Grenoble:
Museum of Dauphiné
p.169

19 Grésy-sur-Isère:
Coteaux du Salin
ecological museum
p.147

20 Mens: Trièves museum
p.171

21 La Mure:
Matheysine museum
p.171

22 Saint-Gingolph:
Museum of Geneva's
traditions and boats
p.113

23 Villard-de-Lans:
Heritage museum
p.164

24 Viuz-en-Sallaz:
Museum of rural life
p.107

13 Saint-Romain-en-Gal:
Museum and archaeological
site
p.183

14 Vassieux-en-Vercors:
Resistance memorial;
museum of the Resistance;
prehistoric museum
p.165

15 Vizille: Museum of the
French Revolution
p. 170

Other sites

25 La Balme-les-Grottes:
Palaeolithic caves
p.136

26 Col des Glières:
Historic discovery trail
p.120

27 Vienne: Temple of
Augustus and Livia
p.182

A *who's* who of the area

T he Savoie and Dauphiné region has its saints, such as François de Sales, who established Annecy as the centre of the Counter-Reformation, and soldiers, such as Bayard, whose château lies hidden in the backwoods of

the Grésivaudan. There have also been inventors, such as Aristide Bergès, and heroines, such as Marie Reynoard, who helped Grenoble become the capital of the French Resistance during World War II.

Château Bayard at Pontcharra

Humbert II
(1312-1355)
In 1349, Dauphiné was the subject of a sale or, rather, a 'transfer'. Having lost his only son, the flamboyant Humbert II decided to sell his land. The king of France seized the opportunity to acquire the Dauphiné for just 200,000 florins. From this time onwards the title of Dauphin went to

the eldest son of the Valois family, and it later came to mean 'heir'.

Amadeus VIII
(1383-1451)
Although physically unattractive – he had a squint – and fervently religious, Amadeus VIII was an accomplished diplomat who strengthened Savoy's position

in Piedmont.
He became duke when Savoy was made a duchy by Emperor Sigismund in 1416. His administrative and legislative skills were unsurpassed and he was responsible for the famous Statutes of Savoy (1430). He withdrew from his château retreat at Ripaille (p.111) when elected Pope under the name of Felix V (1439-49).

Bayard
(1475-1524)
Bayard featured prominently in the wars against Italy waged by Charles VIII, Louis XII and François I, and famously took part in the battles of Marignan and Garigliano bridge. Born Pierre Terrail, the son of a country squire, he became a legendary military figure. His greatest fear was to 'die in his bed like a virgin'. As luck

Statue of Bayard in Place Saint-André, Grenoble

would have it, he was killed in battle by a shot from an *arquebus*, a firearm which, ironically, he despised, having been brought up on tales of chivalry as a young page at the court of Savoy.

St François de Sales (1567-1622)

Encouraged by his father to dedicate his life to religion, François de Sales (p.120), born at Thorens, near Annecy, obtained a degree in civil and canon law. He was a gentle but tireless preacher of the gospel in the

Chablais at a time when the region was almost entirely given over to Calvinism. He became Bishop of Geneva and Annecy and was also the author of a bestselling book, *Introduction à la Vie Dévote* (An introduction to religious life), which reached its 40th edition in his own lifetime.

Aristide Bergès (1833-1904)

Aristide Bergès may not have been a man of means but he was a man of ideas. Born into a family of paper-makers, he became an engineer, and ultimately played an important role in introducing hydro-electric power to France. He showed great skills of improvisation, for example, siphoning water from Lake Crozet for his wood pulp factory at La Combe de Lancey (p.177) and using a pressure pipeline, turbines and a double dynamo.

Marie Reynoard (1897-1945)

For the part it played in the French Resistance, the city of Grenoble was awarded the title of *Companion de la Libération* in May 1944. It's not known if news of this ever reached Marie Reynoard in the concentration camp at Ravensbrück, but it was in her apartment on Rue Fourier in November 1941 that the resistance network was set up. Formerly a professor of literature at the Lycée Stendhal, she would recite excerpts from *Tristan and Yseult* to her fellow prisoners. Her portrait hangs in the Museum of the Resistance and Deportation in Grenoble (14, Rue Hébert, ☎ 04 76 42 38 53).

Savoyard Baroque,

the faith that moves mountains

Savoyard Baroque, intended to astonish and dazzle the faithful, began at the start of the 17thC., at the same time as the Counter-Reformation and the revival of the Catholic church. The austere exteriors of the churches of the Tarentaise and Maurienne, the Arly valley or the Beaufortain hide magnificent altarpieces that testify to a golden age of religious fervour in the Alps.

Saint Grat, church of Cordon

Church of Saint-Michel, Lanslevillard

Crusading art

At the end of the 16thC., the Catholic church underwent severe self-scrutiny following the Council of Trent (1545-63) and turned its attention to the recovery of those followers who had been tempted away by the teachings of Calvin and Luther. The Savoy region was prominent in the fight against Protestantism, which had its headquarters in Geneva. High-profile bishops such as François de Sales played an important part. Subsequently, from 1650 to 1720, practically every church in the Maurienne and Tarentaise region was renovated with an abundance of ornamentation, in direct contrast to the austerity of Protestantism.

A taste of paradise

Every church was built around the highly-ornate altarpiece, its focal point. The idea was to give the faithful a foretaste of paradise, where poverty and misery did not exist. The altarpiece was sculpted and painted, representing an illustrated guide to the life of Christ. The lower part was conceived as a kind of

miniature temple, affirming the presence of Christ, which was central to the dogma of the Counter-Reformation. At the next level were the intercessors, or intermediaries,

Church of Saint-Nicolas-de-Véroce

such as the saints and the Virgin Mary. At the top the sky unfolded, revealing God the Father in all his glory, surrounded by his cherubim.

Bright colours and gold

The altarpieces were sculpted from Arolla pine, which is easy to work, and the bright colours used to decorate it symbolised specific virtues

Church of the Holy Trinity at Peisey-Nancroix

Cherubs on the 'dancing altarpiece' at Hauteville-Gordon

communities established a fixed rate for sculptors and painters, and in the Maurienne, this period gave rise to dynasties of local painters and sculptors – the Simon family at Bramans, the Clappier family at Bessans, and the Flandin and Rey families at Termignon. In the Tarentaise, the villages called in the artists of Valsesia, a valley on the Italian side, including Martel and his son, and Jacques-Antoine Todesco.

Angel faces

Baroque altarpieces are covered with cherubs, cheerful and chubby. Jacques Clérant's altarpiece (1710) in the church of Saint-Sigismond at Champagny-le-Bas (Tarentaise) has 160. Joseph-Marie Martel's cherubs are legendary, especially those on the altarpiece at Hauteville-Gondon (1732), who are executing an angelic *pas-de-deux* so lifelike that to this day the work is referred to as the 'dancing altarpiece'.

– green for hope, blue for faith, red for charity, etc. The brightly-coloured approach was gradually replaced by the use of gold leaf, sometimes to excess, as in the altarpiece at the church of the Holy Trinity, at Peisey-Nancroix (in the Tarentaise). Unsurprisingly, the altarpiece could end up costing as much as the rest of the church.

A high price to pay

The building and decoration of a church could cost more than 4,000 florins, or around the price of a herd of 100 cattle. The church at Peisey-Nancroix, for instance cost 4,550 florins. The peasant

CROSSES OF THE PASSION

There are still several 'crosses of the Passion' in Haute-Maurienne, which serve as a reminder of Savoy's Catholicism. Dating from the 19thC., they stand by the wayside, as at Aussois, or in front of the church, as at Bessans. They are covered with painted wooden artefacts, each evoking a scene from the crucifixion, such as the crowing cock that recalls Peter's denial, the purse for Judas's 30 pieces of silver, the crown of thorns, the hammer and the three nails, the sponge, the lance and the ladder.

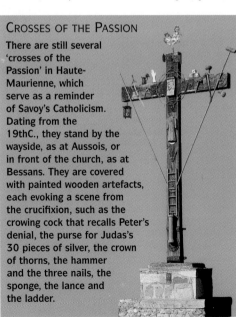

The Olympic Games

Chamonix at the beginning of the 20thC.

The northern Alps have hosted the Winter Olympic Games three times – Chamonix in 1924, Grenoble in 1968 and Albertville in 1992. The events at Chamonix were originally considered as a 'village festival', and it wasn't until May 1925 that the first-ever Winter Olympic Games were declared (retrospectively) to have taken place. And furthermore, Alpine skiing was not accepted as a Winter Olympic sport until 1936!

Baron Pierre de Coubertin

A trial run

Creating the Winter Olympics was not easy – Norway and Sweden, who already had their Nordic Games, opposed the idea. Even Baron Pierre de Coubertin, who had reinstated the concept of the Olympic Games, was not entirely convinced. He reluctantly agreed to organise an international week of winter sports, under the patronage of the IOC (International Olympic Committee), at the end of January 1924. Chamonix was chosen as the location and only the 'Nordic' sports were featured – cross-country skiing, ski jumping, ice-skating, hockey and the bobsleigh.

A solemn oath

On the appointed day, Chamonix prepared itself to welcome 293 athletes (13 of them women), representing 17 nations. Comte de Clary, president of the French committee, directed the standard bearer of the French delegation – most of whom were from Chamonix – to take the Olympic oath. Chamonix was later recognised as having hosting the first Winter Olympics, but in that year the French did not win a single medal.

'A billion francs'

In 1968 it was the turn of Grenoble to host the Winter Olympic Games. 'You will get

Comte Justinien Clary

The Olympic bowl at Grenoble

A NEW KIND OF OPENING CEREMONY
Grenoble may have had a reputation for stuffiness, but in 1992, the opening ceremony of the Winter Games was a magical spectacle, seen on television by 2 billion people. The director was 30-year-old Philippe Decouflé, a graduate of the school of Jean-Paul Goude, a designer who is legendary in France for his astonishing and innovative public ceremonies and processions. As soon as Decouflé had waved his magic wand, rave press reviews dubbed him 'Albertville's little prince'.

a billion francs,' General de Gaulle promised his dashing Minister for Youth and Sports, Maurice Herzog. This money was a godsend that revolutionised the capital of the Dauphiné, where many upper-floor dwellings still did not have running water. A new railway station and a brand-new airport were built, motorways were laid and an arts centre was constructed, inaugurated by André Malraux. The games also made Autrans and cross-country skiing famous.

The legendary 'Jet Man'

When legendary skier Jean-Claude Killy arrived at Grenoble his confidence was at an all-time low, but he went on to win the grand slam – three gold medals in the downhill, slalom and giant slalom. He came to be known as 'Jet Man'. His final test took place at Chamrousse, on 17 February 1968, in dense fog. The president of the IOC, Avery Brundage, did not agree with some athletes wearing sponsors' names on their clothing and threatened to confiscate their medals. 'Let him come to Val d'Isère and get them,' was Killy's reply. This was just the beginning of what was to become the great debate about amateur status.

Albertville

Jean-Claude Killy and Michel Barnier – who had been the youngest-ever deputy and then departmental councillor – first had the idea of holding the Winter Olympics at Albertville (p.148) in 1981. The idea snowballed and eventually 335,000 local people became involved in the event. On 17 October 1986, to great Savoyard celebrations, Albertville was awarded the games of 1992. According to Killy, the committee had 'worked for 10 years for the sake of just 16 days'.

Moguls, a new challenge

Albertville was the first Winter Olympic venue to introduce new events and a

more 'freestyle' approach to the competitions. Local skier Edgar Grospiron, known as the 'master of moguls', had the reputation of being flamboyant, arrogant and a little wild, but he undoubtedly had legs of steel. At Tignes on 15 February 1992, in a blinding snowstorm, he attacked the bumps on the mogul course, aiming for 'gold or nothing', and was rewarded by becoming the first man to win the title of Olympic mogul champion.

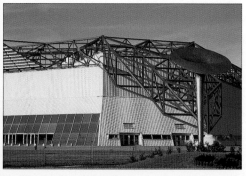

The Olympic stadium at Albertville

Writers and the Alps

J ean-Jacques Rousseau, devoted lover of nature, was one of the first to recognise the appeal of this region for tourists. Before long, the Alps had become a fashionable place to visit, particularly for the Romantics. Hordes of people arrived on foot, by mule, or by stagecoach to marvel at the panoramic landscape. Writers also enjoyed the theatrical atmosphere of the spa towns, with their stucco façades, and waltzes and foxtrots.

A new literary genre

The travelogue was born in the 19thC. Discovering the natural world was the kind of ritual that fitted so well with the Romantic ideal, and there

Stendhal

were many who took to the highways and byways, including Chateaubriand and Alexandre Dumas senior. In 1838, Stendhal wrote *Les Mémoires d'un Touriste*, which first popularised the word 'tourist', with around 100 pages describing northern Dauphiné, seen through the eyes of an iron merchant.

He also satirised his birthplace Grenoble in *La Vie de Henri Brulard*. The real Julien Sorel (from Stendhal's *Le Rouge et le Noir*) was executed in the town in 1827 but the fictional character fared somewhat better.

Pilgrimages to Chartreuse

A description of the landscape of the Chartreuse region under stormy skies was an obligatory feature of 19thC. French travel writing (p.178). Chateaubriand conjures up 'a sudden downpour and torrents of water gushing down, roaring, from the ravines'. Stendhal evokes a similarly 'sublime spectacle', describing the 'extraordinary moaning of the pines, the magnificent claps

of thunder' (*Les Mémoires d'un Touriste*), and his fond memories of Brother Jean-Marie (a lay monk) and his fried carp. Alexandre Dumas recalls the monks' liqueur, which put 'fire' into his blood: 'We started running around the room like men possessed' (*Les Alpes de la Grande Chartreuse à Chamonix*).

Lamartine

DANGEROUS LIAISONS

At the end of the reign of Louis XV, Grenoble was the 'merriest garrison in France', where games, balls, theatre and fine dining were the order of the day. Army officer Pierre-Ambroise Choderlos de Laclos (1741-1803) had plenty of time to observe Dauphinois society from 1769-75, and depicted it mercilessly in *Les Liaisons Dangereuses* (1782). This book was a key work, and Madame de Merteuil, Valmont and Cécile were apparently real people in Grenoble society in the 18thC.

Writers and the spa towns

Writers came to the spa towns to soothe body and spirit. It's difficult to imagine the poet Verlaine treating his rheumatism at Aix, or Colette visiting Uriage for her arthritis, yet these experiences had a positive effect on both their correspondence and their work. Lamartine describes Aix as 'full of smoke and full of the smell of the hot sulphurous waters' (*Raphaël*), while Alphonse Daudet recalls Allevard (in *Numa Roumestan*, 1881), with its 'racking coughs, audible through the hotel walls'.

Ode to Lake B.

Lake Bourget features frequently in literature. Balzac describes the famous Cercle, predecessor of the Aix casino, in *La Peau de Chagrin*, although he had never actually been there. George Sand sets *Mademoiselle la*

Julie Charles

Quintinie in the Château de Bourdeau. The lake also owes its fame to Lamartine's *Méditations Poétiques* (1820). The poem 'Lac' was originally entitled 'Ode to Lake B.', and was dedicated to Julie Charles, the poet's muse, a TB sufferer whom he met at the Pension Perrier at Aix.

À la Recherche...

Balbec, described by Proust in *À la Recherche du Temps Perdu*, is often identified as Cabourg, in Normandy, but in fact the young Marcel Proust (1871-1922) also visited Évian in order to treat his asthma. Between treatments, the writer would have dined at Villa Bessaraba, located on the road to Amphion, where Princess Brancovan – Anna de Noailles – held soirées for members of high society. She was equally obsessed with the passage of time. In her poetry, she described 'the smell of seaweed and fisheries, musty tar and painted boats lapping against the shore' as typical of Lake Geneva (*Le Livre de ma Vie*).

Anna de Noailles

Art and design in the Alps,
mountains in the frame

L andscape painting was for a long time a neglected, even denigrated, art form. At best, the works were produced in a conventional style, and finished off in the studio. In the 19thC., at the height of the Romantic era, the genre came into its own. New generations of painters and engravers braved freezing temperatures, discomfort and fatigue in their efforts to capture the Alpine landscape on canvas.

Turner's sketchbooks

In 1802, JMW Turner (1775-1851) took the Alpine route, accompanied by Newby Lawson, a gentleman farmer and one of his clients. Turner sketched prolifically on the trip. On his return to London, he reworked the sketches in crayon, watercolour and gouache and put them together as a portfolio, in the hope of receiving commissions. Turner's later style, both dramatic and melancholy, owes much to his journey through the Alps. He went on to become a specialist in atmospheric landscapes; in his paintings, the light seems to emanate from the canvas.

Climbers and their art

While the Alpine landscape may have inspired artistry in many, the opposite is also true. Before conquering the Cervin peak (1865) and several others, Edward Whymper was an engraver. The original purpose of his visit to the Alps was to work on book illustration. At the suggestion of the French Alpine Club a society of mountain painters was created in 1898; Gabriel Loppé (1825-1913), who climbed Mont Blanc more than 40 times, was a leading

Gabriel Loppé: Au Montenvers

light in the society. His paintings (including *Sunset on Mont Blanc*) are normally on show in the Alpine museum at Chamonix (p.126), but are currently undergoing restoration.

'To relieve my boredom, I paint. It is not very exciting, but the lake is very nice, surrounded by high hills,' he wrote. The tedium did eventually result in a small masterpiece, entitled *Le Lac*

Painters of the lakes

Originally from Annecy, Prosper Dunant (1790-1878) was a gentleman and father of five, with a penchant for the arts. His oil paintings and engravings, such as *La Barque aux Musicians* (the musicians' boat), are full of serenity and calm. His son-in-law, Firmin Salabert (1811-95), a former pupil of Ingres, also produced over 100 paintings seeking to portray the 'fleeting light' of Lake Annecy.

Paul Cézanne

In 1896, Cézanne (1839-1906) stayed at the abbey of Tailloires, which had been converted into a hotel, but he was bored to distraction.

d'Annecy: Le Château de Duingt vu de Talloires, a clear predecessor of the Cubist movement, with its use of geometric lines.

Samivel

The writing and watercolours of Paul Gayet, also known as Samivel (1907-92), reflect the 'searing nearness of lost

innocence'. The humour is savage, and the plots are highly comical. Much of Samivel's work is set in the mountains, which he discovered while at school in Chambéry, where he would escape at weekends to ski on the Revard slopes.

Posters – a new form of art

The appearance of the first advertising posters coincided with the development of tourism, around 1880, with artists selling their talents to tourist associations and train operators. To depict Savoy, the Paris-Lyon-Méditerranée railway company employed François Cachoud (1866-1943), otherwise known as the 'Corot of the night' or the 'sleepwalking painter'.

Cézanne: Le Bac à Bonnières

Arts and crafts

Silverware from the Bauges, glazed pottery, little carved wooden devils from Bessans… Visit some of the workshops of the region, where craftsmen keep local skills and the traditional of high-quality workmanship alive.

Wood-carving

① **Autrans: Vincent André**
p.167

② **Bessans: 'Au Chapoteur'**
p.155

③ **Châtel: L'Atelier de Théo**
p.102

④ **Entre-Deux-Guiers: Bernard Boursier**
p.181

⑤ **La Magne: Jean-Paul Pernet**
p.141

⑥ **Saint-Jean-en-Royans: Desfonds' workshop**
p.167

⑦ **Saint-Laurent-en-Royans: Bérard's workshop**
p.167

⑧ **Thoiry: Jean-Paul Rossi**
p.141

⑨ **Vacheresse: Philippe Bottollier-Depois**
p.103

Pottery

⑩ **Évires: Jean-Christophe Hermann's workshop and shop**
p.121

⑪ **Morzine: The Morzine pottery**
p.104

SWITZERLAND

Lake Geneva
(Lac Léman)

Thonon-
les-Bains **⑨**

③

Geneva

⑪

Grand Mont
Ruan
3,047 m
(9,994 ft)

A1

Dranse

Haute-
Savoie

Bonneville

A9

⑩ ㉑

Arve

A40

㉕

Annecy

㉗

㉖

⑯

Tunnel

Lac
d'Annecy

N508

Mont
Blanc
4,807 m
(15,766 ft)

A5

Arly

⑬

⑫

⑱

Albertville

N90

Isère

Savoie

A43

Arc

Pointe de
la Grande Casse
3,852 m
(12,634 ft)

②

㉒

Saint-Jean-
de-Maurienne

Tunnel
du Fréjus

La Meije
3,983 m
(13,064 ft)

N91

A32

ITALY

⑲

Hautes-
Alpes

PROVENCE-ALPES-
CÔTE D'AZUR

● Gap

0	10	20	30	40	50 Km

0	10	20	30

miles

Various crafts

⑫ Albertville:
Craft shops in medieval
Conflans
p.148

⑬ Arêches:
La Ruine (local craftwork;
exhibitions)
p.142

⑭ Chartreuse: Farming, craft
and horticulture trail
p.179

⑮ Gruffy: La Grange aux
Fleurs (bouquets of dried
flowers)
p.119

⑯ Megève: A. Allard
(stretch ski pants)
p.124

⑰ Saint-André: La Tourne
paper mill
p.147

⑱ Séez: Arpin mill
(Bonneval cloth)
p.150

⑲ Venosc: Craft village
p.174

Museums

⑳ Alby-sur-Chéran:
Shoemaking museum
p.119

㉑ Évires:
Pottery museum
p.121

㉒ Saint-Jean-de-Maurienne:
Opinel (penknife) museum
p.152

㉓ Sevrier: Bell museum
and Paccard bell
foundry
p.117

㉔ Villard-de-Lans: Museum
of santons (crib figures)
p.164

Antiques and flea markets

㉕ Annecy: Flea market (last
Saturday in the month)
p.116

㉖ Saint-Gervais-les-Bains:
Summer flea market
(mid-July to beginning
of September)
p.130

㉗ Thônes: André Veyret
& Sons (antiques)
p.122

Furniture and everyday objects,
folk art of the mountains

The simple furniture and everyday utensils of the mountains had little monetary value in the past, but are now much sought after in flea markets and antique shops. Folk art is back in favour, and though contemporary craftsmen may make reproductions of old pieces, collectors prefer the authentic odour left in a cupboard, the signs of use on an old table, the lingering smell of flour in a kneading trough – the real thing certainly has more soul!

Woodwork

Mountain craftsmen worked on only a few different types of wood: larch, spruce and pine. *Pinus cembra* (the Arolla pine) was prized for its close grain and the hardness of its wood, as well as its aroma of vanilla and cinnamon. For all types of turned wooden utensils (sarcastically referred to as 'Bauges silver'), maple varieties such as sycamore were preferred. Bas-Dauphiné took pride in its walnut trees, and it was the custom for a father to fell his most prized tree to provide the wood for the furniture of his daughter's dowry.

with great pomp and ceremony into her home. Maurienne chests are the most sought after today for the intricate carvings on their front panels. Chests were also used to store grain, but these tended to be much larger (up to 2 m/6.5 ft) and more rustic.

Maintenance

Today, furniture is often polished to a high gloss but in the past the pieces would have been washed down with water once a year. As a result, resinous wood would

look bleached and pale. In the 19thC. this led to the practice of staining with bull's blood, which was also believed to ward off flies. Staining with walnut shells is a more recent method.

Typical motifs

Recurring patterns, pricked out with a compass, carved with a knife or sculpted with a gouge, include rosettes, and rouelles, or circular motifs. These symbolise the sun and are often

Marriage chests

The carved wooden chest, replaced by the cupboard or wardrobe in the 19thC., was given on marriage to a bride to keep her trousseau in, and carried

accompanied in this region by hearts and the *lac d'amour*, both of which

signify love and fidelity. The *lac d'amour* was a type of bow or knot chosen by the House of Savoy as its emblem

La Tarentaise and Chablais, tables were also used as armchairs, and today these have become fascinating museum pieces.

Box beds

In some Alpine valleys people slept in box beds, completely closed in with doors – either to keep out draughts or to maintain privacy. These small cupboard-like boxes look more like children's beds to us today, and it's hard to imagine an adult could sleep in such a limited space. However, in the past, people would sleep sitting in an upright position, superstitious that only the

THE VALUE OF SALT

Salt, in crystal form, was a precious commodity in the past. A small supply was kept by the chimney-piece, in a wooden box that could

be either round or square; boxes in the shape of a chicken are typical of Bessans (p.155). There were also salt chairs or *salins*, in which the family salt could be hidden and which fooled more than one salt-tax collector. The chair was reserved for the eldest member of the family, preferably someone who was as deaf as a post and who could not be disturbed!

Smart furniture

Space in Alpine chalets was at a premium, particularly where cheese was made. This led to the invention of ingenious fold-away or multi-purpose furniture, such as the shepherd's table, which consisted of a plank of wood attached to the wall with a folding leg. Some tables also doubled up as kneading troughs and cupboards (known as *bornandines*). In the regions of Grand-Bornand,

dead lay down completely flat. Pull-out or stowaway beds have also been found throughout the region.

Marking your bread

Bread-making was not done daily but rather once a month or once every three months – even once a year in some parts of the Oisans. This was why the houses had huge trapezoid kneading troughs,

in which up to 400 kg/880 lb of dough was prepared, and where the cooked loaves were kept. Collectors prize the wooden 'bread stamps', which would identify each family's bread (p.122), having been used to stamp the dough before it was taken to the communal village oven for baking.

THE *GROLLA*

This was a round wooden drinking vessel, surrounded with holes. At the end of a meal, it was filled with coffee mixed with various liqueurs, such as Marc de Savoie (Savoyard liqueur), and orange or lemon zest, then set alight. Each person would drink a mouthful, keeping their fingers over the holes at the sides to prevent spillage, and then pass the *grolla* on. Recipes vary from family to family, but the *grolla* is always the same. You can find them in craft shops in Savoie and Haute-Savoie near the Italian border (they apparently originated in Piedmont). A fine example sits on the desk of the tourist office at Bourg-Saint-Maurice (p.149).

The crowned hand

Genuine Opinel knives, generally considered to be the finest in France, have been identified by a crowned hand etched or laser-engraved into the blade, since the trademark was registered in 1909. The symbol was borrowed from the coat of arms of Saint-Jean-de-Maurienne, where the crown represented the first count of Maurienne, Humbert aux Blanches-Mains ('Humphrey of the white hands'), founder of the House of Savoy. The hand represents the patron saint of Saint-Jean-de-Maurienne, St John the Baptist. The cathedral's treasury has a reliquary purporting to contain three of his fingers, brought back from Egypt. The knives are now only available in 10 sizes, numbers 2 to 12 (p.152). Collectors will find it difficult to get hold of numbers

1 or 11 in the Opinel series as they were withdrawn from production in 1937.

Carved doves

Birds (particularly the dove) are potent symbols in the Catholic faith; it was a dove that announced to Noah that land had been found. The bird also embodies the Holy Spirit and has become a symbol of happiness, in marriages, births and celebrations. The traditional method of carving a dove with a penknife is a delicate operation, starting with two blocks of wood, one for the body and tail, another for the wings. According to a local saying, 'it's the wood that makes the bird'. Some craftsmen prefer unseasoned or 'green' wood, while others use dry wood, softened by quick boiling. Spruce – *la pesse* in local dialect – is the favoured material, preferably from a tree that has grown slowly.

Everyday utensils

Old agricultural and Alpine artefacts are highly prized today. You can still find *couloirs* (shovels for flour and grain), spoons for skimming milk, metal cake moulds, and butter moulds used to identify the producer. A little-known object, the 'coffin', was a container made of beech wood, hollowed-out

A 'coffin' for storing a whetstone

decoration, applied with a paintbrush or a dropper. The spot motif is one of the most popular and simple decorations, while birds and stylised flowers require a more elaborate technique.

Bonneval cloth, almost a legend

Since 1817, Bonneval cloth has been manufactured at Séez in the Tarentaise, at the Arpin mill (p.150) on the banks of the Versoyen. In the past, local wool was bought at the markets of Moûtiers or Saint-Jean-de-Maurienne, but today it's collected from the factory after shearing. This legendary fabric, more or less indestructible and waterproof, has equipped more than one expedition to the Arctic or the Himalayas, particularly in the company of polar explorer Paul-Émile Victor.

cow horn or metal. The reapers would keep their whetstone in this 'coffin', which was richly carved with symbols, initials and dates, and sometimes with little sayings.

Local pottery

Most local potters, like Gérard Menu (p.104) or Jean-Christophe Hermann (p.120), import their clay from central France or Tuscany. Savoyard pottery is glazed and decorated earthenware, with superb effects created from a limited range of colours. Only the creamy yellow colour is natural. The brick-brown comes from mixing clay with ferrous oxide, black from manganese oxide, and green from copper oxide. It was not possible to use the colour blue until the 1930s, as cobalt oxide was prohibitively expensive.

Naïve decoration

Many plates and cups were made for displaying on wooden dressers. Other pieces had more down-to-earth uses, as cutlery drainers, jugs for water or oil, or *toupines* (jars) for eggs, butter or lard. The technique has not changed over the years – one

firing in the kiln at 1,000°C/1,832°F, and simple, almost naïve,

Jewellery and traditional costume

'Peasant on weekdays, princess on a Sunday'

I n Savoy today, traditional headdresses, jewellery and costumes are only worn on special occasions – marriages, baptisms, and religious holidays such as 15 August. The dresses are heavy, weighing around 4-7 kg/9-15 lb. Hearts and crosses gleam on silk shawls embroidered with wild flowers. These precious creations are either handed down as heirlooms from mother to daughter, painstakingly restored or simply re-created from scratch.

Coded messages

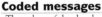

The colour of the shawl, the shape of the headdress, the type of cross, the width of the skirt and the number of its pleats (as many as 40) – all spoke volumes about the woman wearing them. They could reveal where she came from, whether she was single or married and whether she was wealthy or of modest means. If she wore a large bonnet of black silk lace, tied with a large red bow, she definitely came from Bessans (in the Maurienne).

Silver was only worn by young girls or poorer people. The basic fact was that the women were on display, showing their wares.

Savoyard crosses

There are more than a dozen different types of Savoyard cross, from tiny examples (no more than 2cm/1 in in height), to huge ones (up to 40 cm/ 16 in long). The lightest weigh around 1.8 gm/0.5 oz, while some crosses with chains can weigh as much as 120-130 gm/4-5 oz.

with a figure of Christ on the front. There are several local variations of this Latin cross, which has large finials at the ends of each arm. In the Arves, it is worn on a chain of glass beads and the Megève version is remarkably delicate.

tightly back, and rolled into a bun, the *couache*, at the nape of the neck. Short-haired women can cheat by wearing a hairpiece, which has the nickname of 'a fib'.

Lace-making

Lace first arrived in the region towards the end of the 17thC., when the countrywomen of Megève, Tignes and Val d'Isère began to produce beautifully delicate work using *tambours* (small, portable, circular frames).

They later moved on to making lace using a bobbin – a conical spindle on to which the thread was wound. The women of the Beaufortain specialised in needlepoint lace-making. In the traditional costumes of the region, lace is worn both at the wrists and the neck, and may also appear as a *modeste* – a lace insert on the front of the blouse – and, of course, in headdresses. In all cases, it is frilly, pleated and highly-starched.

But the size of the cross did not necessarily reflect the depth of the wearer's devotion. One local priest is reported to have lamented that he had noticed 'the larger the cross, the smaller the faith'.

Personal preferences

One of the most frequently seen crosses is the *Jeanette*, which was popular with farm girls who are said to have bought it on the feast day of Saint-Jean with their first wages. It is also known as the 'cross of the Holy Spirit' as it features a model of a dove, head downwards, with wings folded. The *grille*, or Chambéry cross, is decorated

Delightful headdresses

In Haute Tarentaise, the *frontière* is a headdress that covers the forehead, hence its name. It is distinctive, tapering into three points at the forehead and temples. Richly adorned with gold and silver braid, sometimes embroidered, it is worn with long hair tied

Fairs, festivals and markets

From markets brimming with fresh local produce and rustic agricultural festivals to traditional music and dance – there's always something going on in the Alps.

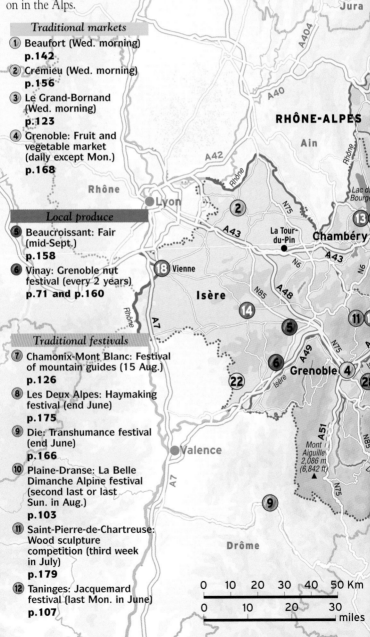

Traditional markets

① Beaufort (Wed. morning)
p.142

② Crémieu (Wed. morning)
p.156

③ Le Grand-Bornand (Wed. morning)
p.123

④ Grenoble: Fruit and vegetable market (daily except Mon.)
p.168

Local produce

⑤ Beaucroissant: Fair (mid-Sept.)
p.158

⑥ Vinay: Grenoble nut festival (every 2 years)
p.71 and p.160

Traditional festivals

⑦ Chamonix-Mont Blanc: Festival of mountain guides (15 Aug.)
p.126

⑧ Les Deux Alpes: Haymaking festival (end June)
p.175

⑨ Die: Transhumance festival (end June)
p.166

⑩ Plaine-Dranse: La Belle Dimanche Alpine festival (second last or last Sun. in Aug.)
p.103

⑪ Saint-Pierre-de-Chartreuse: Wood sculpture competition (third week in July)
p.179

⑫ Taninges: Jacquemard festival (last Mon. in June)
p.107

Jura

A404

A40

RHÔNE-ALPES

Ain

Rhône

A42

Rhône

Lac du Bourge

Rhône

Lyon

②

N75

⑬

N6

La Tour-du-Pin

Chambéry

A43

A43

⑱ Vienne

N6

N85

A48

Isère

⑭

N75

⑪

A49

⑤

Rhône

A7

⑥

Grenoble ④

⑳

Isère

Isère

⑳

Valence

A7

A51

⑳

Mont Aiguille
2,086 m
(6,842 ft)
▲

N85

N75

⑨

Drôme

| 0 | 10 | 20 | 30 | 40 | 50 Km |

| 0 | 10 | 20 | 30 |
miles

SWITZERLAND

*Lake Geneva
(Lac Léman)*

23 **15**
Thonon-
les-Bains

10 Grand Mont
Ruan
3,047 m
(9,994 ft)

**Haute-
Savoie**

Bonneville **12**

A41

3 **21**

:5 **Annecy**

*Lac
d'Annecy*

N508

27

1

● Albertville

17

*Mont
Blanc
4,807 m
(15,766 ft)*

7

Isère

N90

Savoie

Pointe de
la Grande Casse
3,852 m (12,634 ft) ▲

26

Saint-Jean-
● de-Maurienne

A43

Tunnel
du Fréjus

La Meije
3,983 m
(13,064 ft) ▲
N91

8

**Hautes-
Alpes**

ITALY

A32

● **Gap**

16 Saint-Pierre-en-
Chartreuse: Brel festival
(third week in July)
p.179

17 Tarentaise:
Music and heritage
festival (first 2 weeks
in Aug.)
p.151

18 Vienne: Jazz festival
(end June to mid-July)
p.182

Shows and performing arts

19 Chambéry: Musical and
dramatic re-enactments
at Charmettes (July-Aug.)
p.146

20 Vallée de l'Eau d'Olle:
Magic festival (first
2 weeks in Aug.)
p.173

21 Le Grand-Bornand:
Children's festival
(last week in Aug.)
p.123

22 Saint-Antoine-l'Abbaye:
Medieval nights festival
(last 2 weeks in July)
p.160

23 Thonon-les-Bains: Street
festival and fireworks
(second week in Aug.)
p.110

Others

24 Aix-les-Bains:
Flower festival (Aug.);
Navig'Aix (river craft
festival) (end July, every
2 years)
pp.134-135

25 Annecy: Lake festival:
(first Saturday in Aug.)
p.116

26 Haute-Maurienne:
Astronomy festival
(second week in Aug.)
p.154

27 Notre-Dame-de-
Bellecombe: Water festival
(end July and end Aug.)
p.30

28 Uriage-les-Bains: open-air
cinema (in summer)
p.176

Music

13 Aix-les-Bains: Romantic
nights festival (2 weeks
in Oct.)
p.135

14 La Côte-Saint-André:
Berlioz festival
(last 2 weeks in Aug.)
p.159

15 Évian-les-Bains: Music
festival (end June-
beginning of July)
p.112

Mountain festivals,
agriculture, religion and food

All over the Alps, festivals are held that celebrate everyday life – the departure of the shepherd and his flock to summer pastures, woodcutting, the harvest, bread-making, wine and cheese. On saints' days, participants dressed in traditional costume join processions in honour of the Virgin Mary. There is also a long-held tradition of annual fairs; the one at Beaucroissant (p.158), for instance, dates back for centuries.

On the way up or on the way down

Festivities begin with the *transhumance*, when the shepherd and his flock depart for summer pastures, climbing high into the Alps to find fresh grazing. The occasion is celebrated with music, parades of animals through the streets, and tastings of local produce. The *transhumance* festival at Die is one of the biggest (p.166), but there are others at Chambéry (first Saturday in June), Saint-Jean-d'Arves and Passy (third Saturday in June). From August to the beginning

of October, the shepherds and stockmen return from the high pastures, and the partying starts all over again, with local produce, traditional craft markets, folk music and dancing. Some of the best take place at Plaine-Dranse, near Châtel (p.103), at Annecy (second Saturday in October),

at Ugine (first weekend in September) and at La Clusaz (third Sunday in September).

Religious festivals

Feast days are often dedicated to the Virgin Mary, who inspires a great deal of devotion in the Alps. In Savoie, there are countless festivals to celebrate 15 August (the Feast of the Assumption), but the traditional processions and pilgrimages have often been replaced by sporting contests. Pilgrims visit Notre-Dame-de-la-Salette in Corps (Isère) throughout the year, as the Virgin Mary is said to have

appeared to two young shepherds there in September 1846. The 15 August celebrations are very well attended, when a large crowd makes the ascent to the shrine on foot or by car.

Woodcutting

Felling and chopping up a tree is a skill that requires a good deal of practice. Experienced participants compete in local woodcutting contests on 13 and 14 July at Allevard (Isère), on the third and fourth Sunday in July at Villard-de-Lans (Isère), and on the first Sunday in August at Aillon-le-Jeune (Savoie). At Saint-Pierre-de-Chartreuse (p.179), in the third week of July, sculptors are given just five days to create a work of art from a single tree trunk.

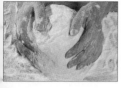

Bread

From May to August, the delicious smell of freshly baked bread fills the village streets. Local communities organise festivals where all types of bread are available for tasting, as well as cooked meats and charcuterie. Visit the bread festivals in La Plagne and

Échelles (Savoie) in July, and La Grave (Isère), Crest-Voland and Saint-Jean-de-Maurienne (Savoie) in August.

Cheese festivals

Every two years, in April, Saint-Marcellin celebrates its cheese with a procession of cows in fancy dress and stands offering cheese tastings. The next one is scheduled for 2002, but if you miss it and can't wait until 2004, console yourself with a visit to the Reblochon festival at La Clusaz (mid-August), the Beaufort festival at Saisies (15 August) or the Tomme festival at Cusy, in Haute-Savoie (October).

Apples and pears

The climate at altitude gives flavour and firmness to many varieties of apples and pears: sweet Golden Delicious, juicy Melrose, crunchy Idared, fine-grained Passe-Crassane and delicious Conference. From La Combe de Savoie to Albanais, 10,000 tonnes of apples and pears are produced in Savoie and Haute-Savoie every year. To sample the harvest, pay a visit to the autumn festivals – the orchard festival at Boussy and Rumilly (Haute-Savoie) in October, Saveurs de l'Épine (tastes of pine) at La Motte-Servolex (Savoie) and the apple festival at Annecy (Haute-Savoie) in November. In summer, locally grown fruit is sold directly from the cooperatives.

GRENOBLE NUT FESTIVAL

The Grenoble nut festival takes place every two years at Vinay (p.160), with producers of nut oils, wines, confectioners (selling delicious nut cake) and cabinet-makers exhibiting and selling their wares. The main attraction is the demonstration of hulling or breaking open the shell and extracting the nut – not as easy as you might think if you don't have a nut-cracker to hand! Start practising now for the next festival, in November 2002.

Good food and gourmet specialities

Cheese, ravioli, ham, special cakes – all these local delicacies can be found on the region's menus or purchased directly from the producers, who will show you how they are made. Gourmets will relish a farmhouse tea, a high-altitude supper or an extravagant banquet.

Good food

1. **Aiguille du Midi:** '3842' restaurant p.**128**

2. **Col des Annes:** La Cheminée (farm-inn) p.**123**

3. **Bourdeau:** Lamartine inn p.**137**

4. **La Chambotte:** La Chambotte restaurant and brasserie p.**136**

5. **Chamonix-Mont Blanc:** Maison Carrier p.**127**

6. **La-Chapelle-d'Abondance:** Les Cornettes restaurant p.**102**

7. **La Compôte:** Châtelain café-restaurant p.**140**

8. **Feissons-sur-Isère:** Château de Feissons restaurant p.**149**

9. **Hauteluce:** Colombe châlet p.**143**

10. **Megève:** Fermes de Marie hotel-restaurant p.**124**

11. **Mens:** Terre Vivante (organic food) p.**171**

12. **Morzine:** La Chamade restaurant p.**105**

13. **Oz:** L'Auberge p.**173**

14. **Pinsot:** Gleyzin farming inn p.**177**

15. **Saint-Hugues:** Brévardière farm-inn p.**180**

16. **Samoëns:** La Fandioleuse restaurant p.**108**

17. **Thonon-les-Bains:** Le Prieuré restaurant p.**111**

18. **Vienne:** La Pyramide restaurant p.**183**

Supper in the Alps

19. **Barbossine:** *soupe au caillou* (vegetable soup) p.**103**

RHÔNE-ALPES

Ain

Lyon

La Tour-du-Pin

Chambéry

Vienne

Isère

Drôme

Grenoble

Farmhouse teas

20 Megève: Calvaire farming inn **p.124**

27 Saint-Joseph-de-Rivière: Plantimay farm **p.179**

28 Thonon-les-Bains: Daniel Boujon dairy **p.110**

Delicatessens and pasta

29 Le Grand-Bornand: Bozon-Liaudet charcuterie **p.123**

30 Saint-Jean-en-Royans: Les Ravioles à l'Ancienne (traditional ravioli) **p.163**

Oil and culinary herbs

31 Chanaz: Nut oils and hazelnut jam **p.136**

32 Chatte: Nut oil **pp.160-161**

33 Le Noyer: Herbal teas, culinary herbs and medicinal herbs **p.141**

Sweet things

34 Annecy: Meyer chocolate factory **p.115**

35 Mieussy: Briffes honey **p.106**

36 Voiron: Bonnat chocolate **p.178**

37 Yenne: 'Au véritable gâteau de Savoie' (Savoyard patisserie) **p.137**

Museums

38 La Côte-Saint-André: Chocolate musuem **p.159**

39 Saint-Marcellin: Cheese museum **p.160**

Gourmet trails

40 Belledonne: Belledonne farm trail **p.177**

41 Chartreuse: Gourmet trail **p.179**

42 Sud-Grésivaudan: Gourmet trail **p.161**

Cheese

21 Aillon-le-Jeune: Val d'Aillon dairy **p.138**

22 Beaufort: Beaufortain milk cooperative **p.142**

23 La Clusaz: GAEC Les Confins dairy **p.122**

24 Mieussy: Hauts-Fleury dairy **p.107**

25 Morzine: Alpage dairy **p.104**

26 Pinsot: Gleyzin farm-inn **p.177**

Map labels

SWITZERLAND
Lake Geneva (Lac Léman)
Thonon-les-Bains
Haute-Savoie
Bonneville
Geneva
Grand Mont Ruan 3,047 m (9,994 ft)
A9
A40
Arve
A41
Annecy
Lac d'Annecy
N508
Arly
Albertville
A43
Mont Blanc 4,807 m (15,766 ft)
Isère
Savoie
Pointe de la Grande Casse 3,852 m (12,634 ft)
Arc
Saint-Jean-de-Maurienne
Tunnel du Fréjus
ITALY
La Meije 3,983 m (13,064 ft)
N91
N90
Hautes-Alpes
Gap

Cheeses
made in rich mountain pastures

Because of the difficulty of communications in the mountains, cheeses needed to keep for a long time and had to be easy to transport. As a result, the region specialises in pressed, compact cheeses, which have become hugely popular. Today, the correct production of cheese is still an art. In dark and silent cellars, the cheeses are washed, scrubbed, salted and turned, and left to mature for several weeks or even months on end.

Cattle and dairies

Four cheeses from the northern Alps have AOC or *Appellation d'Origine Contrôlée* status:

Sassenage-Vercors blue (awarded AOC in 1998), Abondance (1990), Beaufort (1968), and Reblochon (1958). Quality control means that production is limited and the cows are fed only on hay and grass. The producers of Saint-Marcellin (p.160) and Chevrotin des Aravis (p.122) have applied for their AOC. A cheese may be described as *fermier*, or 'from the farm', when the farmer uses the milk from his own cattle, and *laitier*, or 'from the dairy', when a cooperatives uses milk from a variety of different sources. The various cheeses are identified by a stamp made from casein (milk protein) in a particular shape and colour.

Reblochon

The name of this famous cheese is thought to originate from the word *rablassé*, which means 'stolen' in local dialect. The landowners, lords or monks, who rented out the Alpine pastures demanded payment in kind,

COWBELLS

The cowbells worn around the cows' necks (known as *clarines* in some regions) are forged from steel and coated with a layer of bronze. They can weigh as much as 3.5 kg/8 lb and the production of the larger cowbells is a complex affair, reflected in the cost, which can be as high as €380. The last remaining manufacturer of cowbells in the French Alps is based in Chamonix. Gérard Devouassoud only deals with local farmers at present, but plans to open his factory and shop to the public in 2002.

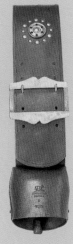

Blue blood

Some rare blue cheeses are naturally blue-veined, including the Aravis and Haute-Tarentaise goat's cheeses and Ternignon cheese (made from cow's milk). There are only five local producers of these cheeses, which are made in the Alpine pastures from June to September only.

Pedigree cows

In Savoy, cows are small, sure-footed and have an impressive pedigree. The Tarine or Tarentaise cows can be recognised by the distinctive black markings around the eyes. The sturdy-legged

calculated according to the quantity of milk produced by the grazing cows. The farmers would carry out a first, incomplete milking for the purposes of measurement, and then would make Reblochon cheeses for their own consumption with milk from a second, unofficial milking. Reblochon is mainly produced in the Thônes region (p.122), in a flat disc shape 13-14 cm/ 5-6 in diameter, weighing around 500 gm/18 oz. It must be matured in cellars for at least two weeks.

On the cheese board

Abondance cheese, promoted by the monks of Abondance (p.102), can weigh 7-12 kg/ 15-25 lb and is produced only in Haute-Savoie. Beneath an amber crust, the cheese is ivory-yellow in colour, with a nutty flavour. Beaufort cheese is produced in the Beaufortain, Maurienne, Tarentaise and Arly valleys. Nicknamed 'the prince of Gruyères' (p.143), it is a mighty cheese, weighing in at 20-70 kg/45-155 lb. The blue cheese of Sassenage-Vercors (Isère), revived by a dozen farms and dairies, weighs 4-4.5 kg/9-10 lb, and

has a sharp, tangy flavour. You can taste it at the Maison du Bleu (house of blue cheese) in Lans-en-Vercors.

The 'Brother in grey'

Tomme cheese was nicknamed '*compagnon en bure grise*' ('Brother in grey') because of the colour of its crust. In the past it was such a common feature of every peasant's evening meal that the word '*fromage*' came to be used to refer to any cheese that was not Tomme. Tomme (spelt 'Tome' in the Bauges, p.138) can be made from goat's milk or cow's milk, and is sometimes flavoured with a variety of ingredients such as white wine or Marc de Savoie (Savoyard liqueur).

Abondance cows are piebald red with markings around their eyes that resemble spectacles. They have been successfully bred for increased milk yield, and a heifer can fetch over €3,000 at auction.

Pork and charcuterie,
nothing goes to waste

I n the mountains there's an entire culture devoted to the pig. Pork in its various forms – such as smoked ham, sausages and salted bacon – guaranteed a year-round supply of meat for mountain-dwellers, who were cut off from the rest of the world during winter. The offal was eaten soon after slaughter, often fricasséd as in the local speciality *fricacha coffa* for example, and potatoes, polenta and *crozets* (a type of pasta) provided an excellent accompaniment to pork of any kind.

The '*caïon*'

Pork is a dominant flavour in mountain cooking. Smoked bacon was used to add flavour to soups, while joints of ham were hung to cure in the attic. Purchased in June when four or five

months old, fed on whey and left-over vegetables, the *caïon* (pig) would be slaughtered in November or December, when the moon was waxing – apparently the best time to obtain top-quality meat. The annual slaughter was an occasion for great feasting, and is still remembered by older inhabitants to this day.

Legendary dishes

Fricassée of *caïon* with *coffe* sauce – *fricacha coffa* – is a legendary dish that fuels the imagination of many French gourmets, but can also be a source of much disappointment. There's no standard way of cooking it, and among the extremely complicated recipes is one that involves using pieces of meat 'in poor condition', and another that requires intestines and loin chops to be simmered separately in Mondeuse wine. The *coffe* sauce (reduced *court-bouillon* and gravy) is added at the end. In Chablais (p.105), *atriaux*, or meatballs, are made with chopped leeks and celery, and herbs (usually chervil and sage).

A variety of sausages

Longeoles and *diots* are little pork sausages weighing around 200 g/7 oz. *Longeoles* have a distinctive flavour imparted by *carvi* (wild

MAGLAND SAUSAGE

Magland sausage may be on sale at the exclusive Parisian food shop of Fauchon, but everyone eats it all year round in the little village of Magland, between Cluses and Sallanches (Haute-Savoie). The smoked and dried sausage is much praised by gourmets, and can be preserved in oil, which softens it. But this means waiting for at least four months before eating it!

cumin), aniseed and fennel, and are slowly simmered in water. *Diots*, however, are simmered in white wine. Toasted cumin seeds are also used to flavour the

murçon sausage from La Mure, which is grilled or baked in the oven.

Herbs and herb-eaters

In the past *'mangeur d'herbes'* ('herb-eater') was used as an insult, meaning 'half-wit'. However, *herbes* (a term that included vegetables such as spinach, chard and leeks, as well as such herbs as chervil and sage) were always used in the tasty *pormoniers* of the Tarentaise and Beaufortain, and the *pormonaises* of Haute-Savoie. Roughly chopped

meat and vegetables were mixed together to make the dishes – the *pormonaise* was originally smoked (although this happens less frequently nowadays) and the smoky flavour was perfectly complemented by its accompaniment of quickly cooked green cabbage.

Traditional hams

It takes from nine months to a year for a traditional ham – known as *jambon 'à l'ancienne'* – to reach the table from the butcher. The meat is hand-rubbed with coarse Guérande salt, flavoured with wild thyme and other spices, and massaged to remove any trace of blood. The ham is then smoked over a wood fire (p.123) which gives it a

beautiful dark red colour, before being left to dry in an attic or drying shed, during which time it loses 50% of its weight.

Crozets

The *crozets* (tiny, greyish pasta shapes) found in the shops today are identical to the *crozets* that were eaten in the time of Louis XIV. Made from flour and buckwheat, they are an ideal accompaniment to pork products. Although they are small in size, they still need to be cooked for at least 30 minutes. Their name derives from the little indentation originally made into the dough with the thumb, to thin it. Allevard housewives would mark their *crozets* with a cross and in the Oisans, on the eve of 2 November, a dish of *crozets* was prepared and left outside on a windowsill for the dead, who were said to rise from their graves on that night.

Local dishes,
country cooking

T oday country cooking is very much in vogue, with top chefs and food critics talking about going back to their roots. The cooking of Savoie-Dauphiné, however, has always been country-style and is basic and nourishing, relying mainly on such ingredients as potatoes, milk and cheese. There are some surprising sweet and sour contrasts, however, such as bacon with dried fruit.

Medieval cuisine

There were two types of medieval cuisine – one for the rich, and one for the poor. Recorded in 1420, the recipes of Master Chiquart, cook at the court of Amadeus VIII of Savoy, are still impressive today (p.111). No doubt they helped to create a reputation for high living for the château of Ripaille, on the banks of Lake Geneva (p.110). The reality was rather different, however, since the lifestyle at Ripaille was somewhat frugal; and the châteaux of Thonon and Chambéry were actually the places for grand courtly feasting.

Herbs and spices

Amadeus VIII was a skilled diplomat who regularly held court; his cook was often required to prepare a feast for up to 1,500 guests at a time. No expense was spared, and costly imported ingredients such as saffron and vanilla were used unstintingly, as a symbol of status and a sign of wealth. Local spices were also important; wild cumin (*carvi*) was particularly suited to use with pork products. A pungent form of wild garlic (*ail des ours*), which has to be picked before it flowers, has recently been rediscovered and is extremely popular with modern chefs.

The humble potato

Potatoes were introduced to the Dauphiné at the end of the 16thC. and were referred to as *tartifle* in local dialect. The renowned *gratin Dauphinois*, consisting of potatoes baked in a rich cream sauce and flavoured with garlic, was a dish made for special occasions, worthy of its appearance on the menu at a 1788 reception hosted by the Count of Clermont-Tonnerre, Lieutenant-General of Dauphiné. Other variations of the dish include *gratin à la savoyarde*, using chicken stock, Tomme or Beaufort cheese, and *gratin du Vercors*, which may not feature either cheese or garlic, but is still extremely

creamy. The town of Autrans still uses the traditional recipe for the Vercors version.

Farçon or farci

Every village in every valley – even every housewife – has her own

Beaufortain, whereas in the Maurienne it is called *farci*.

A RECIPE FOR FARÇON

Ingredients:
1.5 kg/3 lb potatoes, 500 g/1 lb prunes, chopped 200 g/7 oz raisins, a handful of dried bilberries, a tbsp of flour, two eggs, salt, pepper, garlic, a glass of Marc de Savoie liqueur, a pinch of saffron (for colour), 30 rashers of streaky bacon, 100 g/3.5 oz butter.
Grease a mould with the butter and line with the bacon rashers. Grate the potatoes and mix with rest of the ingredients, then place in the mould. Cook in the oven in a bain-marie for 4 hours, ensuring that the water level remains constant.

recipe for this traditional Savoyard dish, a kind of mincemeat used as a stuffing. The ingredients (a list that may reach as high as 19) include potatoes (or bread), bacon, prunes, pears, raisins and eggs. The potatoes may be prepared in a variety of ways, pre-cooked, puréed or grated, and the cooking time may range from 30 minutes to 3 or 4 hours. This festive dish can also be eaten as a dessert, such as *farçon d'Arèges*, which was traditionally eaten lukewarm, after midnight mass at Christmas (p.142). The term *farçon* is used for the dish in the Tarentaise and

Fondues

Everybody thinks of fondue and *raclette* as authentic Savoyard specialities. However, these dishes, which have warmed many a skier and cheered up supper parties around the world, have their origins in Switzerland. Fondue comes from the French-speaking part of Switzerland, while *raclette* – melted Reblochon cheese served with boiled potatoes and cold meats – is from the Valais. One fondue dish does come from the region – *berthoud* (p.102), from the Chablais.

Sweets and desserts
Delicacies of the Alps

Gourmets will be in their element in the Alps, munching sweet specialities in a country café, drooling over the display in a patisserie shop window in Morzine, enjoying rhubarb tart in a fashionable restaurant, or tasting mountain honey straight from the hive, at a market, or as part of a country farmhouse tea. Chocolate lovers will love the tearooms of Chambéry, with their elegant panelled walls and mirrors.

An imperial gâteau

Gâteau de Savoie is a light, airy creation, made from beaten egg white, egg yolk, flour and sugar. It is thought to date from the reign of Amadeus VI (1343-83), the 'Green Count'. According to the stories, it was created by his chef, Pierre de Yenne (p.137), for a reception in Bourget, held in honour of

Charles IV, Emperor of Germany, who appointed Amadeus Vicar-General of the Empire.

Golden mountain honey

There are as many different varieties of honey in the Alps as there are beehives. Mountain honey gets its delicate flavours from the wildflowers found on the slopes, and is produced in an infinite variety of colours – white, tea-coloured, yellow and amber. The taste and colour depend on the type of nectar gathered by the bees, who visit many varieties of plants, from willow herb and golden potentilla, to blue thistle and pink rhododendron. The production of pine honey is a somewhat random affair, depending on the involuntary participation of greenfly, which penetrate the pine needles to drink the sap. The insect prefers very hot or stormy weather.

Rhubarb

Rhubarb has recently made a comeback, and is once more being grown in mountain kitchen gardens and used in traditional desserts such as stewed fruit or tarts (p.126). Only the stalks are edible, and after picking, the leaves

should be trimmed off and the stalks cut into 2-3 cm/ 1 in segments. The best time to pick rhubarb is in June, when the herds head back up to the mountain pastures.

For chocoholics

More than one local chocolate manufacturer goes by the name of 'Le Fidèle Berger' ('the faithful shepherd'), taken from the title of a heart-rending Baroque pastoral work

by Handel. Nearly all have a speciality, whether it be Chambéry truffles (p.145), Annecy roseaux (p.115), or slabs of chocolate from the Vercors (p.178). The recipes are all closely-guarded secrets.

The marvels of Morzine

Morzine is famed for its marvellous desserts, traditionally made to celebrate weddings and christenings. 'These must always be white in colour, to match the bride's dress or the robes of the infant', asserts local chef Thierry Thorens (p.105). This is not always an easy thing to accomplish when frying *bugnes*, a delicate and wonderfully light fritter.

Rissoles

Rissoles (*rézules* or *r'zules* in local dialect) were chiefly eaten during winter, from Christmas to the third Thursday in Lent. They are turnovers, made from shortcrust or puff pastry, and baked or fried. *Rissoles* can be filled with jam or stewed fruit (p.140). When available, Blosson pears are used, which are inedible when raw, but turn red when cooked. Another popular filling is made from small crab-apples known as *croésons*.

COLOMBIER GÂTEAU

In the graveyard of forgotten desserts lie such delights as *pets de nonne* ('nun's farts') – a type of fritter from Chamonix, *Mont-Blanc* (a chestnut-flavoured cone topped with cream) and *nichons,* a kind of dome-shaped meringue from Grésy-sur-Isère. The more agreeably named *colombier* (dove) cake has recently seen a revival in the Chambéry region. The cake is made to celebrate Whit Sunday, and consists of a biscuit base topped with almond paste and crystallized orange zest. A dove charm is slipped into each cake and, according to a local saying, whoever finds it will marry in the coming year.

Wines and spirits

The wines and spirits of Savoy include such classics as Roussette de Savoie, Apremont, Côtes-Rôties, Gentiane and Génépi, enough to tempt the palate of anyone who enjoys a drink. Here are some addresses not to miss, where a warm welcome is guaranteed.

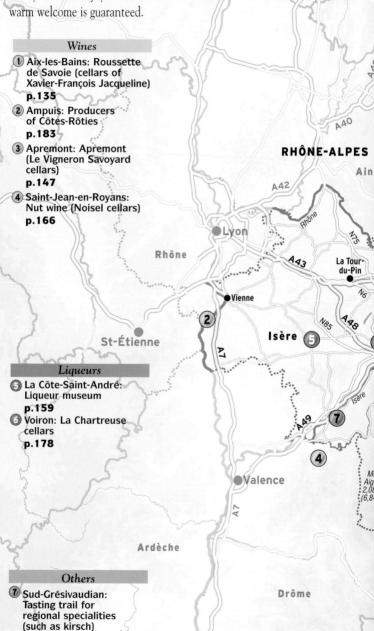

Wines

1. **Aix-les-Bains: Roussette de Savoie (cellars of Xavier-François Jacqueline)** p.135
2. **Ampuis: Producers of Côtes-Rôties** p.183
3. **Apremont: Apremont (Le Vigneron Savoyard cellars)** p.147
4. **Saint-Jean-en-Royans: Nut wine (Noisel cellars)** p.166

Liqueurs

5. **La Côte-Saint-André: Liqueur museum** p.159
6. **Voiron: La Chartreuse cellars** p.178

Others

7. **Sud-Grésivaudian: Tasting trail for regional specialities (such as kirsch)** p.161

RHÔNE-ALPES

Ain

A42

A40

A404

Rhône

N75

Lyon

Rhône

A43

La Tour-du-Pin

N6

Vienne

N85

A48

St-Étienne

A7

Isère

Isère

A49

Valence

A7

Ardèche

Drôme

Mo
Aigu
2,08
(6,84

**Wines of Chautagne
and Jongieux**

Seyssel, Frangy, Chautagne,
Jongieux, Marestel,
Monthoux

**Wines of the Geneva
and Arve valleys**

Marin, Ripaille, Marignan,
Crépy, Ayze

Lake Geneva
(Lac Léman)

Thonon-
les-Bains

SWITZERLAND

Grand Mont
Ruan
3,047 m
(9,994 ft)

Jura

Geneva

Bonneville

Arve

**Haute-
Savoie**

Annecy

Lac
d'Annecy

N508

Arly

Mont
Blanc
4,807 m
(15,766 ft)

Tunnel

Lac du
Bourget

Albertville

Chambéry

N90

Savoie

Isère

ITALY

Arc

Pointe de
la Grande Casse
3,852 m (12,634 ft)

Arc

Saint-Jean-
de-Maurienne

Grenoble

A43

Tunnel
du Fréjus

A32

La Meije
3,983 m
(13,064 ft)

N91

Wines of la Combe de Savoie

Monterminod, Apremont,
Abymes, Saint-Jeoire-
Prieuré, Chignin, Chignin-
Bergeron, Arbin, Cruet,
Montlélian, Saint-Jean-de-
la-Porte

**Hautes-
Alpes**

Gap

**PROVENCE-ALPES-
CÔTE D'AZUR**

0 10 20 30 40 50 Km

0   10   20   30
miles

Savoyard wines,
the taste of the country

The wines of Savoy are virtually unknown to the rest of the world – 80% are consumed within the region itself, when they are young. The Mondeuse, Chignin-Bergeron and Roussette wines do age well, however. Follow the little paths that wind through the vineyards around Chambéry – they are at their most picturesque in autumn when the leaves are changing colour. Right in the middle of the vineyards are the *sartots*, or cabins, where the pressing is carried out.

Whites and reds

From 2,000 ha/4,940 acres of vines, Savoie and Haute-Savoie produce more white wine (around 100,000 hl/ 2,650,000 gallons) than red (25,000-30,000 hl/ 660,500-792,500 gallons). This a fairly recent development, however, dating back to the 1970s. The Romans preferred Allobrogian wine, which took its name from the Celtic population who used to live in the area around Geneva, Grenoble and Vienne. This wine is thought to be the forerunner of Côtes-Rôties (p.183) or Mondeuse wine.

Vines of the region

Of around 20 types of vine planted in the region, two are indigenous to the Combe de Savoie, on the outskirts of

Chambéry: the Jacquère vine produces white wine such as Apremont (p.147), with hints of lime, honeysuckle and fern, and makes a delicious apéritif.

The other local grape, the Mondeuse, produces robust reds, with undertones of violet, pepper, caramel and myrtle. The Arbin Mondeuse is the most famous.

Wine cellars

Sciez, near Thonon-les-Bains (Haute-Savoie), has the oldest cellar in Savoy. It's a beautiful sight, with walls over 2 m/ 6.5 ft thick and old oak beams. According to its current proprietor, Bernard Canelli-Suchet, the cellar dates from 1000 AD. This is actually believable because this ancient fortress, known as the Tour de Marignan, was a dependency of the Abbey of

Filly, established in 930 AD, where the monks clearly knew a thing or two about winemaking.

Wine on the rocks

Marestel wine, produced on the slopes of the Chat mountain, near Aix-les-Bains and Jongieux, takes its name from Claude Mareste, who was adviser to Emmanuel-Philibert, a 16th-C. Duke of Savoy. At the time it was known as the 'table wine of princes'. The Altesse vine was also renowned. Originally from Cyprus, it produces a highly rated, elegant white wine. Today pneumatic drills are used to replant vines on the high, rocky slopes.

High-altitude vineyards

At Marin, near Thonon-les-Bains, some vines are grown up the tall trunks of dead chestnut trees. During the grape harvest in September the grape pickers have to use ladders that are 6 m/20 ft high. The method was probably

introduced from northern Italy by demobilised soldiers returning from the Napoleonic Wars. There used to be as many as 5,000 such vines in

the region, but today only around 150 remain, and the wine that is produced from them is used for local consumption only.

Happy marriages

The wines from the banks of Lake Geneva – Crépy, Ripaille, Marin and Marignan – make an ideal accompaniment to the many varieties of freshwater fish found in the lakes. Another good combination is a Chautagne (Gamay red) with charcuterie and *diots* (sausages). Game and red meat go well with Mondeuse grape varieties such as Arbin and Cruet. As for dessert wines, follow the Savoyards' example and choose a sparkling Ayze.

READING A LABEL

The bottle, also known as a *savoyarde*, should bear a cross of Savoy on its 'shoulder' and the label should confirm that the wine has AOC (*Appellation d'Origine Contrôlée*) status, if this is the case. There are four AOC Savoyard wines: Vin de Savoie, mainly from the Chambéry region; Roussette de Savoie, from the shores of Lake Bourget; Seyssel, from both the Ain and Haute-Savoie regions, and Crépy, from the shores of Lake Geneva. After the AOC the grape variety, of which there are 22, is mentioned, for example, 'Vin de Savoie', followed by 'Apremont' or 'Arbin' or 'Ayze', or 'Roussette de Savoie', followed by 'Marestel'. 'Mondeuse' sometimes appears in large letters, but it is in fact a grape variety. As for the vin de pays d'Allobrogie, this is a modest table wine, but very drinkable none the less.

Distilleries and liqueurs,

secret recipes and medicinal elixirs

The herbs and plants of the Alps have been used for centuries to make elixirs and liqueurs. This is a world of well-guarded recipes using secret, natural ingredients, distilled in temporary stills. The elixirs now enjoyed as apéritifs were originally intended for medicinal purposes, and the recipes are regarded as the 'province of the angels' – one abbot would reveal no more than that they are 'a traditional mixture of aromatic plants and alcohol'.

Old wives' remedies

The Nord-Dauphiné was often referred to as the 'garden of the apothecaries of Lyons', and every family had a herb cupboard. The plants were picked seasonally, following a strict calendar which even specified the time of day – flowers at the summer solstice, roots and rhizomes at nightfall. Only women were allowed to prepare and administer the remedies, hence the saying 'old wives' remedies'. Some preparations are still in use today, such as expectorant herbal teas made from infusions of white stock, marshmallow, mallow or violet.

Secrets of the cloisters

Monks excelled in the production of liqueurs for a number of reasons. They understood Greek and Latin, and could therefore draw upon the botanical knowledge of antiquity. They tended herb gardens, where the cultivation of 88 species of medicinal plants was recommended, including those such as aniseed, foxglove, fennel, mint and lemon balm. The Grand Chartreuse elixir (p.178), which was 71° proof, was sold in the markets of Grenoble and Chambéry as a universal panacea. Officially for purging worms, it could also be taken for fainting fits, asphyxia, 'women's troubles' and fever, amongst other complaints.

MOUNTAIN LIQUEUR

Each family in the region has its own recipe for *génépi* liqueur (absinthe), as well as its own secret spots for picking this dwarf plant that belongs to the *artemisia* family. The plant, which grows at high altitude in only the most inaccessible places, is harvested, then steeped in brandy for 40 days along with 40 cubes of sugar to every 40 sprigs of *génépi* (as few as 25 cubes is acceptable, however). The end product is an aromatic liqueur, greenish-yellow in colour.

Famous old elixirs

The museum of liqueurs (p.159) at La-Côte-Saint-André (Isère), in the region famous for *Ratafia* (cherry liqueur), is a reminder of the days when liqueurs with names such as the 'milk of old age' and 'perfect love' were enjoyed. Barthélemy Rocher (1645-1747) called his first medicinal elixir *'Eau de la Côte'* (coastal water), and the local bandit chief Mandrin is known to have requested it on his deathbed in 1755. Mont-Corbier liqueur, from Saint-Jean-de-Maurienne, is still relatively in its adolescence – it was invented by Abbot Guille as recently as 1888.

'Arise and walk!'

At Pralognan-la-Valoise (Savoie), Gentian liqueur goes by the nickname of 'arise and walk', a reference to its supposed powers to bring the dead back to life. At 50-55° proof, with a distinctive bitter

Dent d'Oche distillery

taste, it's not surprising that it has this reputation. The liqueur is generally given as a gift, or drunk at home or among friends. It's made from the roots of yellow gentian, *Gentiana lutea*, a plant of exceptional longevity (as long as 50 years), which grows at up to 2,500 m/8,200 ft. To produce 1 litre/2 pints of alcohol, 80 kg/175 lb of roots are required, and these have to be dug up at the end of the year.

The travelling stills

In the winter, travelling distillers such as Jean-Baptiste Dupraux or François Baud (better known as *François-de-la-Goutte*, or 'François of the drop') visit the Abondance and Aulps valleys. They turn up without warning, but as a thousand different aromas permeate the air, the village soon knows that the still has arrived. All kinds of fruit – apples, plums and William pears – are distilled, even pine cones. Crushed, fermented fruit is distilled to make brandy, which is then taken home. The client pays the distiller by the litre, on delivery.

Architectural heritage

Little villages pepper the Alpine slopes, while convents and fortresses cling to rocky outcrops high in the mountains. There's plenty of architectural interest to discover in the northern Alps, from rustic churches to lavish Baroque altarpieces, medieval cities and spa towns.

0   10   20   30   40   50 Km

0   10   20   30
                        miles

Pretty villages

1. Bonneval-sur-Arc
   and the hamlet of Ecot
   p.155
2. La Compôte
   p.139
3. Conflans
   p.148
4. Pont-en-Royans
   p.167
5. Samoëns and the hamlet
   of Chantemerle
   p.109
6. Villard-Reculas
   p.175

Old towns

7. Chambéry
   pp.144-146
8. Chamonix-Mont Blanc
   pp.126-127
9. Crémieu
   p.156
10. Grenoble
    pp.168-169
11. Mens
    p.171
12. Montmélian
    p.147
13. La Roche-sur-Foron
    p.121
14. Vienne
    pp.182-183

Belle Époque architecture

15. Aix-les-Bains:
    Palaces, Astoria hotel,
    Grand Cercle casino
    pp.132-133
16. Évian-les-Bains:
    The old Cachat pump
    room and town hall
    pp.112-113

Châteaux

17. Annecy:
    Palais de l'Île and
    château d'Annecy
    pp.114-115
18. Le Bourget-du-Lac:
    Château Thomas II
    of Savoy
    p.137

RHÔNE-ALPES

Jura

Ain

Rhône

Lyon

Rhône

La Tour-
du-Pin

Chambéry

Vienne

Isère

Grenoble

Valence

Mont
Aiguille
2,086 m
(6,842 ft)

Drôme

Picture-postcard chalets

Boudin-en-Beaufortain, 'the land of a thousand chalets'

The Savoyard chalets come straight out of a pretty postcard, with wooden balconies (*galeries* or *loges*) laden with geraniums or begonias, honey-coloured walls, scorched by the sun, and russet-brown or moss-covered roofs, they perch dramatically on the green slopes of the mountains and foothills of the Alpine region. But, however charming their appearance, the chalets are also extremely practical places to live.

A place of work and an animal shelter

The word 'chalet' was originally imported from Switzerland. In Savoy, there were only two types of dwelling – mountain shelters and village houses. Houses were built using any material available – wood, stone, sandstone rock from Chablais, or *cargnieule* (a type of tufa or limestone) from the Maurienne. They were planned according to the lie of the mountain slope and the direction of the sun, protected from the rigours of the winter by thick walls and openings that were kept as small as possible. The chalet was primarily a place of work, where the majority of the space was handed over to the animals and their fodder – every winter, three tons of hay needed to be stored per head of cattle.

Spruce or larch roof tiles?

In the Aravis mountains (p.122) and in the Beaufortain region (p.142), farmhouses

Wooden roof of spruce tiles

retain their wooden roofs, with spruce or larch tiles. The difference lies essentially in the size – spruce tiles are 70-90 cm/25-35 in, whereas

larch tiles are half this size. But the difference in size is not immediately apparent as the rows of spruce tiles are not nailed down but overlapped. Larch tiles are particularly appropriate for areas exposed to damp winds. Chartreuse-style houses (p.178) have four-sided roofs of overlapping planks of larch or other wood, known as *essendoles*.

Slate roofs

A revival in the use of traditional materials has led to an increasing demand for slate, which has been good for the business of the Morzine slate-quarry workers (p.104).

Slate is quarried in galleries up to 300 m/980 ft deep in the cold and damp Séraussaix cliffs, where the temperature is a constant 7°C/45°F. The slate-quarry worker emerges from these tomb-like

box beds against one wall, under which there was space for housing the sheep and goats. The cows and the manger were against another wall, and a waste channel ran down the centre of the room.

conditions into the fresh mountain air, and uses his skills to cut between four and six tiles from each piece of slate.

Protection against the elements
In Haute-Maurienne, particularly at Bessans, the old houses are half-buried in the ground for maximum protection against the elements. In winter, both the inhabitants and their beasts would take refuge in the cellar. This single room had

Traditional fireplaces
In the northern Alps, some farms still have their traditional fireplace, a huge pyramid-shaped wooden structure, occupying an area of up to 6 sq m/65 sq ft. The flue could be opened or closed as required. These fireplaces are no longer used for cooking but they are still occasionally used for smoking ham.

Finding a safe place
Salted meat, butter stored in *toupines*, or pots (p.65), summer clothes, seeds, official documents – anything and everything that was of any value and needed to be protected, particularly from rodents and fire (which was

LONG WINTER NIGHTS
Winter evenings were often spent in the warmth of the cowsheds, which helped to save on fuel. The neighbours would be invited round and young men and women could enjoy each other's company. Everyone helped with the tasks, such as shelling and crushing nuts for oil, or stripping the bark from hemp (which was cultivated up until the 20thC.), telling jokes or ghost stories as they worked.

always a threat) – was taken up to the attic, or to the *mazot*, a miniature windowless hut, separate from the main chalet, and secured with sturdy padlocks.

Mountain strongholds
under threat of war

Esseillon fortress (Fort Charles-Félix)

From the 16thC. to the end of the 19thC., Savoy, which was under Italian rule until 1860, and Dauphiné, which belonged to France, both undertook the construction of huge, impenetrable fortresses to ensure the safety of their borders. Few of these buildings ever saw service, but today they provide hikers with magnificent views across the Alpine valleys.

The Maurienne frontier

Numerous fortifications – 42 in total – sprang up in the Maurienne in the 19thC. This region, used as a buffer between France and Italy, was used to being on the defensive. Before the outbreak of World War II, an 'Alpine Maginot line' was constructed along the complete length of the Maurienne valley. Like its counterpart in the north,

it would prove to be of no practical use. Located between Modane and Aussois, the fortress of Saint-Gobin is another example of this defence system. However, the stone forts of Esseillon are much more impressive, spreading out over an area covering several hundred metres (p.153).

A well-protected pass

The Mont Cenis stronghold, perched at a height of over 2,000 m/6,500 ft between France and Italy, witnessed

Ronce fortres.

Esseillon fortress (The Marie-Thérèse redoubt)

Variselle fortress

the passage of many armies, including those of Charlemagne and Napoleon. At the end of the 19thC., tension between France and Italy was such that, fearing the worst, the French built the fort at La Turra and then Montfroid. The Italians meanwhile, were similarly occupied – Variselle, La Cassa, Malamot, Pattacreuse and the Ronce fortress were all built over a period of 20 years. Perched on a promontory opposite Lake Clair, the Ronce site can be reached with a walk of 30 minutes or so (p.154).

Séré de Rivières

Perched above Bourg-Saint-Maurice, at 2,000 m/6,560 ft, the fort of La Platte, built between 1892 and 1894, illustrates the defence system conceived by General Séré de Rivières. The fort, perfectly adapted to the terrain, lies on a ridge opposite the Petit-Saint-Bernard pass, providing a viewpoint for observing troop movements, which enabled the defenders to prevent enemies from entering the access routes to Haute-Tarentaise. In the Tarentaise, the 'ruined redoubt' above Montvalezan is another outpost set on a ridge, using Séré de Rivières' system. It was reinforced just before World War II and played a vital role in the battle of the Alps in 1940.

Fort Barraux

Between Isère and Savoie, this defensive bastion was built right at the end of the 16thC.

by Charles-Emmanuel of Savoy. The duke had little regard for the legitimacy of borders and chose a location that was actually in France, at Barraux. As soon as the fort was completed, the Duke of Lesdiguières reclaimed it for the French king, Henri IV. With its barracks, arsenal, chapel and cesspit, Barraux was revamped by the military engineer Vauban in the 17thC., and remains a superb example of military architecture to this day.

Grenoble's Bastille

This building was designed by the Duke of Lesdiguières, governor

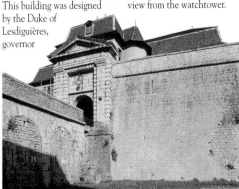

of Dauphiné from the end of the 16thC. to the beginning of the 17thC. The great military architect Vauban was unimpressed, and the fortified site was eventually restored by General Haxo in the 19thC. Today you can take a very pretty walk among ramparts, fortifications, ditches and ladders from the Bastille in the direction of Grenoble (the site can be reached by a cable-car, built in 1934 and renovated in 1976, p.169). Visit the fort of Saint-Eynard at Sappey-en-Chartreuse, on the outskirts of Grenoble, for the magnificent view from the watchtower.

DISCOVER SAVOY'S FORTS

Not content with the 'Baroque trails', for which the organisation is famous, the *Fondation pour l'Action Culturelle en Montagne* (FACIM), an active cultural association, has turned its attention to Savoy's fortifications, creating 18 themed discovery trails known as '*Pierres fortes de Savoie*' undertaken with the close attention of a trained guide. Some of these are particularly suitable for children, such as the treasure trail at fort Tamié, where the participants can join forces in a hunt for 'secret documents'. For a brochure and further information contact FACIM ☎ 04 79 96 74 37.

Abbeys and monasteries,
peace and tranquillity

O ver a period of less than 20 years, between the end of the 11thC. and the beginning of the 12thC., three monastic orders – Carthusians, Antonians (Dominicans) and Chalaisians (no longer in existence) – were founded in Isère. In search of isolation and tranquillity, they sought to build their monasteries in stark, unwelcoming terrain, amid impressive landscapes high in the mountains, where they could feel close to God.

Notre-Dame d'Aulps

The Grande Chartreuse

In 1084, seven shabbily-dressed men arrived at the door of Hugues, Bishop of Grenoble. Originally from Germany, Bruno and his companions had come in search of a place in which to live in solitude as hermits. Inspired by a vision, Hugues led them to a dark forest, located a few miles from Grenoble, which had a mysterious atmosphere – the Chartreuse valley. It was here

that the Grande Chartreuse, the first Carthusian monastery, was built (p.178). Two years later, Hugues blessed the monastery and the Carthusian order was established.

Carthusian monasteries

There are around 20 Carthusian monasteries world-wide. In the Alps, further Carthusian monasteries were built, such as Saint-Hugon in the Belledonne mountains, a dependency of the Grande Chartreuse in the 12thC. The remains of this ancient monastery today house part of a Tibetan centre. At Taninges, the monastery

built by Béatrice de Faucigny is a venue for concerts and exhibitions (p.106). At Aravis, the Carthusian monastery of Reposoir has maintained its beautiful buildings thanks to careful restoration work (p.123).

The Franciscans

Founded by St Francis of Assisi in Italy in the 13thC., the Franciscan Order practises a life of poverty. In the Musée Savoisien de Chambéry (Savoyard museum of

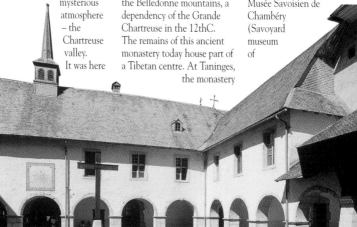

La Chartreuse du Reposoir

Chambéry, p.144), housed in one of the first Franciscan monasteries to be established in France in around 1220 AD, you'll find that peace still reigns in the beautiful cloister with its original arches, and in some of the rooms, such as the chapterhouse, refectory and upper gallery of the cloister.

The order of St Anthony

Nobody would have heard of the village of La Motte-au-Bois if a certain Frenchman had not brought back the relics of St Anthony on his return from the Crusades in 1070. A church was built to house and protect the sacred bones, and to give pilgrims a

place to worship. An almshouse was built to treat the sick, and the hospital Order of St Anthony was born. The monks specialised in the treatment of *mal des ardents* (ergot), a poisoning of the blood caused by eating contaminated rye. The ancient abbey (renamed Sainte-Antoine-l'Abbaye) still stands on its promontory overlooking the village (p.160).

The Benedictines

The Order of St Benedict sought inaccessible locations. At Domène (in the Isère) the old priory lies in ruins, but two distinct types of architecture can still be identified – Roman and Gothic. At Talloires, the ancient Benedictine abbey has been converted into a luxury hotel. The convent of Notre-Dame-de-Chalais, near Voreppe, has been taken over by the Dominicans.

SILENCE

Silence is golden in the Carthusian order, and in order to encourage solitude each monk has his own two-storey cell and a little garden. Meals

are taken alone, served through a hatch in the wall of each cell. At the end of the day, at Vespers, and at the midnight service, the monks assemble for prayers. You can visit the cloisters of the Grande Chartreuse (p.179) and discover their domestic and spiritual life for yourself.

The Cistercians

This order, founded in the 11thC., adhered strictly to the rules of the Benedictines, which had been founded centuries earlier. The splendour of their churches lies in their architectural simplicity, with a single nave and minimal adornment. The abbey of Léoncel (p.166), built at the foot of the Vercors mountains, is a magnificent example of this simple, understated elegance.

Léoncel

The abbey of Tamié, built on the mountain slope, has lost its Romanesque character, as have the ancient Benedictine

abbey of Hautecombe (p.137) and Notre-Dame d'Aulps (p.105), which are predominantly Gothic.

The Augustinians

Abondance, Sixt-Fer-à-Cheval and Entremont are three abbeys founded by the Augustinian Order, whose monks were inspired by the prolific writings of St Augustine.

The abbey of Abondance is the most interesting of the three, with its splendid cloister housing some beautiful 15th-C. paintings (p.102).

Family outings

Children can be safely introduced to rafting or venturing on to the glaciers.
They can enjoy learning about Alpine flora and fauna, or the secrets of
cheese-making, and should have plenty to talk about when they get back
to school.

Sporting activities

1. **Aussois: Fort Victor-Emmanuel** *via ferrata*
   p.153
2. **Autrans: Cross-country skiing (January)**
   p.163
3. **Bourg-Saint-Maurice: Rafting**
   p.150
4. **Megève: Pony rides**
   p.125
5. **Saint-Gervais-les-Bains: Ice-skating rink**
   p. 130
6. **Samoëns: Rafting**
   p.109
7. **Sëez: Adventure playground**
   p.151
8. **La Toussuire: Mountain biking**
   p.155

Leisure parks

9. **Autrans: Adventure park**
   p.164
10. **Les Avenières: Walibi adventure park**
    p.157
11. **Montalieu-Vercieu: Vallée Bleue leisure park**
    p.157

Nature trails

12. **Argentières: Glaciers**
    p.129
13. **Chambéry: Galerie Eurêka (Jean-Jacques Rousseau exhibition)**
    p.146
14. **Megève: Grouse trail**
    p.125

Festivals and entertainment

20 Aix-les-Bains:
Navig'Aix boating event
(end August, held every
2 years)
p.135

21 Vallée de l'Eau d'Oile:
Magic festival
(1st 2 weeks in August)
p.173

22 Le Grand-Bornand:
Children's festival
(last week in August)
p.123

23 Haute-Maurienne:
Astronomy festival
(2nd week in August)
p.154

24 Sciez: Aigles du Léman
(eagles in full flight)
p.111

Museums

25 Lans-en-Vercors:
Mechanical toys museum
p.162

26 Villard-de-Lans: museum
of *santons* (crib figures)
p.164

27 Viuz-en-Sallaz:
Peasant museum
p.107

Others

28 Aillon-le-Jeune:
Tour of Val d'Aillon
cheesemakers
p.138

29 Chatte: Miniature railway
p.161

30 Hauteluce: Baroque
churches and chapels
discovery trail
p.143

31 Megève:
Tea at Calvaire
farm-inn
p.124

32 Morzine: Ardoisière
des 7 Pieds slate quarry
p.105

15 Col des Montets:
Nature trail
p.129

16 Le Pin:
Fishing lessons and
discovering aquatic life
p.158

17 Pralognan-la-Valoise:
Glière forest nature
trail
p.149

18 Sallanches:
Mountain nature
centre
p.131

19 Villard-de-Lans:
Enchanted hideaway
p.164

The French Alps in detail

Isère   156

Index   185

The French Alps in detail

The following pages contain all the information you need for finding your way around Savoie, Haute-Savoie and Isère. Each *département* has been given a different colour code for easy identification.

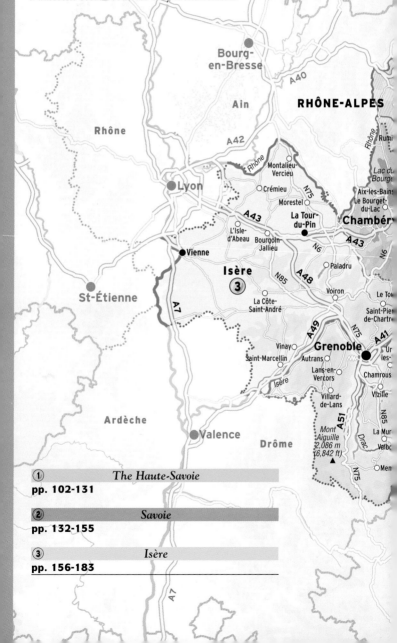

SWITZERLAND

Lausanne

Sion

Lake Geneva
(Lac Léman)
Évian-
les-Bains
Saint-
Gingolph
Thonon-
les-Bains
Yvoire
Abondance
Châtel
Saint-Jean-
d'Aulps
Grand Mont
Ruan
3,047 m
(9,994 ft)
Haute-
Savoie
Avoriaz
Morzine
neva
①
Annemasse
Taninges
Samoëns
Bonneville
La Roche-
sur-Foron
Sixt-Fer-
à-Cheval
Chamonix-
Mont-Blanc
Thonens-
Glières
Le Grand-
Bornand
Flaine
Saint-Gervais-
les-Bains
nnecy
La Clusaz
Menthon
Thônes
Megève
Tunnel
Mont Blanc
4,807 m
(15,766 ft)
rier
Talloires
Lac
d'Annecy
Ugine
N508
Les Saisies
Arly
Beaufort
Aoste
A5
Le Châtelard
La Compôte
Albertville
Bourg-
St-Maurice
La Rosière
Savoie
②
Arc
N90
Les Arcs
Isère
A3
Moûtiers
Tignes
La Plagne
ntmélian
Valmorel
Courchevel
Val-d'Isère
ITALY
Méribel
Bonneval-
sur-Arc
A43
vard
Pralognan-
la-Vanoise
Les Ménuires
Lanslebourg-
Mont-Cenis
Val-Thorens
Saint-Jean-
de-Maurienne
Arc
Modane
Valloire
Tunnel
du Fréjus
L'Alpe
d'Huez
N91
La Meije
3,983 m
(13,064 ft)
A32
Turin
ourg-
isans
La Bérarde
Hautes-
Alpes

PROVENCE-ALPES-
CÔTE D'AZUR

Gap

Alpes-de-
Haute-Provence

| 0 | 10 | 20 | 30 | 40 | 50 Km |

| 0 | 10 | 20 | 30 |
miles

Abondance valley

Apart from tourism, the chief source of revenue in this little valley is the famous Abondance breed of cow, described as 'bespectacled', because of the markings around its eyes. The Alpine surroundings of the valley – rushing streams and meadows dotted with wildflowers – are quite delightful.

Abondance

28 km (17 miles)
SE of Thonon-les-
Bains
Cloître de l'Abbaye Notre-Dame
☎ 04 50 81 60 54
Open daily, 10am-noon and 2-6pm; 5pm in winter. Closed mid-Oct. to mid-Dec.
Admission charge.
Guided tours available.
The paintings in the cloisters of the abbey of Notre-Dame are attributed to Giacomo Jaquerio (c. 1430), a Piedmontese painter popular at the court of Savoy. The paint was applied using a method known as tempera, in which the pigments were mixed with egg yolk diluted with water to produce a quick-drying, long-lasting paint. The principal subject is the Virgin Mary, but you'll also notice some Savoyard motifs in the background, including a ham curing in the fireplace.

La Chapelle-d'Abondance

6 km (4 miles)
NE of Abondance
Local fondue
Restaurant
Les Cornettes
☎ 04 50 73 50 24
Open daily exc. 20 Oct.-20 Dec.
Berthoud, a type of Savoyard fondue, has been made in this restaurant by the Trincaz family for four generations. The recipe is a simple one – rub a cast-iron fondue dish with garlic, add cubes of Abondance cheese, some Savoyard white wine, a dash of Madeira and heat in the oven until melted. Served with potatoes, cooked meats, and pickled chanterelle mushrooms, it's quite delicious.

L'Atelier de Théo
Rte des Freinets, Châtel
☎ 04 50 73 30 86
Open daily except Wed. and Sun., 10am-noon and 3-7pm.

These doves, carved in spruce with an Opinel knife, are a good luck charm. Their feathers are as fine as tissue paper, almost like lace. The carvings are never signed but experts can immediately recognise the work of particular craftsmen, among them members of the David family, where Jean-Pierre has taken over from his father Théo.

Spotcheck
D1

Things to do

Cloisters of Abondance abbey
Trout fishing
Supper in the alpine meadows

With children

La Belle Dimanche (festival)

Within easy reach

Morzine (p.104)
Thonon-les-Bains (p.110)

Tourist offices

Abondance: ☎ 04 50 73 02 90
Châtel: ☎ 04 50 73 22 44

Châtel and its surroundings

*6 km (4 miles) SE of
La Chapelle-d'Abondance*

Tickling trout
La Tanière
☎ 04 50 73 33 59
Open daily 8.30am-
12.30pm and 2-7.30pm;
1 May-15 June and 15
Sept.-end Dec. open daily
except Sun., 10am-noon
and 4-7pm.
Fishing permits on sale.
Abondance valley has over
85 km (55 miles) of streams
and rivers and the wild *fario*
trout (sometimes known as
'Mediterranean') has adapted
to mountain waters such as
the Chevenne and the Eau
Noire. The fishing season is
from the second weekend in
March to the second weekend
in October.

Blessing the herd

La Belle Dimanche
Plaine-Dranse
*9 km (6 miles) S of Châtel
penultimate/last Sun.
in Aug. Free admission.
Shuttle service from Châtel
or Pierre-Longue ski-lift
from Pré-de-la-Joux (5 km/
3 miles SW of Châtel).*

La Belle Dimanche ('beautiful
Sunday') festival has been
celebrated at Plaine-Dranse
for centuries. Age-old
traditions have been revived,
such as the blessing of
the herds and the
playing of Alpine
horns. There are
demonstrations by
rope-makers and
other regional
craftsmen,
along with
plenty of
Abondance cheeses
and local white wines
to be sampled.

Alpine supper
Barbossine
**Information from
Châtel tourist office**
*Admission charge with
guide. Departure from
Petit Châtel (1 km/
0.5 miles E of Châtel).*
Climb to the Alpine meadows
(1 hr 15 mins trip each way)
to enjoy a supper of such
specialities as *soupe au caillou*,
an ancient recipe using a stone
to press down the vegetables
during cooking, and a fruits of
the forest tart. The return trip
down the mountain is an
atmospheric journey lit by the
stars and a few torches.

Vacheresse

*10 km (6 miles)
N of Abondance*
Wood carving
**Philippe Bottollier-
Depois**

Écotex hamlet
☎ 04 50 73 10 27
Open daily except Sun.,
June-Sept. 10am-noon
and 3-7pm.
Free admission.
It was Philippe's grandfather
who taught him to carve his
first *rosace*, a sun symbol
thought to be Celtic in origin
and typical of Savoy. Philippe
now works in walnut and
spruce, carving wedding chests,
salt boxes and distaffs (for
threading wool), a traditional
engagement present. A little
museum above the workshop
houses his treasures.

Morzine,
slate country

Morzine, which lies close to the Swiss border, is said to have made its fortune from 'grey gold', or slate. At the beginning of the 20thC. there were 70 slate-workers here but today only a handful remain. The village, fed by the bubbling waters of the River Dranse, is very charming.

Quarry-owner's château
B&B at the Mas de la Coutettaz
Chemin de la Coutettaz
☎ 04 50 79 08 26
Closed 2nd week in May. This authentic quarry-owner's 'château', built in 1771, is one of the oldest houses in Morzine, and is located close to the church. There are five rooms available on a B&B basis, as well as a converted *mazot*, or miniature chalet. The house is built from stone, with a slate roof and still retains its original fireplace.

Mountain cheeses
L'Alpage
Av. Pied-de-La-Plagne
☎04 50 79 12 39
Tours Wed. and Thurs. at 9am.
Free admission.
After two years studying law, Nicolas Baud realised that he preferred the country life and

turned his hand to producing Tomme, Abondance and Reblochon cheeses. You can see him at work in his 'laboratory', underneath the family dairy, where he extends a warm welcome to all visitors.

Hand-made Savoyard pottery
La Poterie de Morzine
Shop on Rue du Bourg, studio in the hamlet of Mernaz
☎ 04 50 79 00 67
Shop open daily in season exc. Sun., 10am-12.30 and 3.30-7.30pm. Studio open in low season daily (exc. Sun.), 8.30-noon and 2-7pm.
Free admission to workshop.
Gérard Menu creates lovely traditional pottery suitable for

modern living, such as fondue plates that are safe to use in a microwave. Visitors to the studio are welcome to watch him throwing and finishing the pieces. The decoration is mostly in shades of blue, green and brown and includes simple, authentically Savoyard motifs, such as spots and stylised birds (p.65).

Mines d'Or lake

Migratory birds
Ornithological discovery trail
Information from
Maison de la Montagne
☎ 04 50 75 96 65
Depart from Mines d'Or lake (from centre, head E, Rte de la Manche, Nyon cable-car); from Bretolet pass head towards the research centre; change in altitude: 550 m (1,805 ft).

Five billion birds migrate from Europe in the autumn, and more than 10,000 fly over the Coux and Bretolet passes. A ringed quail was once traced all the way to Morocco, which means it made a journey of 2,062 km/1,281 miles. September is the ideal time of year to follow this signposted ornithological discovery trail, which takes around half a day.

Good food
La Chamade
La Crusaz
☎ 04 50 79 13 91
Open daily for lunch and dinner (phone out of season). Closed 3 weeks in May-June and Nov.-Dec.
Chef Thierry Thorens is a rising star who has worked at well-known restaurants in and Lyons. Enjoy some of his delicious traditional recipes from the Chablais, such as *atriaux* (made from chopped pig's liver, heart and kidneys) and *merveilles* (light fritters).

saint-Jean-d'Aulps
8 km (5 miles)
N. of Morzine
Saint Guérin's key
Notre-Dame d'Aulps
☎ 04 50 72 15 15
Guided tours May-Sept., Tues., Thurs., Sun. at 4pm (5pm in July-Aug.); mid-Dec. to mid-Apr. Fri. at 11am.
Admission charge.

Construction of this abbey-church was begun in 1138, and today its ruins include the western doorway, surmounted by a *rosace*, which still stands proudly facing the setting sun. Until 1792, it was the resting place of St Guérin, the patron saint and protector of horses, mules, and horned and woolly creatures. Before being driven to their summer pastures, the herds were brought here to be blessed by a touch of the reliquary, St Guérin's key.

Spotcheck
D1

Things to do
Notre-Dame-d'Aulps
L'Alpage dairy

With children
Ardoisière des 7 pieds
(slate workshop))
Bird-watching trail

Within easy reach
Châtel (p.103)
Taninges (p.106)

Tourist office
Morzine: ☎ 04 50 74 72 72

SLATE QUARRIES
Ardoisière des 7 Pieds (Franck Buet)
Les Meuniers (between the centre and the Avoriaz cable-car)
☎ 04 50 79 12 21
Tours Tues. and Fri. 10.30am and 5pm (summer), Fri. 11am (winter).
Admission charge.
Since 1734, slate has been quarried from the cliffs of Séraussaix, which dominate the Meuniers peaks. The slate is deep grey-blue with a bronze lustre that increases with age. A handful of quarries are still in operation, including Franck Buet's, whose workshop is open to the public. Children will find the visit fascinating.

Taninges, the rebellious valley

Viuz-en-Sallaz

Mieussy

Taninges

Flaine

Désert de Platé

The valleys of Giffre and Taninges, between Lake Geneva and Mont Blanc, have often been shaken by revolution. The uprisings were usually directed at the counts of Savoy, who won back the Faucigny region in 1355. The spirit of rebellion is still alive in the valley, celebrated by the 'Jacquemard Baptism' held every June.

Taninges
19 km (12 miles)
SW of Morzine
The founding of a monastery
Chartreuse de Mélan
Av. de Mélan
Information from the tourist office
Open daily July-Aug., 10am-noon and 3-7pm. Guided tours mid-June to mid-Sept. (phone first). *Admission charge.*
This monastery was founded in 1285 by Béatrice, a rich heiress who was inconsolable after the death of her son Jean. Only the austere church remains, with its heavy yellow tufa (limestone) buttresses.

The 16th-C. cloisters are late Gothic in style. In high summer, the site is a venue for concerts and art exhibitions.

Mieussy
7 km (4 miles)
W of Taninges
Mountain honey
Rucher des Briffes
☎ 04 50 43 06 70
Open every afternoon in summer. *Free admission.*

Beekeeper Dominique Chellianne tends his 300 beehives in the mornings, and then in the afternoons he welcomes visitors. Here you can discover for yourself the ruthless world of insects, where the queen bee kills all potential rivals. The end product, however, is a fine quality mountain honey, sweet and aromatic, with a lovely light brown colour.

The birthplace of paragliding
Club Les Choucas
☎ 04 50 43 05 13
Open all year round.
On 27 June 1978, three impoverished parachutists, André Bohn, Jean-Claude Bétemps and Gérard Bosson, decided to jump from the cliffs of Pertuiser (1.5 km/1 mile to the north}, instead of from a plane. In so doing, they invented the thrilling sport

of paragliding, and you can try it for yourself here – if you have the nerve!

Cheese-making
Fruitière des Hauts-Fleury
☎ 04 50 43 17 14
Open Mon.-Sat. 8.30am-noon and 2.30-7pm; and Sun. am in season.
Admission charge for multimedia room.

In the morning, visitors can watch the Reblochon, Tomme or Abondance cheeses being made from the safety of a windowed balcony. This cooperative of cheese-makers has fewer than 20 members, and some still bring their own milk in the morning and evening. The multimedia room is very popular with children, who can't wait to rush in to use the computers.

THE JACQUEMARD BAPTISM

Taninges
Information from the tourist office
Last Mon. in June.
The people of Taninges are referred to as *Jacquemards*, after Jacquou le Croquant, a trouble-maker (and founder of the *marc*, a unit of weight) who was hanged at the end of the 15thC. On the Monday of the feast day of St Jean, Jacquou's statue, dressed in a uniform of the Empire and hoisted on to the local fire engine, is paraded through Taninges. New arrivals to the region are then given a dousing – hence the term 'Jacquemard Baptism'.

Viuz-en-Sallaz
11 km (7 miles)
W of Mieussy
Old lessons
Musée Paysan
Le Crêt de Singe
☎ 04 50 36 89 18
Open daily 9am-noon and 1.30-6.30pm. Closed Mon. and Sun. am May-Sept.
Admission charge.
Amongst the displays in this rural museum you'll find a reconstruction of a 1930s school. The classroom, with its rows of desks that gradually increase in size and a selection of dunces' hats, harks back to a time when moral education was part of the strict curriculum.

Spotcheck
C1-D2

Things to do
Mélan monastery
Paragliding

With children
Rural museum
Hauts-Fleury cheese-making

Within easy reach
Morzine (p. 104)
Samoëns (p. 108)

Tourist offices
Flaine: ☎ 04 50 90 80 01
Mieussy: ☎ 04 50 43 02 72
Taninges: ☎ 04 50 34 25 05

Flaine
27 km (17 miles)
SE of Taninges
A lunar landscape
Le Désert de Platé
☎ 04 50 34 91 90
Access via Grandes Platières cable-car (open daily July-Aug., 10am-noon and 2-5pm. Mountain bikes permitted.)
In just 15 minutes, you can travel back in time 300 million years, when this lunar landscape was first formed. The 'desert', with its vast crevasses, is the largest area of eroded limestone in France (42 sq km/116 sq miles). In summer, guided tours are organised by the Maison de la Réserve in Sixt-Fer-à-Cheval (by appt.: ☎ 04 50 34 91 90).

Samoëns,
limestone and stonemasons

In Samoëns and its neighbouring hamlets, stonemasons or *frahans* have traditionally worked with one of the hardest limestones, bringing out all the different shades of the stone – pearly grey, metallic grey, blue, or bronze tones. This mountainous area also has other attractions, including miles of hiking routes through lush countryside with waterfalls and streams.

from all over the world, some of which are very rare. Marie-Louise employed the services of one of the greatest landscape gardeners of the era – Louis-Jules Allemand – to design the garden and the result is quite delightful.

The good Samaritan
Jardin Botanique Alpin de la Jaÿsinia
Rue du Parc
☎ 04 50 34 49 86
Open daily 8am-noon and 1.30-7.30pm; 5.30pm in winter.
Free admission.
This Alpine botanical garden was created by the authoritarian but public-spirited Marie-Louise Cognac-Jaÿ (1838-1925), founder of *La Samaritaine* department store in Paris. It was opened to visitors in 1906, and contains some 8,000 different plants

A filling soup
Restaurant La Fandioleuse
La Cour
☎ 04 50 34 98 28
Closed May-June and Oct.-Christmas hols., and Wed. in Jan., Mar. and Sept.
Soupe châtrée, or 'solid soup', flavoured with Tomme cheese and containing dry bread and onion, is so thick that it can be cut with a knife. Order it in advance in this restaurant, the name of which comes from the colourful language of the local stonemasons, *fandioleuse* meaning 'dancer'.

Under the stars
Espace Montagne
Pl. de la Grenette
☎ 04 50 34 19 72
Open Mon.-Thurs. 10am-noon and 2-6pm.
Canyoning is a relatively new sport and is even more thrilling at night. By the light of the moon and the stars, all the senses are heightened and the

contrasts in colour and light as you plunge down the waterfalls are magical. The water is quite cold (12-13°C/54-56°F) but protective neoprene clothing will keep you warm. Night-time canyoning can be enjoyed in July and August.

Ecological rafting

Ecolorado Rafting
La Glière
☎ 04 50 34 45 26
Best undertaken in June-July.
Duration approx. 2.5 hrs. Suitable only for children over 7, with good swimming ability.
This is rafting with an ecological slant – a relatively slow descent of the River Giffre, allowing time to observe the wildlife and look out for the tracks of beavers, which thrive on fish. The route cuts through the Tines gorge, a narrow opening (2 m/6.5 ft wide) between two cliffs.

Circular hiking trail

Yellow markings. Depart from town hall at Samoëns; duration approx. 4 hrs; change in altitude: 500 m/1,640 ft. Topoguide Ref. 741 (tour of the Dents Blanches) available in bookshops and newsagents.
This footpath takes walkers through forests and glades, via the hamlet of Chantemerle (3 km/2 miles north of Samoëns), where the Dunoyer and Simond farmhouses have ancient carved lintels. The charming chapel, built in

1684, is dedicated to St François de Sales, the saint to whom farmers would pray to ensure good weather during the harvest.

Cirque du Fer-à-Cheval

13 km (8 miles)
E of Samoëns
Quite a circus!
Cirque du Fer à Cheval discovery trail
Depart from car park at end of route along Giffre river; duration approx.

Spotcheck
D1

Things to do
La Jaÿsinia Alpine garden

With children
Footpath around the Cirque du Fer-à-Cheval
Rafting on the Giffre river

Within easy reach
Taninges (p. 106)

Tourist office
Samoëns: ☎ 04 50 34 40 28

1.5 hrs; easy 2.9 km (2 miles) circuit.
This signposted footpath winds between wild strawberry plants and beech forests, providing spectacular viewpoints over the natural rock amphitheatre of Fer-à-Cheval, which has over 30 waterfalls, descending from one rocky mountain ridge to another. See if you can spot the Méridienne, so called because the source of the water is lit up by the midday sun.

ON THE TRAIL OF THE *FRAHANS*

Samoëns guided tour
Information from the tourist office
Open all year
(min. 5 people).
Admission charge.
This guided tour reveals the talents of the local *frahans* (stonemasons). In Gros-Tilleul square, the ornate four-sided fountain dates from 1763. Restored by Guillaume Bozonnet, one of the few remaining stonemasons in the area, its smallest block weighs 500-600 kg/1,100-1,325 lb. The font of the church of Notre-Dame-de-l'Assomption was carved out of a single block of black Tines marble by master mason Désarnod in 1844.

Thonon-les-Bains,
a relaxed way of life

It's almost impossible not to fall in love with Thonon, which lies on the banks of Lake Geneva. The small port of Rives is as pretty as a picture, and the town boasts some wonderful panoramic views, as well as offering superb trips on the lake. The local inhabitants are famous for their laid-back attitude, which is extremely contagious.

Fishing talk
Écomusée de la Pêche et du Lac
Port de Rives
☎ 04 50 70 26 96
Open Wed.-Sun., June-Sep., 2.30-6.30pm; daily July-Aug., 10am-noon and 2.30-6.30pm.
Admission charge.
The fishing and lake museum is housed in two colourful old fisherman's huts. It has a wealth of information on different types of fishing with nets, from *à la monte* to *au grand pic.* Early risers can

watch the boats come back to the port before 9am, laden with crayfish and mackerel.

Fireworks over the lake
Les Fondus du Macadam festival of street theatre
Information from the tourist office.
Second week in Aug.
Free admission.
Over 30 companies of street performers, with evocative names such as *Tcherno Debyls* and *Les Chercheurs d'air* ('the air seekers'), take part in this annual festival that sets the town alight. After the jugglers and fire-eaters, the evening ends with a spectacular firework display over the lake.

For cheese-lovers
Fromagerie Daniel Boujon
7, Rue Saint-Sébastien

☎ 04 50 71 07 68
Open daily, except Sun., 8am-12.30pm and 2.30-7.30pm.

This welcoming cheese shop has an extraordinary range of cheeses, including Saint-Sigismond de la Vallée de Cluses, Beaufort d'Alpage, Tome des Bauges with a hint of nuts, and goat's cheese from Morzine. You'll even find such rarities as the blue cheese known as *Termingnon en Maurienne.*

Full steam ahead

Compagnie Générale de Navigation
Quai de Rives
☎ 04 50 71 14 71
Cruises Jun.-Sept. (call for days and times).
Destinations: Évian, Lausanne, tour of lake.
Four steamboats still ply their trade on Lake Geneva: *La Suisse* (1910), *La Savoie* (1920), *Le Simplon* (1920) and *Le Rhône* (1927). Take a journey back in time on one of these vessels, where everything is authentic from the wood panelling to the noise of the pistons.

Feathered friends

La Dranse nature reserve
Information from the tourist office, or nature reserve office
☎ 04 50 81 49 79
Guided tour twice weekly July-Aug.
Admission charge.
Thonon-les-Bains lies on the Dranse delta, with a diverse selection of around 800 types of plants and some 220 bird species. Guides from the nature reserve will teach you to recognise the hoarse cry of the warbler that hides in the rose bushes and introduce you to the yellow-chested toad. Don't forget your binoculars.

The spice of life

Restaurant Le Prieuré
68, Grande-Rue
☎ 04 50 71 31 89
Closed Sun. evening and all day Mon.
The spiced recipes devised by Maistre Chiquart, chef at the Savoy court during the 15thC., still inspire chefs today. Charles Plumex, chef at Le Prieuré,

Spotcheck

C1

Things to do

The château at Ripaille
Fishing and lake museum

With children

Cruise on a steamboat
Eagles of the lake

Within easy reach

Évian-les-Bains (p. 112)
Abondance (p. 102)

Tourist offices

Thonon-les-Bains:
☎ 04 50 71 55 55 or
☎ 04 50 26 19 94 (summer)

has come up with some interesting modern-day versions, including roasted pigeon with tomato, cinnamon and aniseed.

CHÂTEAU DE RIPAILLE

Ripaille
☎ 04 50 26 64 44
Open daily, Feb.-Nov., guided tours only (between 1 and 7 per day, call for more information).
Refreshments available in the garden July-Aug.
Admission charge.
From Rives port, in Thonon, follow the Boulevard de la Corniche.
Between the lake and the local vineyards stands the impressive 'castle with seven towers' of the first Duke of Savoy, Amadeus VIII (1383-1451). Only four of the original seven towers are left and, somewhat surprisingly, the décor of the main rooms is Art Nouveau in style.

Sciez
9 km (5.5 miles) SW of Thonon-les-Bains

The eagles of the lake

The Léman eagles
Bonnatrait
☎ 04 50 72 72 26
Open daily, 15 Mar.-beg. Nov. (call for times).
Admission charge.
Children will be enthralled by the sight of falcons capable of flying at 300km/h (185mph) and sharp-eyed eagles that can pinpoint their prey from 2 km/1.25 m. Training birds of prey is a time-consuming and skilled business that can take anything between three weeks and eight months, as well as a great deal of patience.

Évian-les-Bains,
springs and spas

On the banks of Lake Geneva, Évian has that effortless charm typical of all spa towns, where well-heeled 19thC. socialites flocked to take the waters. Many places, such as the Cachat pump room, have retained their Art Nouveau interiors. The recently restored funicular railway operates between the various sights.

Hollywood glamour
Mairie
2, Rue de Clermont
☎ 04 50 83 10 00
Open. Mon.-Fri. 9am-
11.30am and 1pm-5pm.
Free admission.
Self-guided tours; free
leaflet from tourist office,
Place d'Allinges.
The town hall used to belong
to the Lumière brothers,
pioneers of French cinema,
and its interior resembles a
glamorous film set. A bronze
lion guards the
entrance leading
to an enormous

Villa Lumière, now the town hall

sweeping staircase, which
leads to a reception room
lavishly decorated with gold
leaf, silks and onyx.

A romantic promenade
Promenade du Lac
2 km (1.25 miles) walk.
Depart from the tourist
office in Place d'Allinges.
Musical fountain at
Mouettes port: 4 times
per week in Aug.,
5-10pm; free admission.
The lakeside promenade is a
tranquil shady place, popular
with romantic couples, young
families and the retired alike.

(Watch out for rollerbladers
too.) Various boards give
details of items of interest, such
as the Italian poplar trees or
the giant cormorants that have
been known to fish in the lake
to depths of up to 30 m/100 ft.

Music, maestro !
Classical music festival
Information and
reservations
☎ 01 44 35 26 91
End June to beg. July.
Admission charge.
Since the cello virtuoso
Rostropovich visited the town
in 1988, this classical music
festival has grown in

reputation, and international performers such as Isaac Stern, Seiji Ozawa and Lorin Maazel have all featured on its programme. Concerts take place at the Grange-au-Lac, situated in the Royal-Club Park, which seats 1,200 and has superb acoustics.

The Évian gardens

Évian's public gardens – the English Garden, the Lovers' Garden, the Japanese Garden

General Dupas' garden

and General Dupas' garden – are all free to visitors. The town also has a water garden with a protected area known for its Alpine forget-me-nots. The only way to get there is by water bus (timetable from the tourist office).

Take to the water
Boating on Lake Geneva
Information from tourist offices at Évian and Thonon-les-Bains (p.110)
The *Savoie*, with its billowing sails with a surface area of 380 sq m/4,090 sq ft, provides an unforgettable boat trip. Built in 1896 in traditional style, it was used to take quarry stone from Meillerie to Geneva, but now this flat-bottomed craft ferries tourists around the lake.

Amphion-les-Bains
4 km (2.5 miles) from tourist office at Évian-les-Bains
Évian bottling plant
Company of Eaux Minérales d'Évian
☎ 04 50 26 80 29
Visits 3 times per week mid-May to end Sept.
Free admission exc. transport from Évian.

Évian's Art Nouveau pump house, with its tiled cupola, adorned with organic motifs, was designed by prize-winning architect Jean-Albert Ébrard in 1903. Built on the site of the Cachat spring, which was discovered by the Marquis of Lessert in 1790, the old pump room was the centre for many social gatherings and also has a reading room. It is currently undergoing restoration.

WATER TEMPLE
Ex-buvette Cachat (former Cachat pump room)
19, Rue Nationale,
☎ 04 50 26 80 29
Open daily, May-Sept. 2.30-6.30pm; mid-June to mid-Sept. 10.30am-12.30pm and 3-7pm.
Free admission.

Spotcheck
C1

Things to do
Évian bottling plant
Water garden

With children
Lakeside walk

Within easy reach
Abondance (p. 102)
Thonon-les-Bains (p. 110)

Tourist offices
Évian-les-Bains:
☎ 04 50 75 04 26

Over six million bottles leave the Évian bottling plant at Amphion every day. The factory is extremely high-tech and spotless. Visitors can watch the non-stop, frenetic production line from the safety of a windowed gallery.

Saint-Gingolph
17 km (10.5 miles) E of Évian-les-Bains
'Lake pearls'
Musée des Traditions et des Barques du Léman
Rue de la Colombière (at the château)
☎ (00 41) 24 482 70 22
Open Sat. Apr.-Oct. 2-5.30pm; daily exc. Mon. mid-Jun to mid-Sept. 2-5.30pm.
Admission charge.
The third floor of the museum of Lake Geneva's boats and traditions houses 34 scale models (1/25) of brigs, small craft and keelless boats, representing five centuries of merchant shipping on Lake Geneva. Another once-thriving industry was the fabrication of 'lake pearls', made from fish scales dipped in glue.

Annecy and its lake,
'little Venice'

Lying beside the silvery waters of the lake, Annecy richly deserves its nickname. There are romantic footpaths along the River Thiou and the canals, with their flower-decked quays, as well as a Baroque church, old artisans' workshops and fine restaurants. The setting is absolutely charming and much loved by amateur painters.

[map with labels: Annecy, Albigny, Menthon-St-Bernard, Sevrier, Lac d'Annecy, Talloires, Duingt, La Tournette, Doussard]

The old prison
Palais de l'Île
3, Passage de l'Île
☎ 04 50 33 87 30
Open daily except Tues.
10am-noon and 2pm-6pm; daily June-Sept.
10am-6pm.
Admission charge.
Older locals still refer to this island palace as the 'old prison'. Certain parts of the austere buildings date from the 12thC., and the unnerving and formidable dungeons can still be visited. The place has also served as Annecy's law courts in its time, and in the 16thC., the inner courtyard on the western side was filled with lawyers and their clients.

Kitsch corner
Le Balustre d'Or
Square J.-J.-Rousseau
In his work *Confessions*, philosopher Jean-Jacques Rousseau (1712-78) expressed his wish for a tangible memorial to his propitious encounter with Madame de Warens, along the banks of the Notre-Dame canal one Easter Day in 1728. His longed-for 'golden balustrade' was created two centuries later and nothing was left out: miniature hearts, flowers and a bust of the philosopher himself by Houdon.

Monitoring the waters
The banks of the River Thiou
The lake is monitored around the clock, with thirty-one sluice gates over a 6-km (4-mile) sweep, controlling its water

The Logis Perrière

levels, along with those of the River Thiou (an overflow linking the lake with the Fier). Some are operated manually, such as those near the Pont de la République (bridge), laden with geraniums in season. The engineer who was responsible for the introduction of the sluices was Sadi Carnot, future president of the Republic.

Lakes observatory
Château-museum
Pl. du Château
☎ 04 50 33 87 30
Open daily except Tues.
10am-noon and 2-6pm;
June-Sept. daily
10am–6pm.
Admission charge.
Guided tours available
The château, former residence of the counts of Geneva, also served as a medieval fortress and a Renaissance palace. At the end of the paved courtyard, the Logis Perrière (dating from 1487) houses the Alpine lakes regional observatory, the best place to find out about various

fishing techniques and the variety of fish species found in the lakes.

Roseaux du Lac
Meyer Chocolatier
4, Pl. Saint-François-de-Sales
☎ 04 50 45 12 08
Open Tues.-Sat. 9am-12.30pm and 2-7pm.
A sign in this shop window absolves prospective buyers with the message 'chocolate is not mere greed but a sign of sophistication'. The *roseaux*

du lac ('lake reeds') are a local speciality filled with 12 different liqueurs, such as Génépi and Chartreuse.

Ring out the bells
Monastère de la Visitation
11, Av. de la Visitation
☎ 04 50 66 17 37
Bell ringing on Sat. from 4pm, mid-June to mid-Aug. and in Sept.
Admission charge.

Spotcheck
C2

Things to do
Palais de l'Ile
Bell museum and Paccard foundry
Roc de Chère walk

With children
Albigny beach
Annecy lakeside bus ride
Alpine lakes observatory

Within easy reach
L'Albanais (p. 118)
Les Aravis (p. 122)

Tourist offices
Annecy: ☎ 04 50 45 00 33/56 66
Sevrier: ☎ 04 50 52 40 56
Talloires: ☎ 04 50 60 70 64

LE PONT DES AMOURS
Quai Jules-Philippe, Annecy
The 'lovers' bridge', a single-span bridge (1907) over the Vasse canal, where the water gently laps against rowing boats, epitomises the most romantic image of Annecy. Unfortunately, like many of the canals of this 'little Venice', which flowed along the old fortifications, it was partially covered over in 19thC. Part of it still remains hidden under Rue Vaugelas.

This monastery has a total of 37 bells, and its repertoire is impressive, playing a variety of tunes from Brel to Bach. The head bell-ringer conducts visitors to his lair (a climb of 152 steps) and introduces them to *Karol*, a bell bought in Paccard (p.117) in honour of the Pope's visit.

Albigny beach
Avenue d'Albigny (past the Impérial Hotel)
At the end of the Pâquier ('pasture') common lies the lake. The local inhabitants head out here on fine days, but at a much later hour than the tourists. They bring their picnics and come to relax on the shore at sunset and swim at Albigny between June and the end of September, when the water temperature is around 20°C/68°F. It can reach 23°C/73°F in July and August.

Lake festival
Information from the tourist office
1st Sat. in Aug.
Admission charge (for reserved seating and enclosures).
The whole of Annecy turns out for the 'Fête du Lac', which has been held since the Savoy region was returned to France in 1860. The Empress Eugénie was one high-profile visitor to this dazzling Venetian-style water festival. The sky over the lake is lit up by a spectacular firework display at 1.30am.

Antiques and flea market
Old Town
Last Sat. of the month 8am-7pm.
This market is a bit of a scrum; even the Quibert fountain in Rue Sainte-Claire disappears beneath the crowds. The banks of the Thiou are packed and the Morens bridge is often hidden from view. Look out for butter moulds and postcards showing the old steamboats on the lake, as well as some nice pieces of furniture.

Water buses
Lake Annecy boat company
2, Pl. aux Bois
☎ **04 50 51 08 40**
Open end Apr.-mid-Sept. (3 departures per day).
Admission charge
(children under 5 free). Bikes permitted.
The water bus provides a pleasant way to cross the lake at Annecy, stopping at several places such as Talloires and Doussard on the way. Take your time and have a good look around while you wait for the next ferry.

On your bike
Annecy-Doussard cycle path
17 km (10.5 miles) along the western bank; depart from Rue des Marquisats (1.5 km/1 mile from the centre) towards Albertville.
Avoid the traffic jams by hiring a bike (Sports Passion, 3, Avenue du Parmelan ☎ 04 50 51 46 28). This track follows the bank, passing some beautiful scenery on the way, and goes through a tunnel at Duingt. Do watch out for rollerbladers and pushchairs.

Menthon-Saint-Bernard
9 km (5.5 miles) SE Annecy on the eastern bank
Sleeping Beauty's castle
Château Menthon-St-Bernard
☎ **04 50 60 12 05**
Open Thurs. and week-ends, May-June 2pm-6pm daily July-Aug. noon-6pm
Admission charge.

Birthplace of the patron saint of Alpinists, St Bernard de Menthon, this 500-roomed castle has been in his family since the 11thC. The castle, straight from the pages of a fairy tale book, is still inhabited and richly furnished. Eight rooms are on show, including the pilgrims' room, a library and the bedroom belonging to the lady of the house.

LE CHEMIN DES BELVÉDÈRES ('VIEWPOINTS WAY')
Accompanied walk (in summer, otherwise unaccompanied)
Information from the Réserves Naturelles (nature reserve) office
☎ 04 50 64 44 03
Depart from front of the Talloires golf course; approx 1-hr loop; change of altitude: 110 m/330 ft.
This trail is lovely, with views across the bay at Talloires to the Ruphy château. The path leads through the Roc de Chère nature reserve (69 ha/160 acres), where Mediterranean flowers grow alongside plants from the time of the Ice Age, and rhododendrons bloom in a canyon that rarely sees the sun.

Talloires

2 km (1.25miles) S of Menthon Saint-Bernard
The 19th hole
Lake Annecy golf club
Écharvines
☎ 04 50 60 12 89
Open daily Apr.-Oct. 8am-6pm (7pm Aug.); Nov.-Mar. 8am-5pm. Closed Christmas.
Admission charge.
Situated on the Roc de Chère promontory, on the edge of the nature reserve that bears the same name, this golf course at the foot of the Tournette mountain (2,351 m/7,713 ft) is one for the gourmets. Each year, the first player to get a hole-in-one on the sixth hole wins a free meal for two at Le Père Bise, a high-quality hotel-restaurant in Talloires (Route du Port ☎ 04 50 60 72 01; closed Tues. and Wed. exc. Easter-Nov.; closed first weekend in Nov.-10 Feb.).

Sevrier

5 km (3 miles) S of Annecy west bank
Bell foundry
Musée de la Cloche et Fonderie Paccard
RN508
☎ 04 50 52 47 11
Museum: open daily exc. Mon. and Sun. am, 10am-noon and 2.30pm-5.30pm; June-Aug. daily exc. Sun. until 6.30pm. Foundry: guided tours at weekend, Apr.-Oct.; daily in Aug.
Admission charge..
The bell foundry at Paccard is more than 200 years old and has produced some real heavy-weights, such as the Savoyarde in the Sacré-Cœur in Paris (nearly 19 tonnes/ 21 tons), or the millennium clock (30 tonnes/33 tons) that was shipped across the Atlantic to Newport, Kentucky.

Jacquet lakeside promenade, Annecy

The Albanais,
a secret region

B etween the Bourget and Annecy lakes is a plain with gentle valleys shaped by the unpredictable Chéran and the raging Fier rivers. This unspoilt countryside, full of orchards, fortified manors and mills, was once known for its shoemakers. It has welcomed its share of prospectors panning for gold, too. The largest nugget found here weighed 43.5 grams/153 oz.

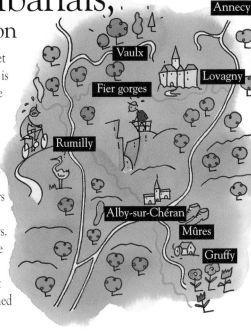

strange shadowy world between two rock faces, riddled with potholes. Water gushes from these holes at rates of between 5 cubic m/175 cubic ft and 1,000 cubic m/35,300 cubic ft per second. The noise is deafening. The walkways through the gorge were created by Lyonnais architect Marius Vallin (1842-89).

Fortress
Château de Montrottier
1.5 km (1 mile)
S of Lovagny
☎ 04 50 46 23 02
Open daily except Tues. mid-Mar. to mid-Oct, 10am-

1pm and 2-6pm (closed Oct. mornings); daily June-Aug., 10am-1pm and 2-7pm.
Admission charge; guided tours only.
This fortress, part of which dates from the 13thC., once effectively blocked the road from Chambéry to Geneva. Today its military days are long gone, and it's home to an eclectic collection of furniture earthenware and other objects acquired in the 19thC. by one of it former owners, Léon Marès. If you tackle the 82 steps up to the castle keep, you can visit the maiden's prison and the alchemist's chamber.

Lovagny
10 km (6 miles)
W of Annecy
Gushing potholes
Fier gorges
☎ 04 50 46 23 07
Open daily mid-Mar. to mid-Oct. 9am-noon and 2-6pm; mid-Jun. to mid-Sept. 9am-7pm.
Admission charge.
A wooden footbridge spanning the River Fier at a height of 20-30 m/65-100 ft leads into a

Rumilly

15 km (9 miles)
SW of Lovagny
Tour of the ponds
Mountain bike circuit
Info. from tourist office
and Mont-Blanc Nature
☎ 06 86 18 40 80
*Depart from the well-
maintained path on the
right before the Madrid
campsite, S of Rumilly;
easy signposted circuit.*
There's plenty to see on this
peaceful mountain bike nature
trail, with wide paths and few
climbs. Take care not to disturb
birdlife and to respect the
banks of the Crosagny ponds,
a refuge for the crimson heron
and the white wader.

Alby-sur-Chéran

10km (6 miles)
SE of Rumilly
Savoy shoemakers
**Musée de la
Cordonnerie**
Pl. du Trophée
☎ 04 50 68 39 44
Open Tues. to Sat., 8.30
am-noon and 2-5.30pm;
June-Sept., 8.30am-noon
and 1.30-6pm.

Free admission.
From the 14thC. to the 19thC.,
Savoy shoemakers plied their
trade underneath the arches of
this charming little town. At
its peak, Alby had 300 cobblers
as well as other tradesmen
who made their living from
re-conditioning old shoes. The
museum retraces the history of
shoemaking in the area.

Mûres

2 km (1 mile)
S of Alby-sur-Chéran
The Miller's tale
Old grain mill
Rte de Gruffy
☎ 04 50 68 16 57
Open weekend afternoons,
May-Sept. (by appt).
Admission charge.

There are plenty of ruined and
restored mills in the Albanais.
This former grain mill by the
Chéran river is one of the few
still open to the public.

Gruffy

3 km (2 miles)
S of Mûres
**A delicious
bouquet**
La Grange aux Fleurs
Le Buisson

Spotcheck
B2-C2

Things to do

Château de Montrottier
Shoemakers' museum
(Musée de la Cordonnerie)

With children

Bike ride around the ponds
Fier gorges

Within easy reach

Aix-les-Bains (p. 132)
Annecy (p. 114)

Tourist offices

L'Albanais (Rumilly):
☎ 04 50 64 58 32
Maison de pays (Alby-sur-
Chéran): ☎ 04 50 68 11 99

☎ 04 50 77 51 18
or 56 43
Displays and sales daily
except Sun. 9am-noon
and 3-7pm.
Admission charge.
For 30 years, Yvette Valero
has been growing and drying
all sorts of flowers and plants,
from gypsophila and statice,
to grasses and yarrow. The
blooms and stems are hung in
bunches head down in her
drying barns, before being
transformed into beautiful
bouquets and floral
arrangements.

SECRET GARDENS

Vaulx, Lagnat hamlet
5 km (3 miles) NW of Lavagny
☎ 04 50 60 53 18
Open daily, end June-Sept., 1.30-7pm; mid-Apr.-end
June, weekend and hols., 1.30-7pm; mid-Sept.-mid-
Oct., 1.30-6pm.
Admission charge. Guided tours.
Originally a run-down old farm, this place has been
lovingly and patiently restored by the Moumen family.
The first impression is of a unique cross between
East and West, laid out in a series of galleries, patios
and gardens. It's like a world tour, all on one site,
where all your senses are stimulated.

Bornes and Filière,
storming the citadel

J ust north of Annecy, the Bornes mountain range rises up like a limestone fortress, its grey cliffs pounded daily by the River Filière. Eagles wheel in the sky above this wild and unspoilt region, and the *sabot-de-Venus* orchid ('Venus' clog') lies hidden in the undergrowth. It may be beautiful, but the area has also had its share of grim history.

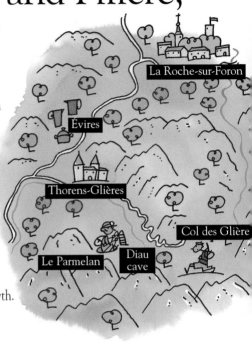

La Roche-sur-Foron

Évires

Thorens-Glières

Le Parmelan

Diau cave

Col des Glière

Col des Glières

14 km (8.5 miles) SE of Thorens-Glières

A voyage of discovery

5-km (3-miles) level circuit. Depart from Monument des Glières car park (at 1,440 m/ 4,725 ft).

In summer the Glières plateau is a pleasant sight, with its poppy fields and herds of grazing cows. But this was the scene of a tragedy in March 1944. Having lost their leader, Tom Morel, 465 Resistance fighters found themselves encircled in this natural fortress by 12,000 German soldiers, helped by 2,500 French militia. More than 160 *maquisards* were killed or deported. Today the site is marked by a man-made footpath that winds past relics of the past, including a former command post and a food depot.

Thorens-Glières

17 km (10.5 miles) NE of Annecy

A local Casanova

Château de Thorens

☎ 04 50 22 42 02

Open Sun. and hols., June-Sept., 2-6pm. *Admission charge.*

Since 1559 the Sales family have owned much of the land around here. Prominent family members have included St Francis and Camille de Cavour (1810-61), architect of Italian unification and

grandson of Philippine de [...]ales. The château displays [...]avour's desk, on which the [...]reaty of Turin was signed [...]n 1860, which lead to the [...]nnexation of Savoy to France [...]p.51). The desk also played [...]s own part in Cavour's [...]orrespondence with his [...]arious mistresses.

POTHOLING IN THE DIAU CAVE

5 km (3 miles) SE of Thorens-Glières. Follow the D55 towards Glières; at Nant-Sec turn right for Verrerie.
Instructor Philippe Durdilly
☎ 04 50 25 88 63
By appt only in winter. *Admission charge (includes gear). Not suitable for children under 10.*

All keen European potholers dream of adding Diau to their list of achievements, with its subterranean descents of over 700 m/2,300 ft below the Parmelan (the highest peak in the Bornes mountain range, at 1,832 m/6,010 ft). By way of initiation you can spend half a day exploring this strange underground world, where the noise of running water follows you along the twists and turns. Fossilised oysters and sea urchins can be found along the way.

Évires
12 km (7.5 miles) N of Thorens-Glières
Évires pottery
Musée de la Poterie La Côte (near the railway track)
☎ 04 50 62 01 90
Open daily Easter to 1 Nov, 2pm-6pm. Guided tours (about 1 hr). *Admission charge.*
Over 2,000 ceramic pieces, dating from the 12thC. to the present day, are beautifully displayed in this museum attached to the studio of Jean-Christophe Hermann. Among them are heart-shaped cheese drainers and milk churns. The pipe-smoking potter exports his work as far afield as New York, and you can see him at work in his studio every day (8-11am and 2-7pm). Ask to see his wood-fired kiln, too.

La Roche-sur-Foron
12km (7.5 miles) NE of Évires
The city with three châteaux
Information from the tourist office.
Guided tours (1.5 hrs,

Things to do
Roche-sur-Foron walk
Pottery museum

With children
Glières plateau footpath
Potholing

Within easy reach
Annecy (p. 114)
Aravis (p. 122)

Tourist offices
La Roche-sur-Foron:
☎ 04 50 03 36 68
Thorens-Glières:
☎ 04 50 22 40 31

admission charge), mid-June to mid-Sept., daily from 3pm (meet at tourist office, Pl Andreventan); self-guided tour (brochure on sale at tourist office) The former capital of the dukes of Geneva (from 11thC.-13thC.), famous for the remains of three châteaux, is strikingly pretty. Painted in Mediterranean colours, from yellow ochre to almond green, and with a network of twisting alleyways, it's a marvellous place for a wander. Near the Falquet gateway, you may be able to spot the grain merchant's bench dating from 1558, with marks for the equivalent of 82, 20 and 5 litres cut into the stone.

Les Aravis,
Reblochon cheese

This giant natural fortress, north of Annecy, is a land of beautiful mountain chalets, little chapels and the famous Reblochon cheese. Made, in part, with condensed milk, it was first created in this region at the Col des Annes on the slopes of the Chartreuse du Reposoir.

Le Reposoir

Col des Anne

Le Grand-Borna

Les Plans

Les Confins

La Clusaz

Thônes

Thônes
16 km (10 miles)
E of Annecy
Hammers and saws
Écomusée du Bois et de la Forêt (forest and woodworking museum)

Les Étouvières
Towards Montremont valley
☎ 04 50 32 18 10
Guided tours Apr.-Sept. twice a week.; July-Aug., 4-5 times a week
Admission charge.
In times gone by, the Thônes valley reverberated to the sound of hammering and sawing. There were once 64 sawmills in the valley, and the Etouvières mill, near Malnant, which closed for business in 1970, is now open to visitors.

Mountain antiques
André Veyret & Son
Route d'Annecy
☎ 04 50 02 15 56
Open daily, except Sun. am and public hols., 8am-noon and 2.30-7pm.
Mountain arts and crafts have made something of a comeback recently, especially with decorative pieces such as bread stamps (p.63) or salt boxes, as well as

furniture, including chests an *bonnetières* (wardrobes with a single door). All the pieces on sale in this antique dealers are certified authentic.

La Clusaz
11km (7 miles)
NE of Thônes
Cheese galore
GAEC les Confins
(Georges and Didier Agnellet)
Les Confins-d'En-Haut
Towards Les Confins, on the right
☎ 04 50 02 61 54
M. Agnellet senior has a fine herd of cows and his son raise goats with such cute names as Plum and Tipsy. Not surprisingly, you'll find an enormous selection of cheese on sale here, including Reblochon, Chevrotin, Arav (sprinkled with chopped parsley) and Sérac.

Le Grand-Bornand

7 km (4.5 miles)
NE of La Clusaz

Heritage centre
Maison du Patrimoine
☎ 04 50 02 79 18
Open July-Aug., Tues.-
Sat., 10am-noon and
3-5.30pm; Sun., 4-7pm.
For guided tours and out
of season, please ring.
Admission charge.

These splendid farm buildings,
dating from 1830, are typical
of the region, with their huge
spruce wood fireplace, used for
smoking meat. You can also
see the cow shed where the
family would gather for
warmth in winter, as well as a
couronne de mariée (wedding
crown) and various old family
portraits.

Son of the Gaul
**Charcuterie
Bozon-Liaudet**
Résidence La Forclaz
☎ 04 50 02 32 13

Open daily, 15 Dec.-Apr.
and 20 June-Sept., 9am-
12.30pm and 3-7.30pm
Régis Bozon, known as the
'son of the Gaul', is a master of
his trade. His raw hams are
cured with Guérande rock salt
and smoked in the traditional
way at his Alpine chalet at
Manigod. He sells his wares at
the Wednesday morning
village market.

One for the children
**Information from the
tourist office**
Last Sat. in Aug.
*Admission charge,
except for the outdoor
entertainments.*
At the end of August, Le
Grand-Bornand becomes a
huge leisure park, with a
whole range of entertaining

ON THE ALPINE PASTURES

**Ferme-auberge
La Cheminée**
Col des Annes
*At Le Grand-Bornand,
head for the Bouchet
valley; turn left at Les
Plans*
☎ 04 50 27 03 87
Open daily mid-June
to mid-Sept., lunchtime
and evening.
**Leave the car by the
La Duche chapel and
climb the 3km/2 miles
to the pass at 1,722 m
(7,650 ft) on foot.
Your reward is a seat
on the terrace of the
La Cheminée auberge,
where you can enjoy
potato fritters and
fresh white Tomme
cheese, to the sound
of tinkling cowbells.**

Things to do
Heritage centre at Le Grand-
Bornand
La Cheminée auberge

With children
Children's festival at
Le Grand-Bornand

Within easy reach
Annecy (p. 114)
Taninges (p. 106)

Tourist offices
La Clusaz: ☎ 04 50 32 65 00
Le Grand-Bornand:
☎ 04 50 02 78 06
Le Reposoir:
☎ 04 50 98 18 01
Thônes: ☎ 04 50 02 00 26

shows, as well as fascinating
children's workshops teaching
everything from bread-making
to magic tricks. Some hotels
or self-catering studios offer a
tariff that includes entrance
to five shows.

Le Reposoir

18km (11 miles)
NE of Grand-Bornand
The silence of the Carmelites
Carmel
Vallon
☎ 04 50 98 15 01
Open daily, 8am-noon
and 2.30-6.30pm (shop
and video presentation).
'Take great care to speak only
when necessary.' Since 1932
this is the rule by which the
Carmelites (who replaced the
Carthusian monks here) have
lived. Only the church and
the first set of cloisters are
open to the public. In the
shop you can buy rhubarb and
angelica jam, sachets of tea
and napkins embroidered
with gentian flowers.

Megève,
the village of the Baroness

I n the heart of the
Arly valley, Megève
has plenty of appeal.
Not only is it a typical
mountain village, with
cows, forests and nearly
50 working farms in the
area, it has also been a
jet-set ski resort since the
1920s, when it was 'discovered' by Baroness
Naomi de Rothschild.

The Calvary trail
**Information from
the tourist office**
Guided tours from
Dec. to mid-March
twice a week (3 hrs).
*Leave from Croix-Saint
Michel, Route E. de
Rothschild
Admission charge.*
This unusual Calvary trail is
a former place of pilgrimage,
a replica of the Way of the
Cross in Jerusalem. It ascends
into the heights of the village
and is dotted with oratories
and eight chapels, whose
impressive interiors, trompe-
l'oeil paintings and wooden
sculptures can be enjoyed
on a guided tour, or on the
Feast of the Assumption,
15 August.

Charming chalets
**Hôtel-Restaurant
Fermes de Marie**
163, Ch. de Riante-
Colline
☎ 04 50 93 03 10
Closed end Mar.-beg.
June and end Sept.-
beg. Dec.
Mixing the old with the new
is definitely in vogue in
Megève, and old wood
salvaged from abandoned
chalets is more expensive than
mahogany! The Fermes de
Marie hotel has reused parts
taken from over 60 farms in
the Abondance, Arly,
Beaufortain, Manigod and
Megève valleys in its
construction. Treat
yourself to a luxury
meal here.
It's pricey, but
worth it.

Stretch ski pants
Boutiques A. Allard
148, Pl. de l'Église and
37, Quai du Prieuré
☎ 04 50 21 03 85
Open Tues.-Sat. (Sun. in
season), 9.30am-
12.30pm and 3-7.30pm.
Closed May-15 June.
In 1929, Armand Allard had
a stroke of genius, coming up
with the idea of a pair of
stretch ski trousers that would
fit snugly and smartly inside a
ski boot. His son, Jean-Paul,
now makes them in flannel,
gabardine and velvet, plain or
tartan, and even offers a
luminous version for night time

Tea-time
**Le Calvaire Ferme-
Auberge**
Chemin du Calvaire
*Near church of
Notre-Dame
des Vertus*
☎ 04 50
21 13 58
Open
daily
except
Tues., mid-
June to
mid-Sept. and
from Christmas
to mid-Apr.

Spotcheck
D2

Things to do

Hot-air balloon ride

With children

Nature trail
Tea at Le Calvaire auberge
Pony trekking

Within easy reach

Chamonix-Mont-Blanc
(p. 126)
Saint-Gervais-les-Bains
(p. 130)

Tourist offices

Megève: ☎ 04 50 21 27 28

This *auberge*, dating from 1780, is owned by the village. At tea-time they serve plenty of treats, such as frothy hot chocolate, light gâteau de Savoie, brown bread and mountain honey – all good comfort food!

Horses for courses
Les Coudrettes
Equestrian Centre
200, Rte Sur le Meu
(towards Rochebrune)
☎ 04 50 21 16 52
Open 20 June to Sept.
Children from age 4.
Horse-breeding is a tradition in Megève, famous for supplying the dukes of Savoy with their mounts, which were said to be feisty and elegant. This riding centre caters for all standards and activities, including family treks and lessons for beginners.

Say 'hello' to Hugo
Nature trail
Information from the
tourist office
Depart from Les Frasses car park (1,550 m/
5,085 ft) or the top of the Le Jaillet cable-car; climb of 220 m/720 ft.
Hugo, the mascot of the nature trail, is a small member of the pheasant family, who lives in the forests between 1,500 and 2,000 m (4,920 and 6,560 ft). In spring, the mating season, he is very noticable. The male has a black plumage and a red 'cap' (a sort of fleshy growth), and

struts around. Information points along the trail explain all you need to know about his life and habits.

Wind travellers
Mont Blanc Balloons
91, Rue d'Arly
☎ 04 50 21 03 07
Daily, weather permitting. Discovery flight (half-day).
Follow in the footsteps of the Montgolfier brothers and take to the skies in a hot-air balloon. They take off from Praz-sur-Arly (4.5 km/3 miles SW of Megève) at first light and climb up to 2,500 m/8,200 ft, or even as high as 3,500 m/ 11,480 ft. The scenery is spectacular, with wonderful panoramic views of the Aravis mountains and Mont Blanc.

TAXI!
Place de l'Église
In Megève, 50 coachmen await your command. It's usually the late-risers and exhausted tourists who hire the horse-drawn carriages like taxis, or take a special trip around the village. More than half a century ago, a young actress named Naomi took a romantic carriage ride in Rochebrune, the southern part of Megève, and ended up as the bride of the Baron de Rothschild.

Chamonix-Mont-Blanc,
the magic mountain

L ocated on the border with Switzerland and Italy, Chamonix (or, rather, its mountain) is one of the three most frequently visited sites in the world (along with Niagara Falls and Japan's Mount Fuji). It has many nicknames, some rather ironic, such as 'The Mountaineering Mecca' or 'Lourdes of the Ice-picks, but those who know it well refer to it simply as 'Cham', and consider it one of the greatest wintersports playgrounds.

Vallorcine

Col des Montets

Argentière

Planpraz

Mer de Glace

Chamonix

Les Bossons

Aiguille du Midi

Balmat and Saussure

Chamonix-Mont-Blanc

18km (11 miles) E of Saint-Gervais-les-Bains

The scientist and his guide

Town visit (with or without a guide)
Information from the tourist office
15 June-15 Sept.
Balmat and Saussure, the first to conquer Mont Blanc in 1786, are immortalised in Place Balmat with a bronze statue by Jean-Jules Salmson (1823-1902). Balmat (1762-1834), a collector of crystals and a sturdy mountaineer, plotted the route and Saussare, a scientist from Geneva (1740-99) who suffered from vertigo, inspired the expedition.

Alpine Mass
Fête des Guides
Information from Compagnie des Guides
☎ 04 50 53 00 88
Maison de la Montagne, 190, Pl. de l'Église
15 Aug.
This festival is the biggest annual gathering of mountain guides, who turn up in their Sunday best: Jacquard socks, beige breeches, black jackets and white shirts. The traditional blessing of their ropes and ice-picks takes place in front of the Saint-Michel church. In the evening, there's a *son et lumière* show to rock music, which takes place at the Les Gaillands climbing site (to the west of the town).

From kitchen garden to table
Maison Carrier
44, Rte du Bouchet
☎ 04 50 53 00 03
Closed Mon., 15 days in June, and mid-Nov. to mid-Dec.
This is the more affordable annexe of the legendary Albert 1er restaurant. The cuisine is strictly regional, with pork in all its guises (even the ears). There's a mouth-watering selection of desserts, including rhubarb tart, which uses fruit from the kitchen garden, right in the centre of Chamonix.

View of Mont Blanc

Mont Blanc memories
Musée Alpin
89, Av. Michel-Croz
☎ 04 50 53 25 93
Open daily, June-15 Oct., 2-7pm; 20 Dec.-1 May, 3-7pm.
Admission charge.
Cham's Alpine museum has many fascinating objects on display, including mountain guides' notebooks, Balmat's ice-pick, and a reconstruction of the Chinese sitting room from Joseph Vallot's 4,400-m/ 14,435-ft observatory, where he would sit in comfort during storms. The whole history of the area is covered, right back to the origins of the village, as the site of a priory in 1091.

Art Nouveau café
Café La Terrasse
Pl. Balmat
☎ 04 50 53 09 95
Open daily, 11am-1.30am
People who complain that Chamonix has no architectural style will be amazed by this café

on the banks of the River Arve, with its highly ornate design. Dating from the early 20thC., it was originally an exhibition hall and was brought from Innsbruck in Austria to be rebuilt here. The wood-panelled top room is worth a look.

Paragliding
Summits
Le Mummery
28, Imp. Primevère
☎ 04 50 53 50 14
Closed mid-Nov.-Dec.

Spotcheck
D1-D2

Things to do
Exploring the mountains
Rock climbing
Paragliding

With children
Aiguille du Midi cable-car
Montenvers area and the Mer de Glace
Chalet at the Montets pass
Argentière glacier

Within easy reach
Megève (p. 124)
Saint-Gervais-les-Bains (p. 130)

Tourist offices
Argentière:
☎ 04 50 54 02 14
Chamonix-Mont-Blanc:
☎ 04 50 53 00 24

At around 9-10am, Planpraz (reached by the Le Brévent cable-car) is crowded, because the morning is an ideal time to try out two-seater paragliding. While waiting in the queue, try to overcome your nerves long enough to appreciate one of the most beautiful panoramas in the world – Mont Blanc and the Aiguille du Midi. If you're lucky, you might have your first flight in the company of Sandie Cochepain, the 1998 and 1999 world paragliding champion.

RARE STONES
Bourse aux Cristaux
Centre Sportif, Chamonix-Mont-Blanc
Information from Club de Minéralogie
☎ 04 50 53 03 38 Early Aug.
The market in crystals operates largely through word of mouth, but crystal collectors and dealers of Chamonix all turn out for this occasion. Around 40 well-respected exhibitors gather in the village sports centre, coming from all over. Experts look for pink fluorite and smoked quartz – two stones for which the region is famous.

Mer de Glace
Tourist train
Gare du Montenvers
35, Pl. de la Mer-de-Glace
Chamonix-Mont-Blanc
☎ 04 50 53 12 54
Daily, 15 Dec.-Feb., 10am-4pm; Mar.-Apr., 10am-4.30pm; May-June, 21 Aug.-Sept., 8.30am-5pm; July-20 Aug. 7am-6pm; Oct.-15 Nov. 9am-4pm.
Admission charge.
This little electric train only takes 20 minutes to cover the 5,141 m/16,866 ft route to the foot of the Mer de Glace. Since 1909, it has carried visitors on the 871 m/2857 ft climb to enjoy fantastic views of the glacier, as well as the panorama of the Drus and the Grandes Jorasses peaks.

A sea of ice
In 1741, two eccentric Englishmen, William Wyndham and Richard Pococke, arrived in Chamonix and climbed to the Glacier des Bois, now known as the Mer de Glace. The largest glacier in France (7 km/4.5 miles long, 200 m/656 ft thick), it fascinates onlookers and sports enthusiasts alike. In summer, the traditional hike across the glacier to the *moulins* ('windmills', or chasms formed by water erosion) is a must, but you will need proper hiking equipment and beginners must

be accompanied by a guide (information from Compagnie des Guides, p.19 and p.126).

The Mer de Glace

Retro charm
Hôtel du Montenvers
☎ 04 50 53 87 70
Open July-Aug.
This traditional and charming hotel, built in 1880, has 24 distinctive wood-panelled rooms, some with views over

the Mer de Glace. They are extremely popular, with visitors coming from all over the world. Alternatively, dormitory accommodation (30 beds) is available, which has been recently refurbished. The restaurant is open all year at lunchtime (except mid-Oct.-mid-Dec.).

Aiguille du Midi
Wine at its peak
Le 3842
gourmet restaurant
Access by Aiguille-du-Midi cable-car (admission charge), 100, Pl. de l'Aiguille-du-Midi, Chamonix-Mont Blanc
☎ 04 50 55 82 23
Open daily from noon depending on the weather (exc. 15 days at end Nov. to early Dec.). This is the highest gourmet restaurant in Europe, decked out with linen tablecloths and

silverware. Although its location causes problems in the kitchen, with water boiling at around 80°C/176°F due to the altitude, it does mean that the wines age better. You'll find Le 3842 has all the best vintages – Château Mouton-Rothschild, Pauillac, Mondeuse and Chignin-Bergeron – on its wine list.

ROCK CLIMBING AT 1,500 M/4,900 FT
Vallorcine
*4 km/2.5 miles
N of Col des Montets*

Close to the Italian border, the Barberine cliff, hundreds of metres high, is a renowned rock-climbing site. There's a beginners' area and other, more difficult routes such as *La guerre du feu* (classified 6b) and *Gros mignons et vieilles dentelles* (4 +).

Les Bossons
1 km/0.6 miles SW of Chamonix-Mont Blanc, towards Les Houches

Snack bars
Chalet du Glacier des Bossons
Access: Glacier des Bossons chairlift (admission charge) or by foot from the bottom of the same chairlift (25-40 minutes).
☎ 04 50 53 03 89
Open daily May-Sept.

There are high-altitude snack bars all over the Chamonix area, where walkers and climbers can relax and have a drink or something to eat. Stéphane Ruby's chalet, at 1,425 m/4,675 ft, loaded down with a mass of flowers, looks out over the Glacier des Bossons. One of the fastest-moving glaciers in the Alps, it travels between 200 and 250 m (655 and 820 ft) every year. There's also an open-air exhibition on the evolution of the biggest frozen waterfall in Europe (with a 3,500 m/ 11,480 ft drop).

Argentière
8 km N of Chamonix-Mont Blanc
The secrets of the glaciers
Information
☎ 04 50 54 00 71
(Les Grands-Montets cable-car)
Daily, July-Sept.
Admission charge.
Luc Moreau knows the Alpine glaciers like the back of his hand. He organises day-long (9am-3pm) family trips to the glaciers (children must be at least 4 years old), which include a visit to the Aiguille des Grands Montets (3,300 m/10,826 ft), and, following an easy walking route, a closer look at the Argentière glacier, which is 10km/6 miles long and up to 250 m/820 ft thick.

Col des Montets
3.5 km/2 miles from Argentière
The cry of the wood warbler
Chalet du Col des Montets
☎ 04 50 54 02 24
Open daily, June-15 Sept., 9.30-12.30am and 1.30-7pm.
Discovery trail (a loop of 2km/1.2 miles); charge for guidebook.
In the middle of the Aiguilles Rouges nature reserve, this virtually flat path meanders among columbines and ferruginous rhododendrons (their red colour due to the iron in the soil). Step back in time on this nostalgic, now disused route, once used by stagecoaches. At the chalet, an information centre allows younger visitors to listen to different birdcalls, though you may find that they are more interested in the computers.

Saint-Gervais-les-Bains, the source of pleasure

Located between the Arve valley and Mont Blanc, Saint-Gervais is a spa resort and the starting point for the Mont Blanc tramway, which climbs towards the highest peak in Europe. The town owes its fortune to a foresighted lawyer, Joseph-Marie Gontard, who in 1806 speculated on the healing powers of the thermal waters, which spring from the mountains at around 40°C/104°F.

Plateau-d'Assy
Sallanches
Combloux
St-Gervais
Les Houches
Nid d'Aigle
Mont Blanc
N.-D. de la Gorge

TRAMWAY DU MONT-BLANC

Saint-Gervais-les-Bains

22 km (14 miles) W of Chamonix-Mont Blanc

Mountain climber

Tramway du Mont-Blanc
Le Fayet
4 km (2 miles) N of Saint-Gervais-les-Bains
☎ 04 50 47 51 83
Open daily, mid-Jun to end Sept. and mid-Dec. to mid-Apr.; mountain bikes permitted on the 3.40pm train.
Admission charge.
Engineers have always seen Mont Blanc as a challenge. Originally, the TMB (Mont Blanc Tramway) was meant to climb to over 4,500 m/14,700 ft, but the ambitious project stopped short at the Nid d'Aigle (2,372 m/7,782 ft) in 1912. The journey still offers magnificent views, winding between rocky needles and jagged peaks.

Ice hockey

Patinoire (ice rink)
77, Imp. Cascade
☎ 04 50 93 50 02
Open daily 5-7pm and 9-11pm, July; 10am-noon, 5-7pm and 9-11pm, Aug.; phone for information out of season.

Ice hockey is sacred here, attracting the same fanatical interest as football does elsewhere. On match days the atmosphere at the ice rink is electric, particularly when Saint-Gervais meet local rivals Megève. If you want to try your hand at this fast-moving sport, there's an ice-hockey school in July (☎ 04 50 78 11 19).

Summer flea markets

Pl. du Mont-Blanc
Information
☎ 04 50 93 66 01
Mid-July to early Sept.
Once a fortnight in summer, around 40 antiques and bric-a-brac merchants set up their stalls in the Place du Mont-Blanc, selling folk art, furniture and all kinds of odds and ends. Join in the search for a bargain.

Things to do
Baroque walking trail
Health and fitness cures

With children
Nature centre
Mont Blanc tramway

Within easy reach
*Chamonix-Mont-Blanc
(p. 126)
Megève (p. 124)*

Tourist offices
Combloux: ☎ 04 50 58 60 49
Les Houches:
☎ 04 50 55 50 62
Plateau-d'Assy:
☎ 04 50 58 80 52
Saint-Gervais-les-Bains:
☎ 04 50 47 76 08

Sallanches
*11 km (7 miles) NW of
Saint-Gervais-les-Bains*
Nature centre
**Centre d'Initiation à la
Nature Montagnarde
Château des Rubins
105, Montée des Rubins
☎ 04 50 58 32 13**
Open daily (exc. Sun. am)
9am-noon and 2-6pm;
daily 9am-6.30pm, July-
Aug. *Admission charge.*
This centre, housed in the
14thC. Château des Rubins,
offers an entertaining introduction to the natural Alpine
world, using videos, CD-
ROMS and touch-sensitive
screens. Find out all about the
region's natural heritage,
including the habits of the
magnificent bearded vulture.

Plateau-d'Assy
*17 km (11 miles) N of
Saint-Gervais-les-Bains*
Sacred art
**Notre-Dame-
de-Toute-Grâce
Information from the
tourist office**
Open all year round.
*Free admission; charge
for guided tour.*
This church, designed by
Maurice Novarina and built
using the local speckled
sandstone, was consecrated in
August 1950. It was worked on
by an extraordinary collection
of celebrated artists (not all
religiously inclined), including
Rouault, Matisse, Braque,
Bonnard, Chagall and Léger.

Combloux
*10 km (6 miles) W of
Saint-Gervais-les-Bains*
The Baroque trail
Sentier du Baroque
*Booklet guide on sale in
tourist offices.*
The *Sentier du Baroque* is a
walking and mountain-biking
trail that explores the rich
Baroque heritage of the area,
taking in some 16 churches,
chapels and shrines *en route*
to Notre-Dame-de-la-Gorge
(20 km/12 miles; total climb
of 200 m/650 ft). These jewels
of Baroque architecture, with
onion-domed belltowers and
ornate altarpieces, have long
been places of pilgrimage for
locals. On 15 August, there's a
splendid *son et lumière* show at
the Notre-Dame-de-la-Gorge
church (information from
Contamines-Montjoie Tourist
office ☎ 04 50 47 01 58).

Les Houches
*16 km (10 miles) E of
Saint-Gervais-les-Bains*
Animal park
Parc de Merlet

On the road to Coupeau
☎ 04 50 53 47 89
Open daily 10am-6pm,
May-Sept.; 9.30am-
7.30pm, July-Aug.
Admission charge.
On the highlands around Les
Houches, Apollon the ibex
and the stags, Tito and
Romeo, rule the roost. They
share the 23 ha/57 acres of
this wildlife park with
chamois, deer, marmots and
wild sheep. Host Thérèse
Cachat will explain all about
her miniature mountain
kingdom and knows the name
of each animal.

HEALTH AND FITNESS
Rando Alti-Forme
Saint-Gervais-les-Bains
☎ **04 50 93 48 07 (for reservations)**
One-week course.
**This original combination of hiking and health treat-
ments will leave you feeling on top of the world.
During the day, you explore the high meadows of the
Alpage des Communailles and then soothe your
aches and pains under a high-pressure jet shower, or
one of the other health treatments on offer at the
Thermes du Fayet. The resort also has a fine park.**

Aix-les-Bains,
a return to the Belle Époque

Aix-les-Bains, the second most important spa resort in France, oozes the luxurious charm of the Belle Époque, the period before World War I when the aristocracy of Europe lived a decadent and leisurely existence. From flower fairs to music festivals, the Aixois still know how to celebrate with a touch of class.

Thermal spa resort
Piscine des Thermes Nationaux
Pl. Maurice-Mollard
☎ 04 79 35 38 50
Closed mid-Dec. to mid-Jan.
Admission charge.
The newly-built Thermes Chevalley spa complex lies in the upper part of the town. Architect Stanislas Fiszer, used moulded concrete and slabs of translucent alabaster to create a building that appears to be bathed in sunlight. Even if you're not staying here, you can still visit the luxurious half-covered, half open-air pool (open 2002), which is heated to around 36°C/97°F and has a view over the Dent du Chat peak. The treatments offered at the complex have a modern approach, and are based around health and well-being.

Belle Époque
Les Anciens Palaces
Information from the tourist office

Guided tours Wed. at 3pm, May-Oct.
Admission charge.
The stately homes, or palaces, of the Belle Époque, now mostly converted into flats, epitomise the grandeur and decadence of the era. The former Hôtel Splendide (1884) still retains its original, deep-blue lapis lazuli columns in the entrance hall. Sissi, Empress of Austria, came to stay here in 1895, strictly incognito… with an entourage of 10 servants and 63 pieces of luggage.

The one and only
Hôtel Astoria
Pl. des Thermes
☎ 04 79 35 12 28
Closed Dec.
The gloriously old-fashioned Astoria, built in 1904, still welcomes well-heeled guests

Main hall of the new spa resort

HELL'S WELL

Source d'Alun
Bd Berthollet
Information from
the tourist office
Guided tours only.
Admission charge.
The first spa tourists
were true adventurers.
Early visitors to the
Alun springs were
lowered on a rope into
the *puits de l'enfer*
('hell's well') for a long
soak, emerging lobster-
red from head to toe.
Today, the guided tour
is less demanding,
taking you to the source
via a long tunnel (98 m/
322 ft long), which was
once flooded with the
rich, turquoise waters.
The air is warm and
thick with the distinctive
smell of sulphur.

ɪn search of some old-world
ɡlamour. Soft sunlight streams
through the glass roof of the
monumental reception hall,
and there are numerous small
salons and lounges dotted
discreetly around the hotel.

Impressionist art

Musée Faure
10, bd des Côtes
☎ 04 79 61 06 57
Open daily (exc. Tues.
and public hols.)
10am-noon and 1.30-
6pm.
Admission charge.
Dr Jean Faure (1862-1942), a
successful pharmacist, moved
to Aix and made his fortune
selling a restorative potion
called *Élixir Bonjean*. On his
death, he left to the town a
fine collection of Impressionist
paintings, now housed in the
Faure museum. Among other
masterpieces, the museum
boasts Cézanne's *Le Bac à
Bonnières* and Degas' *Les
Danseuses Mauves*.

Place your bets!

Casino Grand Cercle
200, Rue du Casino
☎ 04 79 35 16 16
Gaming floor open 8pm-
3am (until 4am on Fri.,
Sat. and the eve of public
hols.). *Admission charge.*

Degas: Les Danseuses Mauves

Spotcheck
B2

Things to do

Thermes Chevalley spa resort
Belle Époque palaces
Music festival

With children

Visit the aquarium
Boating festival

Within easy reach

L'Albanais (p. 118)
Chambéry (p. 144)
Lac du Bourget (p. 136)

Tourist office

Aix-les-Bains:
☎ 04 79 88 68 10

Contact the tourist office for
information about guided
tours, or drop into the casino
during the tea dances (daily
except Tuesday), for a night
of action on the gaming
tables, or to take in a light
opera. The opulent ceiling of
the traditional gaming hall
was designed by Antonio
Salviati in 1883, using some
3,500,000 coloured glass
mosaic tiles. Past performers in
the casino's horseshoe theatre,
upholstered in scarlet, include
the celebrated French actress
Sarah Bernhardt and the
legendary singer Édith Piaf.

Lake Bourget Aquarium
La Maison du Lac du Bourget
200, Av. du Petit-Port
☎ 04 79 61 08 22
Open Wed. 2-4pm, week-ends and public hols.
2-5pm, Feb.-Apr. and Oct.-Nov.; daily 2-6pm, May-June; daily 10-11am and 2-6pm, July-Aug.; Mon.-Fri. 2-4pm, week-ends 2-5pm, Sept.
Admission charge.
This freshwater fish aquarium is one of the largest in France. There are some 57 different species of fish on display, more than 30 of which can be found in Lake Bourget, including the Alpine pollan, charfish and pike.

Garden city
Serres Municipales
Av. de Saint-Simon
Information from the tourist office.
Guided tours May-Oct.

Admission charge.
The municipal greenhouses produce some 400,000 plants each year, used to decorate the town. In spring, Aix's public areas are carpeted with pansies, daisies, buttercups and forget-me-nots, replaced in summer by begonias, petunias and geraniums. In August asters, in shades varying from white to lilac-blue, are the star attraction at the flower festival (Fête des Fleurs). For advice and garden-ing tips, just ask the friendly green-fingered gardeners at the greenhouses.

Boat trips
Bateaux du Lac du Bourget et du Haut-Rhône
Jardin des Belles Rives, Le Grand Port
☎ 04 79 88 92 09
Cruises daily; Fri. and Sun., Nov.-Mar.
Admission charge.
Run by a Breton family, this company has its own fleet on Lac du Bourget, recently swelled by the addition of an ultra-modern 18 m/60 ft catamaran, the *Alain Prud'homme*. They offer a range of excursions, including a three-hour tour of the lake and a cruise with a stopover at Hautecombe abbey.

Hoist the mainsail!
Club Nautique Voile
Le Grand Port
Bd Barrier
☎ 04 79 34 10 74
One-week sailing courses and boat hire in season. Keen freshwater sailors, whether old hands or beginners, should head for this sailing club in Aix-les-Bains. It has produced more than its fair share of national champions, and finished fourth in the last French cup, behind the clubs of three Atlantic ports. If you're taking to the water, note

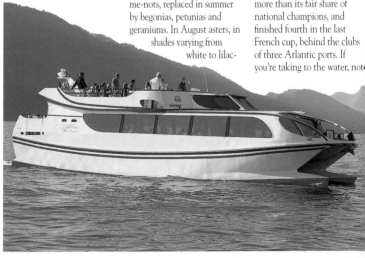

...hat the dominant wind comes from the north, with a powerful nd challenging westerly that icks up in the late afternoon.

Lake fishing
Pêche Passion (fishing store)
20, Av. du Grand-Port
☎ 04 79 61 64 12
Open daily (exc. Sun. pm)
*.30am-noon and 2-*pm, in season; closed or a fortnight in Dec. Sells one-day and vacances' (15 day) ishing permits, and orga-ises demonstrations and

fishing expeditions.
On Lake Bourget, the locals fish *au gig-gig* (with a lure of artificial bait), *à la gambe* (for perch and Alpine pollan), or *au plombier* (to land charfish and trout). The lake attracts large numbers of enthusiastic beginners and experienced anglers, whose boats, laden with spoonbaits, look like jewellery stalls.

Boating festival
Navig'Aix
Le Grand Port
Information from the tourist office
Late Aug.
The Navig'Aix festival is a wonderful display of old wooden boats, with brightly-decorated paintwork and gleaming copper trimmings. The last festival attracted over 70 motor and steamboats, including some made by Riva, the favourite boat builder for celebrities and royalty in the 1960s. Some boats welcome passengers on board, to take a cruise around the lake and help out on deck. Children over five will enjoy skippering their own electric boat, miniature replicas of a steamship or an oil tanker.

Wine cellar
Cave Xavier-François Jacqueline
7, Ch. Saint-Simond
☎ 04 79 35 03 23
Open Wed. and Sat. afternoon; by appt at other times.
The son of a doctor, Xavier-François Jacqueline chose a different career, and now cultivates vines. On 6 ha/15 acres around the Baie de Grésine he produces fruity wines, notably the *Cuvée Romantique* white wine, made from the Roussette de Savoie grape. This wine has a suitably romantic label – an old engraving showing Princess Marie de Solms out boating with writer François Ponsard.

The enchanted forest
Forêt de Corsuet
2 km (1 mile) N of the centre of Aix-les-Bains
The Corsuet oak forest, covering an area of 116 ha/287 acres, lies just outside Aix-les-Bains. There are walking trails to suit all levels of ability, including a 1.5-hour tour that's perfect for families, who can search in the forest for periwinkles, mushrooms, cedar, medlar and even fig trees (total climb of 150 m/500 ft). For more seasoned walkers, there's a 3-hour circuit (total climb of 550 m/1,800 ft), to the Grotte des Fées (fairytale cave) and the Croix de Meyrieu. The forest has a car park and picnic areas, and you can pick up a free map of the footpaths from the tourist office in Aix (*45 Randonnées autour du Lac du Bourget*).

MUSICAL NIGHTS

Information:
☎ 04 79 88 46 20
Tickets:
☎ 04 79 88 09 99
(open 10am-12.30pm).
A fortnight in Oct.
Admission charge.
The *Nuits Romantiques* ('nights of romance') music festival has a different theme each year. Concerts are held in the most evocative settings in the town, from the Hautecombe boathouse to the horseshoe theatre at the casino. For a perfect evening, take a walk in the priory gardens in Bourget-du-Lac before the concert, and end with a late supper.

OFFICE NATIONAL DES FORETS
FORET DE CORSUET

SENTIER BOTANIQUE

Lake Bourget
the Romantics' lake

The 19thC. Romantic poet Alphonse de Lamartine fell deeply in love with Lake Bourget and it's obvious why – magnificent scenery, tiny harbours, châteaux perched on hilltops or lost in the marshland, and the lake's Côte Sauvage (wild coast), bathed in the sweet scent of honeysuckle. While away an hour, an afternoon or a week here – the beauty of the Lac du Bourget is timeless.

La Chambotte

12 km (7 miles)
N of Aix-les-Bains
A taste of royalty
Restaurant-Brasserie
La Chambotte
☎ 04 79 63 11 76
Open daily, Easter to 1 Nov.
When Queen Victoria visited La Chambotte, she was carried up the hill in a sedan chair. Today, visitors are more likely to make the trip on foot (the main footpath starts at Brison-Saint-Innocent, 2 km/1 mile north of Aix-les-Bains), or by car. At the top (724 m/2,375ft) you'll find wonderful views as well as the Lansard family's home-made scones. Dishes fit for a queen are served all day.

Chanaz

12 km (7 miles) NW of La Chambotte
Scenic cruise
Le Chautagnard
☎ 04 79 54 51 80
Departures daily at 3pm, May to end Sep.
Admission charge.
For 10 months of the year, the overflow from Lake Bourget runs into the River Rhône. For the other two months, water is fed back into the lake via the Canal de Savières, which is the route taken by the *Le Chautagnard* pleasure boat. This scenic cruise takes you through the canal locks and past Châtillon, the final resting place of the poet Lamartine. Keep an eye open for the birdlife, which include coots and crested grebes.

Oil mill
Moulin à Huile
☎ 04 79 54 56 32
or 04 79 81 53 77
Open daily 10.30am-noon and 2.30-5.30pm, May-Sept.; 2.30-5.30pm Apr. and Oct.; out of season, by appt.
Free admission;
45-minute guided tour.
When Chanaz town council decided to recruit a new miller in 1990, this oil mill, dating from 1868, hadn't turned in 40 years. The Rozwadowzky family took over, and visitors

Map labels: Chanaz, St-Pierre-de-Curtille, La Chamb[...], Abbaye d'Hautecombe, Brison-St-Innocent, Yenne, Bourdeau, Aix-les-Ba[...], Le Bourget-du-Lac

...an now watch the picturesque ...ill in action once again, and ...ample walnut oil, hazelnut oil ...nd hazelnut jams, all made in ...he traditional manner.

Saint-Pierre-de-Curtille

...km (3 miles)
... of Chanaz

Tomb of princes

Abbaye d'Hautecombe
...km (3 miles) S of
...aint-Pierre-de-Curtille
☎ 04 79 54 26 12
Open daily (exc. Tues.)
...0-11.30am and 2-5pm.
...ree admission.
Over 40 princes were buried ...n the church of the Cistercian ...bbey of Hautecombe, includ...ng the celebrated Comte

KING OF THE LAKE

Auberge Lamartine
Rte du Tunnel,
Bourdeau
10 km (6 miles)
W of Yenne
☎ 04 79 25 01 03
Closed Sun. evening
and Mon. lunchtime.
At lunchtime this
hotel-restaurant has a
reasonably-priced set
menu (€23) which
includes the 'king of
the lake', *lavaret* (Alpine
pollan). You'll also find
another local star,
pianist Pierre Marin,
who has returned
home after stints at
Pierre Orsi in Lyon,
among other venues.

Rouge and the Comte Vert of the House of Savoy. Thereafter, the noble family chose the Italian city of Turin as their final resting place, except for the last and short-lived king of Italy, Umberto II. The sanctuary was restored in 1824 in a style known as 'Gothic troubadour'. Only the church is open to visitors and there's a small café.

Yenne

12 km (7 miles) SW of
Saint-Pierre-de-Curtille

The real gâteau de Savoie

Au Véritable Gâteau de Savoie Patisserie
2, Rue des Prêtres

☎ 04 79 36 70 02
Open Tues.-Fri. 9am-
noon and 3-7pm; week-
ends 8.30am-12.30pm
and 3-7pm.
Gâteau de Savoie is said to have been invented here around 1348 by Pierre de Yenne, chef to the court of the kings of Savoy. At this Yenne pâtisserie, the famous cake is still prepared according to the original, secret recipe, and baked in the traditional wood-fired oven.

Le Bourget-du-Lac

13 km (8 miles)
SE of Yenne

Marshland château

Château Thomas II de Savoie
Information from the tourist office.
Guided tour twice weekly in July-Aug.

Spotcheck
B2

Things to do
Visit Hautecombe abbey

With children
Try the real gâteau de Savoie
Scenic cruise

Within easy reach
Aix-les-Bains (p. 132)

Tourist offices
**Le Bourget-du-Lac and
Bourdeau:** ☎ 04 79 25 01 99
**Chautagne (Chanaz, Saint-
Pierre-de-Curtille, etc.):**
☎ 04 79 54 54 72
Yenne: ☎ 04 79 36 71 54

Admission charge.
This unusual château is hidden in the marshes at the southern end of Lake Bourget, at the mouth of the Leysse river. In the 13thC., the château was used as a hunting lodge by Thomas II of Savoy, but it then became one of the favourite residences of the itinerant royal court until 1427. A course of restoration work is planned.

Les Bauges, 'little Austria'

There are five gateways to the mountainous Les Bauges region, five winding passes leading to the heart of this green highland citadel. Lying just east of Chambéry, the Massif des Bauges is popular with caving and hiking enthusiasts. This regional nature park retains its original rural character, and many local farms still have huge wooden doors and traditional bread ovens.

Col de Leschaux
Broissieux
Bellecombe-en-B.
Pont du Diable
Lescheraines
Le Nant-Fou
Le Noyer
Le Châtelard
La Magne
La Compôte
Plateau du Margeriaz
Ecole
Aillon-le-Jeune
N.-D. de Bellevaux
Le Couvent
Thoiry

Aillon-le-Jeune
22 km (14 miles)
NE of Chambéry
Creamy Tomme cheese
Fromagerie du Val d'Aillon
☎ 04 79 54 60 28
Open daily 9am-noon and 3-8pm.
Admission charge (exc. shop).

This is one of the smallest dairies in the Savoy region, but it still processes some 650,000 litres/143,000 gallons of milk each year. If you visit in the morning, you can see them making Tomme cheese, which is 75% of the dairy's output. There are also children's games and workshops, where they can learn all about dairy farming and the cheese manufacturing process.

On the orchid trail
Sentier des Orchidées
Signposted from the road to Aillon-Station.
1-hour loop.
There are around 100 species of orchids in France and half of them can be found in the Massif des Bauges. They include the burnt orchid, which takes 14 years to reach its full size, and the spider orchid, so called because of its distinctive shape. The best time to see them in all their glory is between mid-May and mid-July. For further

MASSIF DES BAUGES
NATURE RESERVE

Maison du Parc
Le Châtelard
3 km (2 miles)
N of La Compôte
☎ 04 79 54 86 40
Open Mon.-Fri. 8am-
noon and 1.30-5.30pm.
The Parc Naturel
Régional du Massif des
Bauges, established in
1995, covers an area
of 86,000 ha/215,000
acres, and takes in some
58 local *communes*.
Work on a variety of
themed exhibitions is
currently in progress at
the Maison du Parc
information centre, but
meanwhile, you can find
out information on the
nature reserve's plant
and animal life at the
Maison de la Faune et
de la Flore in École.

nformation and to pick up a
ooklet about the walking trail,
isit the tourist office in
Aillon-le-Jeune.

Charterhouse
Le Couvent
Take the D32 towards
Aillon-Station.
Information from tourist
office in Aillon-le-Jeune
Weekly guided tours
2 hrs) in July-Aug.
Admission charge.

hurch doorway at Aillon-le-Jeune

La Chartreuse (charterhouse),
founded in 1178 by Humbert
III, Count of Maurienne, has
been damaged three times by
fire. The remains – a squat
gatehouse, one gallery of the
cloisters and an ornamental
pond, represents just a tiny
part of the original convent.
Until the proposed Maison du
Patrimoine (heritage centre)
opens on the site, the rest is
left up to your imagination.

sentier
des tannes et
glacières

A natural ice box
Les glacières
du Margériaz
Park at Place à Baban,
N of Aillon-le-Jeune on
the road to Aillon-
Margériaz, then follow
marked circuit trail
(4.5 hrs; total change in
altitude: 420 m/1,380
ft). Topo guide available
from the tourist office or
the Maison du Parc in
Le Châtelard.
Le Margériaz limestone plateau
is riddled with holes, known
locally as *tannes*. The Tanne
aux Cochons, a favourite with
cavers, is the deepest pothole
in the Savoy region, plunging
to a depth of 825 m/2,700 ft.
Some of these chambers once
contained ice, which was
quarried in summer and trans-
ported by the miners or on the
backs of donkeys back to the
cafés and fish merchants of
Chambéry and Aix-les-Bains.

Spotcheck
C2

Things to do
Orchid trail
Canyoning

With children
Val d'Aillon dairy
Donkey treks

Within easy reach
Aix-les-Bains (p. 132)
Chambéry (p. 144)
L'Albanais (p. 118)

Tourist offices
Bauges (Le Châtelard):
☎ 04 79 54 84 28
Les Aillons (Aillon-le-Jeune):
☎ 04 79 54 63 65

La Compôte
14 km (9 miles)
NE of Aillon-le-Jeune
Rustic farms
Information from Les
Bauges tourist office.
Weekly guided tour
(3 hrs, includes *rissole*
tasting), mid-July to
end Aug.
Admission charge.

In the maze of La Compôte's
narrow streets, many of the traditional farm buildings have
tavalans, shelves suspended
from the roof overhang on
poles. These balconies were
used to keep the firewood dry.
The small barns in the meadows
above the Escorchevel bridge,
on the road from Le Châtelard
to École are reminiscent of the
Austrian Tyrol.

Rissoles on Sunday
Café-Restaurant Châtelain
Small street to the right of the church
☎ 04 79 54 82 53
Closed evenings and Sat.
Book in advance.

At this unpretentious bistro, with its rustic wooden tables, you can sample the *menu ouvrier* (workers' lunch) and the charming hospitality of the Châtelains, the elderly couple who own the place. Madame is a skilled *cordon bleu* cook, and her husband plays the part of her long-suffering sidekick. On Sundays, they offer a classic regional dish and speciality of the house: *farçon* (p.79) and *rissoles* (puff-pastry turnovers filled with quince jam).

Around École
3 km (2 miles) S of La Compôte
Sacred fountain
Notre-Dame de Bellevaux
☎ 04 79 54 80 20
Pilgrimage the day after Whit Sunday; mass on Thurs. at 10am in summer.

Accessible via a footpath (30 mins) from the road to Le Chéran, around 3 km/2 miles from École, this 11thC. Benedictine priory, once home to St François de Sales, has long since crumbled to ruins. The Chapelle de la Sainte-Fontaine, however, built in

1865, still attracts pilgrims. It houses one of the site's ancient shrines and a source of spring water, the focus of ancient superstition. According to custom, pilgrims drink only from the inside source, and not from the fountain outside.

Alpine lodge
Chalets d'Orgeval
Car park at Nant-Fourchu, 3 km (2 miles) E of Notre-Dame-de-Bellevaux.
☎ 04 79 54 80 44
(reservations)
Open early June-early Oct.

You have to get up at the crack of dawn to see the chamois and

wild mountain sheep, so spend the night at the Chalets d'Orgeval gîte (30 dormitory beds), located at 1,603 m/5,260 ft, in the shadow of the Pointe d'Arcalod peak. The 600-m/2,000-ft climb to the gîte, at the heart of the Les Bauges wildlife reserve, created in 1950, is demanding in places, but it's a classic family outing.

Around Bellecombe-en-Bauges
13 km (8 miles) N of La Compôte
Pont du Diable
After Lescheraines, head for Col de Leschaux. Par on the left and walk to the bridge (15 mins.) along the right-hand path.
Introduction to canyoning: Gérard Garnier
☎ 04 79 63 30 83
June-Oct.

The impressive Pont du Diable (devil's bridge) is a stone arch spanning a 30 m/100 ft drop into a narrow gorge. The gorge itself is barely 200 m/650 ft long, but makes an excellent site for an introduction to

canyoning, a thrilling sport that combines climbing, rock slides, abseiling and jumping in pools.

Donkey treks

Oxalis
Broissieux
☎ 04 79 63 36 97
Open all year round
One-day and one-week expeditions.
The Oxalis co-operative offers a variety of trekking expeditions, but you can also hire a donkey and strike out on your own, or plan an outing, with or without guides, according to your own schedule. Sidonie, Galopin or Indiana will carry all your bags and picnic supplies and will be happy to follow where you lead.

Sawmills

Les Scieries
Turn right at Bellecombe, follow signs for Les Scieries.
Information from Oxalis
☎ 04 79 63 36 97

Free admission; charge for summer guided tour when mill is in operation.

During the 19thC., four sawmills operated on this site. The Scierie des Mugnier was still in operation right up to 1965, and you can take a guided tour of the mill and see the original machinery, including a huge saw driven by water power. There's also a picnic area in a beautiful countryside setting.

Le Noyer
11 km (7 miles) SW of Bellecombe-en-Bauges
Healing herbs
Benoît and Valérie Claude
Le Crêt farm
☎ 04 79 63 32 42
(book in advance)
Sale of herbs and infusions; botanical walks.
Benoît and Valérie believe fervently in the healing powers of nature. On their farm they grow wormwood, balm and St John's wort, known for its benefits in combating stress and depression. They also offer a guided botanical walk (around 1 hr; charge), explaining about the healing properties of forest plants and gathering sweet woodruff, a natural relaxant, and ramson leaves (wild garlic), used to flavour salads, along the way.

WOOD-TURNING

The wooden dishes and cooking utensils used by the peasants of Les Bauges were once ironically referred to as 'Bauges silverware'. In 1850, there were at least 60 wood-turners working in the town of La Magne (*commune* of Saint-François-de-Sales; around 1 km/0.6 miles from Le Noyer). Now, there's only one: Jean-Paul Pernet (☎ 04 79 63 30 13), who makes practical pieces in his spare time, working in sycamore. Further afield, other artisans keep the tradition alive, including Jean-Paul Rossi in Thoiry (10 km/6 miles SW of Aillon-le-Jeune ☎ 04 79 28 40 85), the only turner still making *pôches*, classic ladles with hooks. This ladle, which demands a high level of skill from the wood-turner, was once the symbol of the region, where soup was often eaten three times a day.

The Beaufortain,
mountain meadows and deep blue lakes

Lying just outside Albertville, this 'land of a thousand chalets' is also a land of traditions, such as the *remues*, when farming families follow their herds to the high mountain pastures, and festivals when locals sport

Roselend lake

traditional dress, including the region's woven linen caps (*berres*). One of its great delicacies is the celebrated Beaufort cheese, with its distinctive hazelnut flavour. The region also has four dams, with reservoirs that create a dramatic and graceful landscape.

Beaufort

20 km (12 miles) NE of Albertville

Farçons and gratarons

Town market

Opposite the co-operative dairy.
Wednesday morning. Beaufort's produce market is one of the best places to sample the local *farçon*. Made to a traditional recipe, with 19 ingredients, such as potato, bread, eggs, figs, raisins and cinnamon (p.79), this regional speciality has a solid, dense consistency and is eaten as a dessert. *Gratarons*, small goat's cheeses from the Beaufortain region, are also sought-after, with their distinctive grey crust.

Arèches

5 km (3 miles) S of Beaufort

Souvenirs of the Beaufortain

La Ruine shop
☎ 04 79 38 19 25
Open daily (exc. Tues.) 10am-noon and 4-7pm. Housed in a former 17th-18thC. miller's house which had fallen into ruin, this

shop has been beautifully restored. The name serves to remind people of its past, but La Ruine is as much a meeting place as a souvenir shop, where locals drop in to share news. The owner, Martine, only sells things that interest her, and you're bound to find a charming and reasonably-priced oddment to take home, such as a salt cellar or a Beaufortain cross.

A head for heights

Roc du Vent *via ferrate*

Information from the guides office
☎ 04 79 38 37 57
Guided circuit walk (4-5 hrs), with a climb of 540 m/1,770 ft. Depart from Plan de la Lai, E of Arèches on the road to Cormet de Roselend, at 1,820 m/5,970 ft.

Classified as 'quite difficult', this new walkway has been designed for appreciation of the scenery, and is suitable for all reasonably-fit walkers. Sufferers of vertigo, however, may find it challenging – one of the most thrilling parts of the trail is a 'Nepalese' bridge, suspended 35 m/115 ft above the valley, overlooking the La Gittaz lake.

Lac de Roselend
12 km (7 miles)
E of Beaufort
In the saddle
Mountain bike trail
no. 14
Information and topo guide from tourist office.

Circuit route around the lake, 12 km/7 miles long, with a climb of 400 m/1,300 ft.
Over 130 km/80 miles of mountain biking trails criss-cross the pastures, forests and mountain ridges of this region. One of the most attractive is circuit no. 14, which runs above Roselend lake, on tarmac and dirt tracks.

Saint-Jacques church

Hauteluce
14 km (9 miles)
N of Beaufort
Baroque heritage
Église et Chapelles guided tour
☎ 04 79 85 78 73
Admission charge; book in advance; open to children over 7.

Spotcheck
C2-D2

Things to do
Mountain biking around Roselend lake
Roc du Vent via ferrata

With children
Hauteluce Baroque tour

Within easy reach
Albertville (p. 148)
Megève (p. 124)
La Tarentaise (p. 148)

Tourist offices
Arèches: ☎ 04 79 38 15 33
Beaufort: ☎ 04 79 38 37 57
Hauteluce: ☎ 04 79 38 81 67

This entertaining and informative tour of the Baroque churches and chapels will fascinate the whole family. Discover the splendid *trompe l'œil* façade of the Église Saint-Jacques-d'Assyrie (1558) and learn about the complex system once used by locals as protection against disaster, using a different saint to guard against each problem – St Sébastien to keep the plague away, St Antoine to keep mules healthy, etc., etc..

Traditional cuisine
Chalet de Colombe
Towards the Col du Joly, entrance on the right after the Col du Joly chairlift
☎ 06 11 09 09 10
Open daily, June-Aug.; weekends, Sept.-Oct.
This restaurant makes a perfect break on the path to the Barrage de la Girotte (dam). The chef, Isabelle, prepares traditional recipes such as *gourres* (small sweet-and-sour meatballs in broth) and *apprestaments* (potatoes *au gratin*). For a list of other recommended restaurants, ask at the tourist office.

BEAUFORTAIN CO-OPERATIVE DAIRY
Coopérative Laitière du Beaufortain
Av. du Capitaine-Bulle, Beaufort
☎ 04 79 38 33 62
Open daily 8am-12.30pm and 2-7pm, May-Sept.; daily (exc. Sun.) 8am-12.30pm and 2-6pm, out of season. *Free guided tour.*
This dairy processes around 9,800 litres/2,200 gallons of milk per year, from 160 farms in the region, producing 920 tons of cheese (around 22,500 'wheels' of Beaufort). Visitors can watch the production process from behind a window and then visit the cellars where the cheeses are matured. The tour ends with a visit to the on-site shop.

Chambéry, capital of Savoie

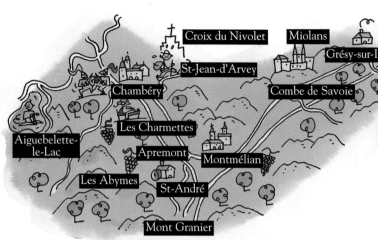

F ormer seat of the House of Savoy, Chambéry's love of the extravagant and the fanciful is well illustrated by its famous Fontaine des Éléphants. A tour of the historic centre is a riot of *trompe l'œil* decorations, brightly coloured façades and wrought-iron embellishments. Lying between the Combe de Savoie valley, Aiguebelette lake and the La Chartreuse and Les Bauges highlands, Chambéry also makes an ideal base from which to explore the region.

Place Saint-Léger

The old town
Guided tours
☎ 04 79 85 93 73
Daily, May-Sept.; Sat.,
Sun. and public hols.,
Oct.-Apr.
Admission charge.
The historic centre of
Chambéry is a conservation
area covering some 17 ha/42
acres, in which the beautiful

townhouses are maintained
in their original glory. The
guided tour takes in the
picturesque alleyways and
interior courtyards of the
old houses, Mediterranean-
style colours, Renaissance
façades, Piedmontese
architecture, *trompe l'œil*
decoration and wrought-
iron detailing. All these
styles come together in

Place Saint-Léger, a lively
and harmonious square.

Savoyard
museum
**Square Lannoy
de Bissy**
☎ 04 79 33 44 48
Open daily (exc. Tues.
10am-noon and
2-6pm. *Admission
charge.*

Fountain of the Elephants

Spotcheck
B2-C2-B3-C3

Things to do
Hike to La Croix du Nivolet
Rousseau museum

With children
Mountain centre
Château de Miolans
Aiguebelette lake

Within easy reach
Aix-les-Bains (p. 132)
Bauges (p. 138)
Chartreuse (p. 178)

Tourist offices
Aiguebelette-le-Lac:
☎ 04 79 36 00 02
ATD Savoie:
☎ 04 79 85 12 45
Chambéry: ☎ 04 79 33 42 47

...oused in a former Franciscan monastery, the Savoyard museum is dedicated to the region's heritage, with scale models of farms typical of the Chartreuse and Maurienne ranges, and traditional clothing and furniture. The Le Cruet wall paintings, over 30 m/100 ... in length and depicting hunting and battle scenes from the 13th and 14thC., were discove-red by chance in 1985 in the hall of a château.

Château des ducs de Savoie
Pl. du Château
☎ 04 79 85 93 73
Guided tours, Sat. at 3pm and 4pm.
Admission charge.
The former residence of the dukes of Savoy now houses local government offices. The guided tour takes in various reception rooms, the covered walkway and the Sainte-Chapelle, where the Turin shroud was displayed before it was returned to Turin in 1578. The belltower contains some extraordinary machinery that operates the château's 70 bronze bells, which have a combined weight of 41 tons. To ensure the sound quality, which is among the best in the world, Paccard (p.117) made all the bells from an identical bronze alloy. There's a dummy set below the tower, that the bellringers use for practice.

GOURMET SWEETS
In 1895 M. Dufour, a pâtissier from Chambéry, invented the chocolate truffle. The town was already known for its sweets – the *Bonbon Mazet*, a round toffee in nine different flavours, dates back to 1820. Since then, *Bouchons d'Apremont, Muscadines, Pavés des Éléphants* (in honour of the fountain) and *zizis* (chocolate-coated morello cherries in kirsch) have all added to the growing list of Chambéry sweet treats.

Madame de Warens' bedchamber

An evening with Rousseau
Musée des Charmettes
Ch. des Charmettes
☎ 04 79 33 39 44
Open daily (exc. Tues. and public hols.) 10am-noon and 2-4.30pm (until 6pm, Apr.-Sept.); historical re-enactments, Wed. and Fri. at 9pm (12-31 July), 8.30pm (2 Aug.-1 Sept.).
Admission charge.
Illustrious 18thC. philosopher Jean-Jacques Rousseau spent some of the happiest days of his life in this beautiful country house, in the company of his mistress, Madame de Warens. On summer evenings, the house is the backdrop for dramatic and musical re-enactments in period costume. Accompanied by readings from his work, the presentations provide a unique insight into the life of a celebrated thinker.

Eureka gallery
Médiathèque Jean-Jacques-Rousseau, Pl. François-Mitterand, Carré Curial
☎ 04 79 60 04 25
Open Tues.-Fri. 2-6pm, Sat. 10am-1pm, July-Aug.; phone for details out of season.
Free admission.
The exhibition at the Galerie Eurêka combines scale models, interactive games and videos to create a uniquely entertaining

learning experience for children and adults alike, dealing with all aspects of the mountain environment.

Saint-Jean-d'Arvey
*9 km (6 miles)
E of Chambéry*
Hike to La Croix du Nivolet
Information and brochure (*Promenades et Randonnées Pédestres en Savoie*) from ATD Savoie
Depart from car park in the hamlet of Lovettaz.
This 5-hour hiking circuit is not suitable for all walkers. It's a challenging route, across mountain pastures, precipitous ledges and slippery terrain, with a tricky climb through the Passage des Échelles (an iron staircase between two rocky outcrops). At the summit (1,547 m/5,076 ft), there's a huge cross (Croix du Nivolet)

and an uninterrupted view ov the Cluse de Chambéry valley and Bourget lake.

Aiguebelette-le-Lac
*21 km (13 miles)
SW of Chambéry*
Aiguebelette lake
Information from the tourist office.
Free admission.
The remarkable emerald-gree waters of Lake Aiguebelette are very mild (22-26°C/72-79°F in high summer), makir it the perfect spot for a swim. The most enjoyable way to

explore the lake, however, is cruising on a 'surfbike', a sort of pedalo, with a saddle that lifts you high above the wate You can rent surfbikes (about €8 per hour) at the beaches, the Plage du Sougey and the Plage de Lépin-le-Lac.

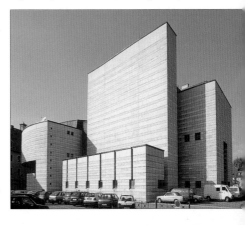

Apremont

* km (6 miles)*
E of Chambéry
**Le Vigneron
Savoyard**
te du Crozet
☎ 04 79 28 33 23
Open Tues.-Fri. 8am-noon
nd 2-6pm (5pm Sat.).
ree admission.
ollowing a huge landslide on
he slopes of Mont Granier in
248, it took ages for the vines
o take root in the damaged
oil. Today, however, the vine-
ards of the Cru des Abymes
nd Apremont wines cover 500
a/1,200 acres, spread over five
ocal *communes*. You can taste
ese crisp, light wines, with
heir distinctive flinty taste, at
e Vigneron Savoyard, a co-
perative cellar that stocks the
ines of various local growers.

Saint-André

km (2 miles)
* of Apremont*
aper mill
**loulin de la Tourne
achat**
☎ 04 79 28 13 31
uided tours daily at
pm and 4pm, May-Sept.;
lon., Wed. and weekends
t 4pm, rest of the year;
osed 15 Dec.-15 Jan.
hop open Mon.-Fri.
0am-noon and 2-6pm.
dmission charge.

In former times, the region's
paper mills were the subject of
numerous bizarre superstitions.
With their huge furnaces that
burned throughout the night,
people believed the paper-
makers were in league with
the devil. On the guided tour
of this ancient mill, you'll
discover the legends and
history of the trade, as well as
its secrets, including how the
raw materials, just a bunch of
old rags, are transformed into
a smooth sheet of paper.

Montmélian

4 km (2 miles)
NE of Saint-André
A fortified town
Guided tour 8pm Thurs.
July-Aug., depart from
the church square.
☎ 04 79 84 07 31
This old fortified Savoyard
town was always in the front
line during clashes with the
neighbouring Dauphiné region.
Traces of Montmélian's power
and prosperity remain in the
town's historic centre, notably
the casement windows of the
Hôtel des Portiers, the spiral
staircase of the Hôtel des

Nicolle de la Place, the 16thC.
Italianate loggia at the Maison
du Gouverneur and the town's
covered passages and gateways.

Miolans

17 km (11 miles)
NE of Montmélian
**Medieval
fortified château**
Château de Miolans
☎ 04 79 28 57 04

Open daily (exc. Sun. am)
10am-noon and 1.30-
7pm, May-Sept.; week-
ends and public hols.
1.30-7pm, Apr.
Admission charge.
The Marquis de Sade,
imprisoned here in 1772, soon
discovered the impossibility of
escape. Perched on a rocky
outcrop, at 550 m/1,800 ft, this
fine fortress was built between
the 11th and 16thC. It's a
real maze of tunnels, secret
chambers, dungeons, covered
passages and turrets, and also
has an attractive garden, with
a view that stretches from the
Chartreuse regional park in the
west to Mont Blanc in the east.

COMBE DE SAVOIE VALLEY
This peaceful valley is
deep and narrow, and
well off the beaten
track. Take the D201,
linking Montmélian
and Albertville, and
allow time to explore
the charming villages
and scenic views over
the valley and its
vineyards. Stop off
at the Écomusée des
Coteaux-du-Salin
(Grésy-sur-Isère, 20
km/12 miles NE of
Montmélian, ☎ 04 79
37 94 36). From the
museum, there's a
500 m/1,600 ft trail
through woodland and
past farms, where you
can catch a glimpse
of the daily life and
work of present-day
inhabitants of the
Combe de Savoie.

Gésy-sur-Isère

Tarentaise,
Olympic valley

The Tarentaise valley follows the course of the Isère river, all the way from Albertville to Val-d'Isère. Synonymous with snow and ski resorts that are famed throughout the world, the attractions of the Tarentaise valley also include its gilded Baroque chapels and the Vanoise national park, with its unspoilt natural beauty.

Albertville

50 km (31 miles)
NE of Chambéry
Maison des Jeux Olympiques d'Hiver
11, Rue Pargoud
☎ 04 79 37 75 71
Open Mon.-Sat. 9am-7pm, Sun. and public hols. 2-7pm, July-Aug.; Mon.-Sat. 9am-noon and 2-6pm, rest of the year.
Admission charge.
This museum recounts the full story of Albertville's hosting of the Winter Olympics, from the thrill of the announcement in 1982, to the staging of the events 10 years later. On two floors, the exhibitions,

including the memories and memorabilia of champions and costumes from the opening ceremony, capture the emotion and excitement of Olympic competition. There are also displays showing the history of winter sports, including the evolution of the ski boot.

Medieval Conflans
Locals often make the 10-minute climb from the centre of Albertville to the charming suburb of Conflans, guarded by the Porte de Savoie the gateway to the former medieval town. Conflans is full of floral squares, beautiful 16thC. houses and former artisans' workshops, now converted into craft shops.

Weddings at the Église Saint-Grat in Conflans are another long-standing tradition, the church's impressive steps providing the ideal spot for photos.

Feissons-sur-Isère

15 km (9 miles)
S of Albertville
**Dining at
the château**
**Restaurant du
Château de Feissons**
☎ 04 79 22 59 59

Open daily (exc. Sun. evening and Mon.).
Perched on a rocky outcrop, the Château de Feissons once guarded the entrance to the Tarentaise valley for the Lords of Briançon. Now this ancient fortress has been faithfully restored, and its restaurant serves classic, refined French cuisine in front of the huge fireplace or out on the terrace, with views of Mont Bellachat in the distance. Set menus from €24; children's set menu €12.

PARC NATIONAL DE LA VANOISE
(NATIONAL PARK)
Administrative headquarters,
135, Rue du Docteur-Julliand, B.P. 705,
73007 Chambéry ☎ 04 79 62 30 54
By the early 1960s, there was growing concern over the ibex, which was fast disappearing from the slopes of the Massif de la Vanoise. As a result, in 1963, the French government created the country's first national park. Today, there are nearly 2,000 ibex roaming the 53,000 ha/131,000 acres of the Vanoise national park, and a total of 6,000 including those in the Gran Paradiso national park in Italy. Together, the two parks form the largest nature reserve in Western Europe. For more information contact the park headquarters or tourist offices in the *communes* within the protected area.

Pralognan-la-Vanoise

Spotcheck
C2-D2-D3

Things to do
White-water rafting on the Haute-Isère
Angling
The Vanoise national park

With children
Museum of the Winter Olympics
Bois de la Glière woodland walk
Treetop adventure
Alpine garden

Within easy reach
Beaufortain (p. 142)
Maurienne (p. 152)

Tourist offices
ADT Savoie
☎ 04 79 85 12 45
Albertville: ☎ 04 79 32 04 22
Bourg-Saint-Maurice:
☎ 04 79 07 12 57
Pralognan-la-Vanoise:
☎ 04 79 08 79 08

Pralognan-la-Vanoise

39 km (24 miles) SE of Feissons-sur-Isère
Woodland walk
Bois de la Glière
Information from the national park (*see box*) or the Pralognan-la-Vanoise tourist office.
Around 1.5 hrs.
Specially designed for children, this discovery trail starts from the Fontanettes car park (eastern side of Pralognan-la-Vanoise) and passes through La Glière woods to the scenic

viewpoint, the Belvédère de l'Arcelin, passing interesting trees, mosses, streams, waterfalls, and animal and insect life.

Notre-Dame-
du-Pré

*25 km (16 miles)
SE of Feissons-sur-Isère*
Angel faces
**Église Notre-Dame-
du-Pré**
The rosy-cheeked angels and opulent altarpieces of the charming Notre-Dame-du-Pré church are a classic example of 17thC. mountain Baroque style. The church was rebuilt in 1647, but the main altarpiece, designed by Pierre-Antoine Marquet in Rococo style, dates from the 19thC. The FACIM conservation association publishes a brochure (*Chemins du Baroque*), with information about opening times and guided tours for 54 Baroque

churches in the Beaufortain, Maurienne and Tarentaise and the Arly valley. For further details, contact the tourist offices or FACIM: ☎ 04 79 96 74 37 or 43.

Bourg-Saint-Maurice

32 km (20 miles) NE of Notre-Dame-du-Pré
White-water rafting
Arc Aventure
☎ 04 79 07 44 64
Coureur de rivières
☎ 04 79 04 11 22
Virages
☎ 04 79 07 78 82
Open all year.
Various companies offer white-water rafting trips along the upper Isère river. You'll be provided with a wetsuit, a lifejacket, helmet and a neoprene jacket (if it's really cold) and then you set off in a team of eight (with a guide) to ride the rapids. The complete descent of the Haute-Isère takes between 2 and 2.5 hours and is open to all those 14 years and over. The less strenuous introductory trip, which covers the first section of the river, lasts just over an hour and is open to children over 10 years of age, provided they can swim.

Séez

4 km (2 miles) E of Bourg-Saint-Maurice
Traditional fabrics
Filature Arpin
La Fabrique
☎ 04 79 07 28 79
Guided tours Mon.-Sat. 8.30-11.30am and 2-5pm (machines do not operate on Sat.); shop open Mon.-Sat. 9am-noon and 2-7pm. *Admission charge.*

Saint-Pierre-d'Extravache chapel

Classed as an historical monument, the old weaving looms at the Filature Arpin factory have been operating since the first fabrics were produced in Séez in 1817. The company is known for *drap de Bonneval* (p.65), a hard-wearing cloth well-suited to the rigours of mountain-life, still used as a furnishing fabric

TARENTAISE BAROQUE FESTIVAL

Association Musique et Patrimoine en Tarentaise
Ancien Évêché, Pl. Saint-Pierre, Moûtiers
9 km (6 miles) S of Feissons-sur-Isère
☎ 04 79 24 47 02
Admission charge.
The Tarentaise music festival serves a double helping of Baroque culture – the chance to see the splendours of the region's Baroque art, while listening to the music of Bach and other Baroque composers. The festival takes place over the first fortnight in August and includes concerts in around 15 of the Baroque churches and chapels of the valley. Each concert is preceded by a talk on the architecture and history of the venue, given by a guide from the Tarentaise heritage assocation.

Treetop adventure
Arc Aventures
Longefoy
☎ 04 79 07 44 64
Advance booking required.
Admission charge.
Arc Aventures has created an adventure playground in the treetops of the Forêt de Malgovert, with 50 platforms connected by a network of rope slides and walkways. This exciting place is open to all children over 1.45 m/4 ft 9 in in height, who are supervised by trained professionals.

Col du Petit-Saint-Bernard
28 km (17 miles) NE of Séez
Hospice du Petit-Saint-Bernard
☎ 06 09 90 26 71
Open daily 9.30am–12.30pm and 2-6pm, mid-Jun. to mid-Sept.
Free admission.
On the border between France and Italy, at an altitude of 2,188 m/7,179 ft, the Petit-Saint-Bernard pass has been a busy crossing point since Roman times. The Petit-Saint-Bernard hospice dates back to the 6thC., and has been repeatedly destroyed and rebuilt over the years. Now being renovated once more, the hospice houses a small museum

and information centre for the Vanoise (French) and Gran Paradiso (Italian) national parks. Plans for the site include a hiking gîte, a European cultural centre, a chapel and an exhibition of regional products.

Jardin Alpin La Chanousia
☎ 04 79 07 43 32
(summer only)
Open daily 9am-1pm and 2-7pm, July to mid-Sept.
Admission charge.
Located next to the Petit-Saint-Bernard hospice, this beautiful Alpine garden was established in 1897 by the green-fingered Abbot Chanoux. Rector of the hospice, he gathered several thousand plants from the neighbouring mountains. Today, the rockeries, flowerbeds and lawns of this 1-ha/2.5-acre garden are home to around 1,200 species, including gentian, primrose and rhododendron.

Les Menuires
38 km (24 miles) S of Feissons-sur-Isère
Angling
Information from ADT Savoie
The beautiful Du Lou mountain lake , lying at an altitude of 2,100 m/6,900 ft, is a great spot for fly fishing, with healthy populations of river trout and charfish. To reach the Lac du Lou, it's about an hour's walk from the car park, on the CD915 just outside Les Menuires (follow the signs for Val-Thorens).

La Chanousia Alpine garden

Maurienne,
the valley of conquerors

L ying between the Tarentaise and Oisans regions, the Maurienne valley is the longest in the Alps. For centuries, it was the main route through the mountains to Italy, trodden by the greatest adventurers and conquerors. Most of today's adventurers attack the mountain passes on bicycles. In the Haute-Maurienne, in the heart of the Vanoise national park, a rich historical heritage comprises Baroque chapels, military fortresses and numerous ancient villages.

Saint-Jean-de-Maurienne

73 km (45 miles) SE of Chambéry

A design classic

Musée de l'Opinel
Av. Henri-Falcoz
☎ 04 79 64 04 78
Open daily (exc. Sun. and public hols.) 9am-noon and 2-7pm.
Free admission.
Created in 1890 by Joseph Opinel, the Opinel knife is an undisputed design classic, with over 200 million originals sold, and a specimen in New York's Museum of Modern Art. Jacques Opinel, a descendant of the pioneering toolmaker, has opened this museum in a former company workshop. Dedicated to the history of the family and the knife that made their name, the museum has a video display showing the manufacturing process. The museum shop displays the full Opinel range, with 10 different blade sizes and a wide variety of models, including utility, customised, highly sharpened and stainless steel.

Modane

32 km (20 miles) SE of Saint-Jean-de-Maurienne

The path of pleasure

This 50-km/31-mile marked route, the *Chemin du Petit Bonheur* ('path of pleasure'), certainly lives up to its name. Winding along the bottom of the valley, through spruce and larch forests, it links all the villages of the upper Maurienne valley, from Modane to Bonneval-sur-Arc in the heart of the Vanoise national park. It's perfect for mountain biking, horse-riding, walking and snowshoe trekking in winter.

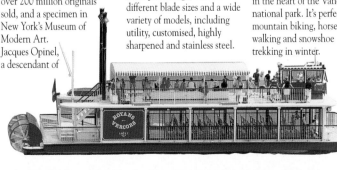

Spotcheck
C3-D3

Things to do
Chemin du Petit Bonheur
Canyoning

With children
The Esseillon forts
Astronomy festival

Within easy reach
Belledonne (p. 176)
Combe de Savoie (p. 147)
Tarentaise (p. 148)

Tourist offices
**Maurienne tourism
committee:** ☎ 04 79 83 23 94
Upper Maurienne valley:
☎ 04 79 05 91 57
Lanslevillard:
☎ 04 79 05 23 66

Valfréjus

2 km (1 mile)
S of Modane
High adventure
Canyoning
Information from the
Maison de la Montagne
☎ 04 79 05 33 76

Starting in Valfréjus and heading downstream 3 km/ miles towards Le Lavoir, this canyoning expedition is the perfect way to explore the Fréjus river. The sport combines abseiling down waterfalls, jumping into pools and sliding down canyons, and should only be carried out in the company of a qualified guide with a good knowledge of the river and the canyoning route.

Aussois

7 km (4 miles)
NE of Modane
The Esseillon forts
☎ 04 79 05 15 23
Open all year round.
Free admission.

Built between 1817 and 1830 by the kingdom of Piedmont-Sardinia to keep the French at bay, the five Forts d'Esseillon are dotted along the side of a rocky outcrop overlooking the Maurienne valley. On the walls you can still see messages carved by the garrisoned soldiers, recalling long, harsh, isolated vigils, followed by sudden flights to safety. The Esseillon forts were never actually called upon to defend the honour of their Italian masters – Savoy was handed over to the French in 1860.

Little angels or little devils?
There are two *via ferrata* walkways at Fort Victor-Emmanuel (one of the five Esseillon forts), which have been specially

designed for children. On the eastern slope, the *Angelots* ('little angels') is for children aged 6 and over, who can climb along the side of the fort to the car park in five small sections 4-20 m/13-66 ft high, accompanied by an adult. The *Diablotins* ('little devils') route is for older children, who scale the slightly steeper western side of the fort.

Sollières-Sardières

11 km (7 miles)
NE of Aussois
The monolith
For years this impressive 93 m/305 ft monolith humbled the climbers of the region, and it was finally conquered only

THE *LOMBARDE*
Before setting off on a hike on Mont Cenis, take time to check the weather forecast. The *Lombarde* is a southeasterly breeze that blows in from Italy, bringing a blanket of cloud that obscures the view. When the clouds cover the mountain, visibility can be less than 30 m/100 ft, but when the *Lombarde* turns, Mont Cenis is simply a paradise.

Open daily (exc. Sat.)
3-7pm (mid-June to mid-Sept.), 3.30-7pm (mid-Dec. to Apr.).
Admission charge.
This information centre, housed in an old church, is dedicated to the rich Baroque heritage of the Maurienne valley. The exhibition retraces the history of Baroque art and architecture in the mountains from the 17th to the 19thC., and is an excellent starting point for a tour of the churches and chapels of the surrounding area.

Fort de Ronce (30 mins). This attractive circular fort, built by the Italians, formed part of the system of defence for the plateau, which remained in Italian hands until 1947.

Col du Mont-Cenis

10 km (6 miles) S of Lanslebourg-Mont-Cenis
Mont-Cenis
After the Mont Cenis pass (2,081 m/6,828 ft), on the N6 road, the views are spectacular, with the rich blue waters of the Lac du Mont-Cenis taking centre stage. Park your car at the 'Parking des Fontainettes', and set off on foot on the marked footpath to the

as recently as 1963. Today, climbing enthusiasts have a choice of three routes to the top. Whether climbing or not, the site is still worth a visit. A signposted trail begins at the church in Sardières and it takes less than an hour to reach the monolith, passing through a beautiful coniferous forest. Lying within the bounds of the Vanoise national park, the site has numerous marked footpaths and is often covered with mountain flowers.

Lanslebourg-Mont-Cenis

8 km (5 miles) NE of Sollières-Sardières
Espace Baroque Maurienne
Old church
☎ 04 79 05 90 42

Astronomy festival
Festival d'Astronomie de Haute-Maurienne
Information from the Upper Maurienne tourist office
Second week in Aug.
Admission charge.
This astronomy festival has been held in the Haute-Maurienne valley for nearly two decades. The festival combines lectures, workshops, observations at the Col du Mont-Cenis and the Col de l'Iseran (14 km/9 miles north of Bonneval-

LA TRANSMAURIENNE
Registrations at the JVO
☎ 04 79 31 65 28
Third weekend in Aug.

The *Transmaurienne* mountain-bike race is regarded as the true test of high-altitude mountain biking. The course links La Toussuire, Saint-Sorlin-d'Arves and Saint-Jean-de-Maurienne over three stages of 25-30 km/16-20 miles. The exact routes change from year to year, but the change in elevation from start to finish always totals more than 1,000 m/ 3,300 ft. There are shortened routes for the women's and children's events, while the *Transmômes* event, for 9- to 14-year-olds, combines tests of cross-country, off-road and downhill biking.

The hamlet of Écot

sur-Arc), events relating to the sun, and courses for children, all of which throw new light on the night sky and the origins of the universe.

Lanslevillard
3 km (2 miles) E of Lanslebourg-Mont-Cenis
Baroque adventure

Information from the tourist office

There are numerous Baroque-style chapels to explore in the meadows around Lanslevillard, including the chapels of Saint-Roch, Saint-Jean-Baptiste and Saint-Sébastien. Each has its own unique character, such as the exquisite frescoes at the Chapelle Saint-Jean and the prayers said at Saint Roch for protection against the plague. Before setting off, remember to pick up the keys to the chapels (refundable deposit of €30).

Bessans
10 km (6 miles) NE of Lanslevillard
Devilishly good
'Au Chapoteur'
Rue du Saint-Esprit
☎ 04 79 05 95 49
Open daily 10am-noon and 3-7pm.

In 1857 Étienne Vincendet carved a small model of a devil holding a curate under his arm, starting a curious local tradition that still continues to this day. These monstrous models are now part of the town's scenery, with a four-horned devil standing in the village square. George Personnaz sculpts a range of brightly-coloured models in the studio next to his shop. If you'd prefer a souvenir that's a little less macabre, but equally characteristic of local wood-working crafts, he also makes chicken-shaped salt cellars.

Bonneval-sur-Arc
7 km (4 miles) NE of Bessans
At the ends of the earth

In former times, Bonneval-sur-Arc, the last village in the Arc valley, at an altitude of over 1,800 m/5,900 ft, was often cut off by avalanches. In one popular Christmas song, the village is called *Bonneval to Solet* ('Bonneval all alone') and it was nicknamed 'the principality' by its neighbours, due to the independent spirit of its inhabitants. Today, the village is easier to reach, and the exposed stonework, *lauze* roof tiles (made from slabs of schist) and tiny windows of the houses, huddled together in the narrow streets, help it maintain a timeless charm. The hamlet of Écot (inaccessible in winter), 5 km/ 3 miles from Bonneval, with its well-preserved architecture, is listed as being of historical interest.

North Isère,
art and light

The beautiful light and colourful palette of northern Isère have long been an inspiration for writers and artists. From the stone-grey limestone cliffs of the Isle-Crémieu range, which climbs to the imposing Jura plateau, and the soft greens of the Bièvre-Valloire countryside around La Côte-Saint-André, to the deep blue of Paladru lake, lying in the shadow of the Chartreuse mountains, the landscape could not be more picturesque.

La Balme-les-Grottes

Montalieu-Vercieu

Crémieu

Morestel

Les Aveniè

Le Pin

Paladru Lak

Charavines

La Côte-St-André

Beaucroissant

St-Pierre-de-Bressieux

Parc naturel animalier de Chambaran

Cloisters of the Augustine convent

Crémieu
70 km (43 miles)
NW of Chambéry
The lower town
Once a frontier town between Dauphiné and Savoie, this fine medieval city remains a lively trading centre. Its regional market on Wednesday morning is held in a superb 15thC. hall boasting a set of grain-weighing scales that predate the French Revolution. In the old town, the 16thC. craft studios and shops in the Rue des Augustins still have the pulley systems used to lift sacks of grain to the upper floors. Other highlights include the town's three fortified gateways, the cloisters of the Augustine convent (Couvent des Augustins), the Rue Porcherie, with its tanners' ('adobeurs') workshops, and townhouses dating back to the 14th and 15thC.

La Balme-les-Grottes
18 km (11 miles)
N of Crémieu
Balme caves
☎ 04 74 90 63 76

Open daily 10am-noon and 2-6pm, Apr.-Sept.; weekends and public hols 11am-noon and 2-6pm, Mar. and Oct.; Sun. and public hols. 2-5pm, Feb. and Nov.-15 Dec.
Admission charge.
The huge arch at the entrance to the Grottes de la Balme was carved from the cliffs over thousands of years. The caves were occupied by prehistoric man from the early Stone Age to the end of the Iron Age, and they contain some beautiful chambers with pools, calcite-rich springs, coloured deposits and a subterranean lake. The *son et lumière* show, which uses

models to recreate scenes from daily life in the Stone Age, really brings the caves to life.

WALIBI RHÔNE-ALPES THEME PARK
Les Avenières
11 km (7 miles) SE of Morestel
☎ 04 74 33 71 80
Open daily 10am-7pm (to 9pm, 15 July-15 Aug.), July-20 Aug.; 10am-6pm, June and 21-31 Aug.; weekends and public hols. 10am-6pm, May and Sept.
Admission charge.

The Walibi Rhône-Alpes theme park has over 30 different rides and attractions, including a rollercoaster, a water park with a wave pool and giant water slides, and a zero-gravity tower that propels you to a height of 55 m/ 180 ft in less than 3 seconds. There are also two spectacular shows – the Acapulco divers and the Treasure of the Pharaohs.

Montalieu-Vercieu
11 km (7 miles) SE of La Balme-les-Grottes
Relaxing in the Blue Valley
Base de Loisirs de la Vallée Bleue
☎ 04 74 88 49 23
Open daily 10.30am-8pm; Wed. and weekends, Nov.-Apr.
Free admission; charge for leisure activities.
At this leisure resort, situated on the banks of the Rhône, you can take a 4-km/2-mile ride on a steam train, or climb aboard the *Dauphin Bleu* for a scenic cruise along the river. The centre also has a marina, with jet skis for hire, 4x4 off-road racing, and a huge variety of other activities, including a giant swimming pool with water slides, a mini adventure park for 2- to 12-year-olds, tennis courts and numerous

Spotcheck
A3-B3

Things to do
Blue Valley leisure resort
Chocolate museum
Paladru lake mountain biking

With children
Walibi theme park
Balme caves
Fishing for beginners

Within easy reach
Chartreuse (p. 178)
Sud Grésivaudan (p. 160)

Tourist offices
Charavines: ☎ 04 76 06 60 31
La Côte-Saint-André:
☎ 04 74 20 61 43
Crémieu: ☎ 04 74 90 45 13

walking and mountain biking trails. It's a perfect day out for the whole family.

Morestel
18 km (11 miles)
S of Montalieu-Vercieu
City of painters
Morestel was home to landscape artist François-Auguste Ravier, an antecedent of Impressionism and leading light of the 19thC. Lyon school of painting. The town remains

a popular centre for art and culture. In Rue François-Auguste-Ravier, Maison Ravier (☎ 04 74 80 06 80) displays works from the Morestel and Lyon schools and stages exhibitions on sculpture, photography and literature. The work of contemporary artists is shown at the 11thC. medieval tower (entrance via the Montée Quinsonnas ☎ 04 75 33 04 51 or 04 74 80 10 51) and there are displays at Galerie Joseph-Romagnol (301, Grande-Rue ☎ 04 74 80 33 86), in the Pictur'Halles centre (Pl. Antonin-Chanoz ☎ 04 74 80 07 80) and at Maison du Pays des Couleurs (84, Place du 8 Mai 1945; information from the tourist office ☎ 04 74 80 19 59).

Around Lake Paladru
35 km (22 miles)
S of Morestel
Biking round the lake
Espace VTT-FFC
Information and topographical guide from Charavines tourist office

The 17 mountain-biking circuits around Lake Paladru are classified by colour, from green to black, according to their level of difficulty. For a family outing, try the blue *Plaine de Blaune*, which covers 14 km/ 9 miles of rolling country with an overall climb of 192 m/ 630 ft. Take a picnic break at Dîmière grange, a farm building

that once belonged to a 17thC. Carthusian monastery and now houses sculpture exhibitions during the summer.

Flooded villages
Musée du Lac de Paladru
Charavines
7.5 km (5 miles)
S of Paladru
☎ 04 76 55 77 47
Open daily 10am-noon and 2-6pm (to 7pm, July-Aug.), Jun-Sept.; weekends 2-6pm, May and Oct.-Nov.
Admission charge.

This museum displays evidence of early man's ancient dwellings around Paladru lake, and reveals how the homes of both prehistoric and medieval inhabitants of the area were flooded, or even buried, by sudden changes in the water level. You can also visit the divers and archaeologists who are conducting underwater excavations at the hamlet of

Colletière (open to visitors, July-Aug.; information from Musée du Lac de Paladru).

Learning to fish
Étangs de la Salamandre
Le Pin
2.5 km (2 miles) N of Charavines. At Le Pin, take the Rue de la Caserne on the right, turning left after 100 m/300 ft.
☎ 06 03 51 92 59
At the Salamandre ponds, Sébastien Vieubled hires out fishing equipment and gives fishing lessons to children aged 6-12 (introductory course: Tues.-Sat. 9am-noon, €8 per session, €30 for 5 sessions). They learn about the different species of fish found in local rivers and lakes, the importance of protecting the environment, how to tell when the fish are about to bite, and, most important of all, how to sit still.

Beaucroissant
17 km (11 miles)
S of Le Pin
Rural traditions
Foire de Beaucroissant
☎ 04 76 91 02 65
Mid-Sept.
In 1219, when Grenoble was flooded, the regional fair moved 30 km/19 miles to

Dîmière grange

BERLIOZ FESTIVAL

Musée Hector-Berlioz
69, Rue de la République, La Côte-Saint-André
☎ 04 74 20 24 88
Open daily (exc. Tues.) 9am-noon and 2-6pm (8pm during the Berlioz festival).
Admission charge.

French composer Berlioz was born here in 1803. His house, built around 1680, is now a museum dedicated to his life and work, with memorabilia, portraits, musical instruments, scores and period furniture. During the second fortnight in August the town hosts a Berlioz festival, with performances of his work, as well as that of his contemporaries. For more information, contact the tourist office.

Saint-Pierre-de-Bressieux

9 km (6 miles) S of
La Côte-Saint-André
Le Parc Naturel Animalier de Chambaran
☎ 04 74 20 14 93
Open Wed., weekends and public hols. (daily during school hols.) 8am-dusk.
Admission charge.
Over 250 animals roam free in the Chambaran wildlife park, a private reserve covering more than 300 ha/750 acres. The fallow deer are the tamest of these wild creatures, often waiting to greet visitors at the entrance, but there are also roe deer, stags, wild sheep and boars. To be sure

of seeing the animals, it's best to come early in the morning or at the end of the afternoon.

Beaucroissant, and has stayed here ever since. The Foire de Beaucroissant is the oldest regional fair in France and one of the most spectacular. Over two or three days this village of 1,250 inhabitants welcomes more than a million visitors. The festivities begin on 14 September with a livestock market, displaying over 5,000 sheep, cattle, goats and horses. There follows a classic autumn fair, with 2,000 exhibitors covering 40 ha/100 acres with food stalls, regional produce, agricultural equipment and all manner of entertainment.

La Côte-Saint-André

9 km (12 miles)
NW of Beaucroissant
Chocolate paradise
Opp. Château Louis XI
Open by appt:
☎ 04 74 20 35 89
Admission charge; guided or self-guided tours.
This pastry and chocolate shop, in the centre of La Côte-

Saint-André, has been run by the Jouvenal family for three generations. Current owner, Pierre, has created a chocolate museum, the Musée du Chocolat, located opposite Château Louis XI, with tours that include tastings. Cherry Rocher, a local liqueur maker, was inspired by this enterprise and has created the Musée des Liqueurs, housed in the town's former distillery (Av. Camille Rocher ☎ 04 74 93 38 10; open daily 3-6pm, except Mon. and public hols., June-Sept.; free admission).

Sud-Grésivaudan,
walnuts and cheese

The Sud-Grésivaudan region, in the shadow of the Vercors mountains, is a land of rolling countryside, where the locals have an appetite for life as well as good food. Enjoy crunchy walnuts, plump cherries, the celebrated St-Marcellin cheese, and make the most of the area's numerous family attractions.

Saint-Antoine-l'Abbaye

60 km (37 miles)
W of Grenoble
Abbey church
Information from the
tourist office
Open daily.
Free admission; charge
for guided tour.
The magnificent Gothic church that rises above the village of Saint-Antoine was the centrepiece of an old abbey founded by the Order of St Anthony (p.95). Inside are many artistic treasures, such as painted frescoes, Aubusson tapestries, a 17thC. organ and a fine ivory sculpture of Christ, dating from the late 16thC.

Medieval festival

☎ 04 76 36 40 68
Every year during the second half of July, the little town of Saint-Antoine-l'Abbaye comes to life for the *Nuits Médiévales* (Medieval nights). This four-day festival brings together musicians, singers, dancers and actors, who, wearing period costume, stage around 20 different shows with medieval themes, creating an authentic atmosphere of the times. Naturally, feasting and drinking are also on the menu.

Saint-Marcellin

12 km (7 miles) E of
Saint-Antoine-l'Abbaye
Cheese museum
2, Av. du Collège
☎ 04 76 38 53 85

Open daily 9am-noon and 2-6pm.
Admission charge.
Housed in a former Ursuline convent, the Musée du Fromage is dedicated to the history of St-Marcellin cheese, with a reputation dating back to the court of Louis XI in the 15thC. Originally made only from goat's milk, its composition has changed over the centuries and in 1980 it was standardised as a cow's milk cheese. There are a number of ways to sample St-Marcellin: on a slice of fresh bread, cooked in a pastry parcel wrapped in smoked bacon (*à la Marcelline*), or very runny, eaten with a spoon (*à la Lyonnaise*).

Around Vinay

9.5 km (6 miles)
NE of Saint-Marcellin
Capital of walnuts
Around Vinay, the capital of Grenoble walnuts (awarded an AOC seal of quality in 1938),

he walnut groves ave been a part of the countryside for centuries. The listed 18th-C. *séchoir* (walnut-drying barn) just outside Cognin-les-Gorges (5 km/3 miles S of Vinay; information from Vinay tourist office) bears witness to this long tradition. Its wooden shelves can hold layers of walnuts up to 15 cm/6 in thick. At the walnut-oil mill in Chatte (4 km/2 miles SW of Saint-Marcellin), you can learn all about the traditional techniques used to produce the oil from the miller, Denis Faure (☎ 04 76 38 07 78).

Christian Abric has been creating this open-air model railway for over 14 years. Now occupying an area of 1,300 sq m/ 14,000 sq ft, the amazing network has over 30 trains, which race through a superbly detailed landscape of lakes, rivers, fields, mountains and villages, all housed in a country garden.

La Sône

5 km (3 miles)
S of Chatte
On the water
Paddle steamer and 'Fossilised Fountains'
Site des Tufières
☎ 04 76 64 43 42

Chatte

4 km/2 miles
SW of Saint-Marcellin
A model garden
2, Rte de Lyon
☎ 04 76 38 54 55
Open daily 9.30am-
6.30pm, Apr.-Sept.; call
for details, out of season.
Admission charge.

Spotcheck
B3

Things to do
Cheese museum
Gourmet farm tour

With children
Isère river cruise and spring
Open-air model railway

Within easy reach
Drôme (p. 165)
Vercors (p. 162)

Tourist offices
Saint-Antoine-l'Abbaye:
☎ 04 76 36 44 46
Saint-Marcellin:
☎ 04 76 38 53 85
Vinay: ☎ 04 76 36 69 90

La Sône park

GOURMET FARM TOUR
Groupement Promotionnel du Sud-Grésivaudan
22, Cours Vallier, Saint-Marcellin
☎ 04 76 38 67 20
This tasting tour takes in around a dozen farms in Sud-Grésivaudan, giving visitors a chance to sample the region's finest farm-produced specialities, including kirsch, cherry juice, cold meats and walnuts. Pick up a free guide to the *Points Fermiers* from the Sud-Grésivaudan association in Saint-Marcellin.

Cruises: daily at 10.30am, 2pm, 3.30pm and 5pm. Gardens open daily 9.30-6.30, June-Aug.; phone for details out of season. *Admission charges.*
Take a trip on the *Royans Vercors* paddle-steamer and see the red rock and volcanic tufa landscapes, marshland and riverside villages of the Isère. The cruise, with commentary, lasts 90 minutes. Overlooking the landing stage, a former landfill site has been turned into a superb park, with over 15,000 species of plants. A calcite-rich spring leaves crystalline deposits on nearby rocks and on any objects left in its flow; the 'petrified' items are then sold in the shop.

Vercors,
a mountain citadel

From gorges, canyons, cliffs and natural rock amphitheatres to green valleys and beautiful forests, the limestone region of the Vercors is packed with spectacular scenery and breathtaking views. The high plateaux, a natural barrier dividing the Vercors mountains in half, are part of a protected area and home to an exceptional variety of wild animals and plants.

Map labels: Gorges du Bruyan · Autrans · Grotte de Choranche · Méaudre · Lans-en-V. · Pont-en-Royans · Villard-de-Lans · St-Jean-en-Royans · Corrençon-en-V. · Léoncel · La Chapelle-en-V. · Lente · Mont Aigu · Die

Lans-en-Vercors
24 km (15 miles) SW of Grenoble
Vercors regional park
Maison du Parc
25, Ch. des Fusillés
☎ 04 76 94 38 26
Open Mon.-Fri. 8.30am-12.30pm and 2-6pm.
Free admission.
Designated as a regional park in 1970, the Vercors range is a protected area where the natural and architectural heritage of the region is carefully preserved.

The Maison du Parc information centre provides leaflets detailing the 2,850 km/1,770 miles of marked trails through the reserve. There are further information centres at Autrans (9.5 km/6 miles northwest of Lans-en-Vercors ☎ 04 76 95 35 01), Prélenfrey (30 km/19 miles south of Grenoble ☎ 04 76 72 34 41) and Chichilianne (50 km/31 miles south of Grenoble ☎ 04 76 34 43 09). You can also pick up park information from the tourist offices of the Vercors region.

Mechanical toy museum
Musée Magie des Automates
Rte de Villard, Père Noël Hamlet
☎ 04 76 95 40 14
Open daily 10am-6pm.
Admission charge.

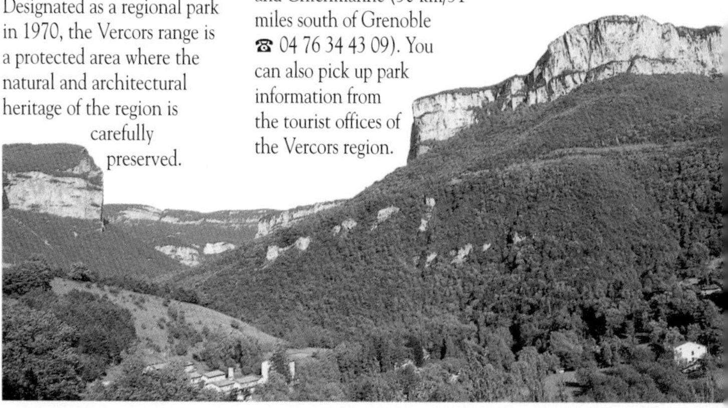

VERCORS RAVIOLI

This distinctive ravioli, filled with Comté (a type of gruyère) and soft white cheeses, parsley and eggs, is said to have been invented by woodcutters from the Piedmont region of Italy. Reluctant to give up their pasta, they simply stuffed it with local ingredients. This traditional regional dish is still made in Saint-Jean-en-Royans (Ravioles à l'Ancienne, Avenue Pionniers du Vercors ☎ 04 75 47 52 50).

Alain Bardo collects and makes automata, and this entertaining museum displays over 300 working pieces, including a family of bears, snake charmers playing flutes, a sorcerer consulting the stars, a circus parade and Father Christmas preparing his toys.

Les Gorges de Bruyant

Discovery trail

Marked trail: 4-hour round trip. Sentiers du Vercors *map (1:40,000), showing the Vercors footpaths, available from tourist offices and park information centres.*

A classified and protected area, the Bruyant gorges are one of the most unspoilt sites in northern Vercors. This trail takes walkers through some spectacular landscape while also helping to explain how the gorges were formed. Start from the central square in Lans-en-Vercors, near the Maison du Parc information centre, on the road to the Hameau des Balcons. The route goes through the gorges, before returning via the *Sentier des Danois*.

Autrans

9.5 km (6 miles) NW of Lans-en-Vercors
Cross-country skiing

La Foulée Blanche
☎ 04 76 95 37 37
Penultimate Sun. in Jan.
Autrans is a cross-country skiing paradise, with 160 km/ 100 miles of pistes. Every January, the resort organises the *Foulée Blanche*, a cross-country skiing competition open to competitors of all ages and all abilities. As well as a race for expert skiers, there are

Spotcheck
B3-B4

Things to do

Villard-de-Lans heritage museum
Bruyant gorges
Try walnut specialities at the Cave Noisel
Underground adventure

With children

Aventure Parc
La Tanière Enchantée wildlife centre
Santons and mechanical toy museums
Museum of prehistory
Choranche cave

Within easy reach

Grenoble (p. 168)
Sud-Dauphiné/Trièves (p. 170)
Sud-Grésivaudan (p. 160)

Tourist offices

ADT Vercors:
☎ 04 76 95 15 99
Bourne gorges:
☎ 04 76 36 09 10
Vercors region:
☎ 04 75 48 22 54
Royans: ☎ 04 75 48 61 39

senior citizens' and children's races over courses of 2-50 km/ 1-30 miles. Arrive before the weekend to see the different races, or go on Sunday to join the crowds for the open race.

Aventure Parc
Stade de Neige
de la Sure
☎ 04 76 94 77 00
Open daily 9.30am-7pm,
July-Aug.; weekends
and public hols. 10am-
6.30pm, Wed. and spring
hols. 11.30am-6.30pm,
Apr.-1 Nov.
Admission charge.
This innovative forest theme
park has four obstacle courses,
varying in difficulty, with over
70 separate challenges, all
suspended between the branches
of trees. One course is specially
designed for children, but they
must be at least 8 years old and
over 1.3 m/4 ft 3 in in height.

Méaudre
6 km (4 miles)
S of Autrans
Grande Traversée
du Vercors trail
Marked trail; route map
(1:60,000) available
from Vercors regional
tourist office, local tourist
offices and park
information centres.
This 150-km/90-mile trail
crosses the Vercors range from
north to south, roughly tracing
a route from Méaudre to Lente,
but also offering a number of
side trails. The path leads
through unspoilt countryside,
forests and over mountain
ridges, and is a must for hiking,
mountain-biking, horse-riding
or skiing enthusiasts. Local
tourist offices can provide lists
of overnight accommodation.

Place de la Libération, Villard-en-Lar

Villard-de-Lans
10 km (6 miles)
S of Méaudre
Maison
du Patrimoine
Pl. de la Libération
☎ 04 76 95 17 31
Open Tues.-Sat.
2-7pm, Wed. 10am-
noon.
Admission charge.
This heritage centre
houses the documents,
artefacts and other
memorabilia bequeathed to
the town by local life-long
collector Jacques Lamoure.
From ploughs to bobsleighs,
from old school photos to ox
yokes and traditional wood-
working tools, all the pieces
are authentic, and give an
insight into the rural way of
life in the region.

Musée
des Santons
Espace Loisirs
☎ 04 76 94 90 94
Open daily 10am-1pm
and 2-6.30pm.
Admission charge.

This museum demonstrates
the skills of the *santonnier*,
who makes traditional crib
figures. Some 2,000 statuettes
made from

There are many images of bears
the villages of the Vercors

materials such as wood, cork,
clay and cloth, are brought to
life in a variety of scenes,
including a nativity crib, a
village square and a cinema.

Tanière Enchantée
Rte de Correncon
☎ 04 76 94 18 40
Open weekends, public
and school hols. 10am-
noon and 2-6pm; 9.30an
6.30pm, May-Sept.;
closed 15 Nov.-15 Dec.
Admission charge.
The last sighting of a bear in
the Vercors (and in the Alps
general) occurred in 1937, bu
this wildlife discovery centre
brings this majestic animal
back to life. An educational
trail takes visitors from one de
to the next, where animated
models reveal the habitats an
habits of mountain fauna, suc
as chamois, marmots, Alpine
grouse (ptarmigan) and foxes.

Les hauts-plateaux du Vercors

Ce vaste espace présente un paysage tabulaire où alternent alpages et forêts. Le hêtre, le sapin et l'épicéa, présents sur les pourtours, laissent la place en altitude au pin à crochets qui s'accommode du froid et de la roche calcaire.

Corrençon-en-Vercors

.5 km (3 miles) of Villard-de-Lans
Hauts Plateaux nature reserve

The Réserve des Hauts Plateaux is the largest nature reserve in mainland France, around 30 km/19 miles long and 6 km/4 miles wide, and covering 17,000 ha/42,000 acres of the Vercors mountains. There are no roads or villages in this unspoilt wilderness, but there are signposted footpaths. At Corrençon-en-Vercors, one of the gateways to the park, pick up the GR 91 trail as it crosses the village, and follow it to the Carrette hut, from which there's a choice of paths. Keep to the marked paths, and remember that it's forbidden to take animals into the park or to pick any flowers and plants.

La Chapelle-en-Vercors (Drôme region)

8 km (17 miles) W of Villard-de-Lans
Underground adventure

Maison de l'Aventure
☎ 04 75 48 22 38
Open all year round
Over 3,000 caves and potholes have been discovered in the limestone rock of the Vercors range, making the area an adventure playground for cavers. Discover the underground world in the company of guides from the Maison de l'Aventure, who organise introductions to cave walking, potholing and well descents on half-day expeditions or courses lasting several days (see p.47).

Vassieux-en-Vercors (Drôme region)

10 km (6 miles) S of La Chapelle-en-Vercors
Memorial to the Resistance
Col de Lachau
☎ 04 75 48 26 00
Open daily 10am-5pm (until 6pm, Apr.-Sept.); closed from 1 Nov. to the New Year.
Admission charge.
More than 600 members of the French Resistance and 200 civilians, including a number of women and children, were killed in the Vercors during World War II. The famous

memorial at the Lachau pass, with its sober architecture, commemorates the sacrifice of these fighters, who waged a tireless guerrilla war against German occupation. A Resistance museum in Vassieux-en-Vercors (Rue Fourna, ☎ 04 75 48 28 46; open daily Apr.-Oct.; free admission) retraces the poignant and often tragic history of the *maquisards* – so called because their secret domain was the wild *maquis* or scrubland of the south.

Musée de la Préhistoire
La Hâle
☎ 04 75 48 27 81
Open daily 10am-12.30pm and 2-5pm (until 6pm, Apr.-June); 10am-6pm, July-Aug.
Admission charge.
In 1970, a Dr Malenfant was out walking when he found some pieces of flint scattered on the ground. They turned

MONT AIGUILLE
Mont Aiguille ('needle mountain') is the highest peak in the Vercors range, overlooking Chichilianne and the Trièves region from its 2,086 m/6,844 ft summit. Its inaccessibility remains a popular myth among climbers, but it was climbed as early as 1492, by Antoine de Ville, and has been conquered often since. Today, there are several routes to the summit.

out to be the remains of a late Stone Age tool-making workshop, dating back some 4,500 years. The find is now the star exhibit at La Hâle's museum of prehistory, built around the archaeological site to protect it. Visitors are introduced to the history of human habitation in the area and the techniques used by Stone Age man to make tools and weapons. In summer there are short courses and workshops..

Die (Drôme region)
32 km (20 miles) S of Vassieux-en-Vercors
Fête de la Transhumance
☎ 04 75 22 00 05
Weekend closest to 21 June.
This annual festival celebrates the *transhumance*, the tradition of moving herds to high pastures for the summer. For three days Die comes alive with shows, exhibitions and events, while thousands of sheep pass through the village to be sheared in the streets, before heading off to graze on the high plateaux.

Léoncel (Drôme region)
43 km (27 miles) W of Vassieux-en-Vercors
Cistercian abbey
☎ 04 75 02 20 21
Open daily
Free admission; charge for guided tour.

Nestled in the foothills of the Vercors range, this abbey-church was part of a 12th-C. Romanesque abbey built by Cistercian monks. A haven of peace for most of the year, in summer it's the venue for concerts and conferences. The village is also the starting point for some attractive walks that cross the Léoncel national forest to the Bataille pass (Col de la Bataille).

Saint-Jean-en-Royans (Drôme region)
18 km (11 miles) NE of Léoncel
Cave Noisel walnuts
☎ 04 75 47 56 54

Open daily 10am-noon and 3-6pm.
Free admission.
At the Cave Noisel, just past the church on the way out of the village, you can discover how walnuts are used to flavour everything from drinks to dessert. Proprietor Jean-Luc Odeyer conducts the tour and offers tastings of his specialities such as walnut wine, pickled walnuts, green walnut jam and walnut oil. There's also a video show, revealing all the stages in the manufacturing process.

Wood-turning and carving

The manufacture of wooden items, such as salad servers, pepper mills and bowls for grinding herbs, was once one of the main industries of the Royans region. Several local artisans continue to turn finely crafted wooden pieces, notably at Desfonds in Saint-Jean-en-Royans (☎ 04 75 48 60 06), Bérard in Saint-Laurent-en-Royans (5 km/3 miles south of Pont-en-Royans ☎ 04 75 47 70 48) and Vincent André in Autrans (☎ 04 76 95 37 55).

Pont-en-Royans
9 km (6 miles) NE of Saint-Jean-en-Royans

Houses in the air

Guided tours: information from the tourist office of the Gorges de la Bourne

Every summer, the narrow streets of Pont-en-Royans are jammed with coaches as visitors flock to see the extraordinary architecture of this village, perched on the side of a cliff, its houses hanging over the river. To escape the crowds, leave your car outside the village and take the stairway leading down from the town centre to the riverside. You can

see the town's old wooden balconies from the gateway to the quayside, but the best view of the picturesque houses, with their yellow and ochre façades, is from the Quai de la Bourne.

La grotte de Choranche
☎ **04 76 36 09 88**
4.5 km (3 miles) E of Pont-en-Royans on the D531
Open daily 9am-6.30pm, July-Aug.; out of season, phone for details
Admission charge.
The Choranche cave, more than 70 million years old, was first discovered in 1875. Starting from the car park, an educational trail on the theme of earth sciences leads to the heart of a magnificent underground world. In the first chamber, a subterranean lake is crowned with thousands of 'angel's-hair' stalactites, unique in Europe. The highlight of the tour is a *son et lumière* show in the final gallery – 'the cathedral' – to the atmospheric music of Purcell's King Arthur. After the tour of the caves, the educational trail continues along the cliffs to the waterfall before returning to the car park. Displays along the way explain the evolution of the Choranche site in the context of the history of the planet.

Grenoble,
active and innovative

Grenoble is dominated by a magnificent ring of Alpine peaks that surround the city. Its resident are an active lot, with a pioneering spirit that led to the creation of the first tourist office in France and the first 'MJC' association for the promotion of youth culture. The city is sophisticated and charming, particularly in the appealing streets of its historic centre.

The historic centre

Start your tour of the old town at the tourist office (14, Rue de la République) and head off along Rue Lafayette, to see a remnant of the fortified walls that encircled the Gallo-Roman town of Cularo. Behind the Place Grenette are the town gardens, with chestnut trees planted in the 17thC. Take a look at the Place Saint-André and the Place aux Herbes, with its fruit and vegetable market (daily exc. Mon.), and continue along Rue Chenoise, one of the oldest streets in Grenoble, with houses dating to the 14thC. (no. 20) and 16thC. (no. 8). End your tour at the Musée de Grenoble, built against the old town ramparts, with its fine selection of ancient and

modern art (5, Pl. de Lavalette ☎ 04 76 63 44 44; open daily exc. Tues., 10am-6pm, to 9pm on Wed.; admission charge; free admission first Sun. of month).

Early Christians
Musée de l'Ancien Évêché
2 Rue Très-Cloîtres
☎ 04 76 03 15 25

Open daily (exc. Tues.) 10am-7pm.
Admission charge.
This museum of regional history, housed in the former bishop's palace, has a tranquil and spiritual atmosphere. It traces the history of civilisatio in the Isère region, from prehistoric times to the preser day, with Gallo-Roman and

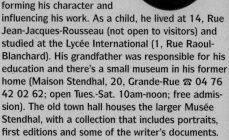

ON THE TRAIL OF STENDHAL

Musée Stendhal
1, Rue Hector-Berlioz
☎ 04 76 54 44 14
Open Tues.-Sun. 2-6pm.
Free admission.
Writer Henry Beyle, better known as Stendhal, was born in Grenoble on 23 January 1783. Although he had no great affection for his native city, he spent his entire youth here and it certainly played its part in forming his character and influencing his work. As a child, he lived at 14, Rue Jean-Jacques-Rousseau (not open to visitors) and studied at the Lycée International (1, Rue Raoul-Blanchard). His grandfather was responsible for his education and there's a small museum in his former home (Maison Stendhal, 20, Grande-Rue ☎ 04 76 42 02 62; open Tues.-Sat. 10am-noon; free admission). The old town hall houses the larger Musée Stendhal, with a collection that includes portraits, first editions and some of the writer's documents.

Legendary warrior Bayard, Place Saint-André

medieval relics on display, particularly the remains of Grenoble's first baptistry.

Saint-Laurent archaeological museum

Église Saint-Laurent
☎ 04 76 44 78 68
Open daily (exc. Tues.)
9am-noon and 2-6pm.
Admission charge.
The 12thC. Saint-Laurent church, which lies at the foot of the Bastille fortress, has a splendid ceiling painted in the early 20thC. The swastikas in the decoration have been ancient Hindu symbols of peace since around 3,500 BC. The church's principal treasure is the 5th-8thC. crypt, where the supporting columns have retained their original Corinthian capitals.

Musée Dauphinois

30, Rue Maurice-Gignoux
☎ 04 76 85 19 01
Open daily (exc. Tues.)
10am-7pm (May-Oct.);
10am-6pm (Nov.-Apr.).
Admission charge.

This former 17th-C. convent, which clings to the side of the Bastille cliff, now houses a museum dedicated to the regional history and heritage of the Dauphiné. In tribute to the neighbouring mountains, it also has a delightful museum devoted to skiing. There are temporary exhibitions, always lively and well presented. Getting there is half the fun – you can reach the convent by taking the cable-car, a distinctive feature of Grenoble, from the Quai Stéphane-Jay.

Via ferrata

Storming the Bastille

Information from the tourist office
This climbing route, the first urban *via ferrata* in France, runs along the rock faces above Grenoble in a series of cables, handrails and ladders. The trail begins from the Parking de l'Esplanade, near the Porte-de-France, takes around 1.5 hours, and climbs 110-120 m/360-

Spotcheck

B3

Things to do

Climb the Bastille cliff

With children

Cycling around the town

Within easy reach

Belledonne (p. 176)
Chartreuse (p. 178)
Sud Dauphiné (p. 170)
Vercors (p. 162)

Tourist offices

Grenoble: ☎ 04 76 42 41 41

390 ft. The final stretch begins 50 m/160 ft below the Bastille fortress, climbing 10 m/30 ft in 30 m/100 ft, and takes just 5 minutes. Beginners must be accompanied by a trained guide.

Cycling in Grenoble

Although surrounded by mountains, Grenoble is actually the flattest city in France, which makes cycling the perfect way to get around and explore it at your own pace. You can hire a bicycle for a day or half-day and set off on one of the four cycle routes themed around snow, water and gardens, heritage and sculpture. For further information, contact the tourist office.

Sud-Dauphiné,
the secret garden

Between the Oisans and Vercors mountains, the Sud-Dauphiné is a garden paradise. From the Matheysine region to the far south of the Trièves region, where the towns and scenery have a distinctly Mediterranean feel, the Sud-Dauphiné is an elegant mix of hills, lakes and valleys, with a variety of cultures and climates.

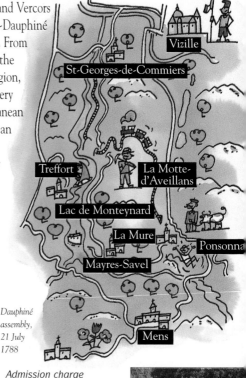

Vizille

St-Georges-de-Commiers

Treffort

La Motte-d'Aveillans

Lac de Monteynard

La Mure

Ponsonna

Mayres-Savel

Mens

Dauphiné assembly, 21 July 1788

Vizille
*16 km (10 miles)
S of Grenoble*
Museum of the French Revolution
Château de Vizille
☎ 04 76 68 07 35
Museum open daily (exc. Tues. and 1 May) 10am-6pm, Apr.-Oct.; park and gardens open daily 9am-8pm, June-Aug.; out of season phone for details.

Admission charge (exc. park and gardens).
The Musée de la Révolution retraces the turbulent history of the château, birthplace of the French Revolution, where on 21 July 1788, the Dauphiné Assembly demanded a meeting of the Estates General to express their grievances against the French crown. The deer park and gardens make a very pleasant place for a walk.

Saint-Georges-de-Commiers
*11 km (7 miles)
SW of Vizille*
La Mure train
☎ 04 76 73 57 35
Departures daily at 9.45am, noon, 2.30pm and 5pm, July-Aug.; 9.45am and 2.30pm, Apr.-Oct.
Admission charge.
The *Petit Train de La Mure* runs on an old coal-mining track between Saint-Georges-de-Commiers and La Mure, and gives passengers a unique

glimpse of the Drac river gorges. The journey (1 hr 45 mins), is colourful, taking in the azure blue river, the deep green forests, and the grey peaks of Mont Aiguille and Pierre Percée in the distance.

La Motte-d'Aveillans
15 km (9 miles) SE of St-Georges-de-Commiers
Mining memories

La Mine Image
Les 4 galeries
☎ 04 76 30 68 74
Open daily, June-Sept.; phone for details of guided tours (1.5 hrs with video presentation). *Admission charge.*
The local miners had a name for the carbon-rich deposits of the area – *le soleil en conserve* ('potted sunshine'). Their working conditions, however, were a lot less poetic. As you explore the tunnels and chambers of this former coal mine, guided by the glow of a miner's lamp, you'll soon see why this was such a dangerous profession.

La Mure
7 km (4 miles) S of La Motte-d'Aveillans
Musée Matheyzin
Maison Caral,
Rue Colonel-Escallon
☎ 04 76 30 98 15
Open daily (exc. Tues.) 1-6.30pm, 2 May-Oct. *Admission charge.*
This museum is dedicated to the history and traditional way of life in the region, illustrated by first-hand accounts and a

selection of everyday objects, such as the blacksmith's tools and glove-maker's iron moulds. There are also archive photos and a video showing how this old province of Dauphiné has changed in recent years.

Ponsonnas
3 km (2 miles) S of La Mure
Bungee jumping
Vertiges Aventure
☎ 04 76 47 42 80
Adrenaline junkies should take the D526 to Ponsonnas, where there's a 103 m/338 ft bungee platform on a bridge above the Drac river. This was the first bungee-jumping centre in Europe and safety is guaranteed.

Mens
16 km (10 miles) SW of Ponsonnas
Living earth
Centre Européen de l'Écologie Pratique
Domaine de Raud
On the D526, towards Prébois
☎ 04 76 34 80 80
Open daily (exc. Tues.) 10am-6pm, 14 June-12 Sept.; Fri.-Sun. and public hols., May-24 Oct. *Admission charge.*
This centre, established 20 years ago, has a 50-ha/125-acre fruit and vegetable garden, cultivated to the centre's own ecological guidelines, and a 'habitat zone' with displays of environmentally-friendly building techniques and

materials. Allow half a day to explore the centre and sample the organic dishes served up in the on-site restaurant.

Lac de Monteynard
NW of Mens
La Mira cruises
☎ 04 76 34 14 56
Mid-May to Oct.
La Mira takes passengers on scenic cruises through the Drac and Ebron gorges. You can board either at Treffort (30 km/19 miles NW of Mens) or at Mayres-Savel (11 km/7 miles SW of La Mure). The 20-km/12-mile long Monteynard lake is renowned as the best windsurfing spot in the region, and it also has beach sports on offer.

Spotcheck
B4

Things to do
Bungee jumping

With children
Ecological centre
Monteynard lake
La Mine Image
Deer park of Vizille château
Petit Train de La Mure

Within easy reach
Grenoble (p. 168)
Oisans (p. 172)
Vercors (p. 162)

Tourist offices
Sud Dauphiné:
☎ 04 76 34 69 99

MEDITERRANEAN FLAVOURS

Mens, capital of the Trièves region, offers a taste of the south of France, with four-sided roofs and curved roof tiles, an ancient covered market, and small shady squares and fountains. The Musée de Trièves, in the old centre, explores the region's heritage, history and architecture (Place de la Halle ☎ 04 76 34 88 28; open daily exc. Mon., 3-7pm, May-Sept. and school hols.; weekends 2-7pm, Oct.-Apr.; admission charge).

Oisans,
on the top of the world

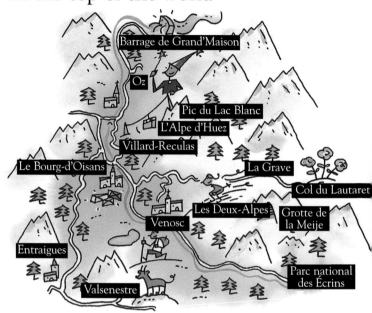

Barrage de Grand'Maison

Oz

Pic du Lac Blanc

L'Alpe d'Huez

Villard-Reculas

Le Bourg-d'Oisans

La Grave

Col du Lautaret

Les Deux-Alpes

Grotte de la Meije

Venosc

Entraigues

Parc national des Écrins

Valsenestre

On the border between the northern and southern Alps, Oisans is a mountain kingdom of precipitous slopes, glaciers, torrents and waterfalls, pierced by six valleys. A large part of the region lies within the boundaries of the Écrins national park, including the 4,103 m/13,462 ft Barre des Écrins and the 3,983 m/13,068 ft Pic de la Meije, making this area a paradise for sports lovers and for all those in search of unspoilt natural beauty.

natural source of energy, from ancient times to the present day. Highly informative and well presented, the exhibition dedicated to the construction of the Grand'Maison dam is a striking illustration of man's inventiveness in attempting to master this elemental force.

La vallée de l'Eau d'Olle

49 km (30 miles) E of Grenoble
Musée Hydrélec
Allemont
☎ 04 76 80 78 00

Open daily 10am-6pm, 15 June-15 Sept.
Free admission.
Located near the Grand' Maison hydro-electric power station, this museum retraces man's relationship with this

Le Bourg-
d'Oisans

Oisans potatoes
L'Auberge
Oz, L'Enversin d'Oz
Hamlet
3 km (2 miles)
NE of Allemont
☎ 04 76 80 73 18
Open daily, May to end
Nov.
Speciality set menu: €65.
Ganèfles is one of the most
typical dishes of the Oisans
region. The celebrated local
potatoes are finely grated and
mixed with eggs and a small
quantity of flour.
The resulting paste
is fried in a hot pan,
a spoonful at a time,
and the small potato cakes are
served with fried onions and
cheese. Try this classic
regional speciality at the
L'Auberge restaurant, which
has a delightful rustic dining
room with a traditional
French-style ceiling.

Festival
de la Magie
**Information from the
Maison d'Eau d'Olle
tourist office**
First fortnight in Aug.
This festival of magic, nearly a
decade old, was the inspiration
of four villages in the Eau
d'Olle valley – Allemont, Oz,
Vaujany (7 km/4 miles north of
Oz) and Villard-Reculas (11
km/7 miles south of Allemont).
During the festival fortnight,
the magical circus moves from
one village to the next, with a
packed programme of free
magic shows, workshops for
beginners, star performers and
up-and-coming talents.

11 km (7 miles)
S of Allemont
Musée des
Minéraux et de
la Faune des Alpes
Pl. de l'Église
☎ 04 76 80 27 54
Open daily 2-6pm;
11am-7pm, July-Aug.;
closed 15 Nov.-15 Dec.,
25 Dec. and 1 Jan.
Admission charge.

Spotcheck
C4

Things to do
Cycle tours
Summer skiing

With children
Meije cave
Chamois walk
Festival of magic
Alpine garden

Within easy reach
Grenoble (p. 168)
Hautes Alpes (p. 175)
Sud Dauphiné (p. 170)

Tourist offices
Allemont:
☎ 04 76 80 71 60
L'Alpe-d'Huez:
☎ 04 76 11 44 44
Le Bourg-d'Oisans:
☎ 04 76 80 03 25
Les Deux-Alpes:
☎ 04 76 79 22 00
Eau d'Olle valley:
☎ 04 76 79 40 10
Venosc: ☎ 04 76 80 06 82

ÉCRINS NATIONAL PARK

Park headquarters
Domaine de Charance
05500 Gap
☎ 04 92 40 20 10
Designated in
1973, the vast,
Parc National des
Écrins covers over
270,000 ha/
670,000 acres of
the Isère and
Hautes-Alpes regions,
with a protected area of
91,000 ha/225,000 acres. It
contains more than 100 peaks over 3,000 m/9,800
ft. The national park in the Oisans and Valbonnais
regions has two official gates with reception centres,
one at Bourg-d'Oisans (☎ 04 76 80 00 51) and the
other at Entriagues (29 km/18 miles S of Bourg-
d'Oisans; ☎ 04 76 30 20 61). There are also
temporary information points in Saint-Christophe-en-
Oisans (8 km/5 miles SE of Venosc) and La Bérarde
(11 km/7 miles SE of Saint-Christophe-en-Oisans).

The mineral deposits of the Oisans region have long attracted prospectors to the park. The trade is now strictly controlled, so you'll have to come to this museum if you want to see some precious gems for yourself. The highlight is a huge piece of jagged gypsum of extraordinary luminosity, quarried in La Gardette. One room is dedicated to the park's wildlife, including around 140 naturalised species, such as the Alpine grouse (ptarmigan), stoat, wolf and golden eagle.

Valsenestre
41 km (25 miles)
S of Bourg-d'Oisans
On the chamois trail
Information from Maison du Parc in Entraigues
☎ 04 76 30 20 61
'*À la rencontre des chamois*' is a hiking trail (2 hrs 15 mins) that gives you the chance to observe the animals of the Valbonnais valley. Get up early, and at Valsenestre, head for the hiking refuge (*gîte d'étape*) and then take the path on the left. After an energetic climb, you'll be rewarded with a view of the whole valley, before returning to the bottom – where the chamois spend the winter – and continuing on to the Valsenestre valley.

L'Alpe-d'Huez
13 km (8 miles)
NE of Bourg-d'Oisans
Top cycling
The 21 hairpin bends of the D211, which climbs from Le Bourg-d'Oisans (720 m/2,360 ft) to L'Alpe-d'Huez (over 1,800 m/5,900 ft), are famous throughout the world. The Alpe-d'Huez stage of the Tour de France cycle race is one of the most demanding parts of the event. Each year, thousands of enthusiasts come here to make their own personal assault on the summit, joining the weekly 'expeditions' organised by the tourist office.

Pic du Lac Blanc
Lifts open daily 8.30am-5.30pm, July-Aug.; 9.15am-3.30pm, Dec.-Jan.; 9.15am-3.45pm, Feb.-Apr.
The Pic du Lac Blanc cable-car climbs to over 3,330 m/10,900 ft and the view at the top takes in three countries and some of the highest and most famous Alpine peaks: Mont Blanc, the Grandes Jorasses, the Aiguilles d'Arves and the Pic de la Meije in France, the Grand Combin in Switzerland, Cervinia between Switzerland and Italy, and the Gran Paraiso and Monte Viso in Italy.

Venosc
25 km (16 miles)
S of Alpe-d'Huez
Crafts village
Information from the tourist office.
The village of Venosc, in the Vénéon valley, is packed with the workshops of local artisans, including silk-screen painter Annie Lavoie (Il Était une Soie), jeweller Bruno Laval (Bijoux Créations), painters and woodturners (Au Gré du Bois) and Michèle Jerez, who makes miniature glassware (Les Trois Lutins). The oldest sundial in Isère adorns a façade in the narrow street known as Le Cours de la Vie ('life's journey'), which has seen the passing of countless marriage and funeral processions.

Les Deux-Alpes
29 km (18 miles)
N of Venosc
Summer skiing
Information from the tourist office.
Ski lifts operate daily 7.15am-3pm, end July to early Sept.
Admission charge.
Here, on the largest skiable glacier in Europe, skiers and snowboarders can enjoy their sport all year round. In high summer, there's plenty of sunshine and the snow is at its best early in the morning.

VILLARD-RECULAS, A VILLAGE THAT ROSE FROM THE DEAD
11 km (7 miles) S of Allemont
Twenty years ago, the population of this resort in the Eau d'Olle valley was just six – and falling. The construction of a second access road and the establishment of a local finance association brought Villard-Reculas back to life. In 1979, a land management plan was agreed, along with a series of architectural guidelines that were followed to the letter by the new inhabitants. These days, Villard-Reculas has a population of 60, a series of beautiful chalets that blend with its traditional style, and some 1,500 hotel beds. There's also a chairlift linking the village with Alpe-d'Huez, providing access to the Grandes Rousses ski area in winter.

La Fête des Foins
Information from the tourist office
Early Aug.
Each August, Les Deux-Alpes hosts a lively celebration of rural life, with traditional costumes and music. The highlight of the festival is a feast of local fare, with 800 places set around a huge table placed on the edge of the golf course. The meal is rounded off with traditional barley coffee. There are also demonstrations of rural activities, such as threshing, carding (preparing wool for spinning), and sheep shearing, with around 800 sheep lining up for a trim.

La Grave
(Hautes-Alpes region)
26 km (16 miles) E of Les Deux-Alpes
Ice cave
Grotte de la Meije
Access from the Glaciers de la Meije cable-car
☎ 04 76 79 91 09
Cable-cars operate daily 9am-3.30pm, end Dec. to early May and end June to 1 Sept.
Admission charge.
The Grotte de la Meije is a man-made ice cave, quarried 30 m/100 ft beneath the surface of the glacier, at an altitude of 3,200 m/10,500 ft. In the cold air and white light of the cave,

natural crevasses and temporary ice sculptures combine to create a work of art. Every three years, however, the movement of the glacier swallows the cave completely, and it has to be reworked by hand.

Col du Lautaret
(Hautes-Alpes region)
11 km (7 miles) E of La Grave
Le Jardin Alpin
☎ 04 92 24 41 62
Open daily 10am-6pm, 25 June-5 Sept.
Admission charge.
Perched at an altitude of 2,100 m/6,900 ft in the Monêtier-les-Bains area, opposite the Meije peak, this Alpine garden is a botanical paradise. Around 2,500 species flourish in the mountain air, including Alpine columbines, lilies, carnations and campanulas. The best time to visit is in early summer (before 15 July), when the flowers are in bloom.

The Belledonne massif,
a magnificent range

The Belledonne massif stretches along 20 km/ 12 miles of the Grésivaudan valley, between Grenoble and Chambéry. This magnificent series of mountains offers a wide variety of attractions, including thermal spas at Allevard and Uriage-les-Bains, winter sports at Collet d'Allevard, Prapoutel-les-Sept-Laux and Chamrousse, and a fascinating industrial heritage. A scenic drive along the Route des Balcons (D280), between Uriage and Allevard, gives unbeatable views of the Grésivaudan valley and the Vercors and Chartreuse mountains.

Uriage-les-Bains
11 km (7 miles)
E of Grenoble
The stars come out at night
Information from the tourist office
Around once a fortnight in summer, the park in Uriage-les-Bains is transformed into an open-air cinema. A screen is installed and the audience arrange their cushions, blankets and picnics on the grassy slopes. The programme includes recent films and, what's more, it's free.

Prémol
10 km (6 miles)
S of Uriage-les-Bains
Réserve Naturelle du Luitel
☎ 04 76 60 23 25
or 04 76 86 39 76
Open all year, free admission.
At this nature reserve, 5 km/ 3 miles from Prémol, you can take a walk through the 1,000-year-old Luitel peat marshes. Learn about this world of carni-

vorous plants by following the informative plaques along the walkway, or by joining one of the tours led by guides from the national forestry office (ONF).

Chamrousse
10 km (6 miles)
NE of Prémol
The highland lakes
The cable-car station at the Col de la Croix (2,250 m/ 7,400 ft) is the starting point

for a number of footpaths linking the high-altitude lakes of the area, including Achard, Robert and Merlat. The GR 549 trail winds past several small lakes, and a gentle 2-hour walk will take you to the impressive Lake Achard, surrounded by forests of Cembro pine that are well adapted to the harsh mountain climate.

Saint-Martin-d'Uriage
16 km (10 miles)
NW of Chamrousse
Blazing saddles
Le Mas de Loutas
Le Pinet
☎ 04 76 89 52 46
Open daily from 2pm, May-15 Oct.
Admission charge.
The Mas de Loutas equestrian centre and lodge runs evening horse-riding expeditions, leaving at 7.30pm and returning around 1.30am, pausing for a campfire barbecue. Non-riders can still join in, riding to the camp in an off-road vehicle

Spotcheck
B3-B4

Things to do

Thermal spas
Belledonne farm tastings
Horse-riding expedition

With children

Luitel nature reserve
Walk up to Achard lake
Sentier du Fer
Open-air cinema in Uriage

Within easy reach

Chartreuse (p. 178)
Grenoble (p. 168)
Sud-Dauphiné (p. 170)

Tourist offices

Allevard: ☎ 04 76 45 10 11
Belledonne resorts:
☎ 04 76 54 90 78
Uriage-les-Bains:
☎ 04 76 89 10 27

Lancey
1 km (13 miles) N of
Saint-Martin-d'Uriage
Musée de
la Houille Blanche
Maison Bergès
☎ 04 76 45 66 81
Open Tues.-Sat. 2-5pm
Admission charge.

THERMAL SPAS
Uriage-les-Bains
☎ 04 76 89 10 17
Allevard
☎ 0 803 038 580
The spa resorts of
Uriage and Allevard,
at opposite ends of
the Grévisuadan valley,
have much in common:
19thC. architecture, a
casino and a number
of famous clients, such
as Alphonse Daudet,
Coco Chanel (Uriage)
and the Bonaparte
family (Allevard). Both
resorts also specialise
in the treatment of
respiratory complaints
and rheumatism.

Uriage-les-Bains

This museum of hydro-electric
power, located near the former
home of Aristide Bergès, traces
the pioneering work of this
engineer from the Grévisaudan
valley, who invented a system
of conduits that could channel
water up a 200 m/650 ft incline.

Allevard
25 km (16 miles)
NE of Lancey
Sentier du Fer
**Information and map
from the tourist office**
*Begins at Montouvrard
(S of Allevard on D108).*
This 'iron trail' (2 hrs) through
the Ayettes forest, retraces the
history of the area's iron and
steel industry, taking you past
former iron-ore mines, furnaces
and stables for the pack mules
which were used to transport
the minerals.

Pinsot
7 km (4 miles)
S of Allevard
Down on the farm
**Ferme-Auberge
du Gleyzin**
4 km (2 miles) from Pinsot
☎ 04 76 97 53 64
Closed Wed., Thurs., Fri.
pm and Sun. pm (exc.
school hols.); gîte closed
Oct. and Christmas week;
guided farm tours by appt.

Monique and Marcel Ferrier
are members of the Belledonne
farms association, which
promotes tourism and tastings
of farm produce (information
from the tourist office or the
Association pour le Développement de l'Agriculture de
Belledonne, ☎ 04 76 20 68 45).
At their farmhouse inn you
can try Tomme (made
with cow's or goat's milk)
and *belledochon* cheese, a
type of Reblochon made with
goat's milk. The restaurant
serves typical farmhouse fare,
with home-produced
vegetables and meat (including
kid goat) and cheeses.

Chartreuse,
the enchanted forest

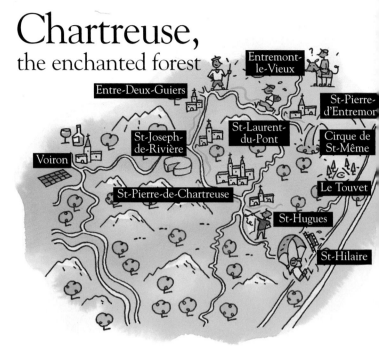

Entremont-le-Vieux

Entre-Deux-Guiers

St-Pierre-d'Entremor

St-Joseph-de-Rivière

St-Laurent-du-Pont

Cirque de St-Même

Voiron

St-Pierre-de-Chartreuse

Le Touvet

St-Hugues

St-Hilaire

Fir, spruce and beech forests form a leafy guard of honour along the Chartreuse mountains, which straddle the border between Isère and Savoie. This medium-altitude area, with few peaks over 2,000 m/6,500 ft, was influenced by the presence of the Carthusian monastic order and remains a place of peace and tranquillity where life proceeds at a gentle pace.

Voiron
26 km (16 miles) NW of Grenoble
Nectar of the gods
Caves de la Chartreuse
10, bd Edgar-Kofler
☎ 04 76 05 81 77
Open daily 9-11.30am and 2-6.30pm, Easter-1 Nov.; 9am-6.30pm, July-Aug.; Mon.-Fri. 9-11.30am and 2-5.30pm, rest of the year. *Admission charge.*
The Carthusian monks of Voiron have been producing the famous Chartreuse liqueur since 1935, following an original recipe that includes 130 different plants. Green or yellow,

on the rocks or 'Alaska' (mixed with gin), Chartreuse is consumed in a variety of ways. In the tasting room of the Caves de la Chartreuse there's a fascinating display of counterfeit drinks which have tried to imitate the celebrated liqueur, such as the imaginative 'Grande Charmeuse'.

Heavenly chocolate
Maison Bonnat
8, Cours Senozan
☎ 04 76 05 28 09
Shop open daily (exc. Mon.) 8am-noon and 2-7pm; tours on Sat. by appt. (exc. end Nov. to early Jan.). *Free admission.*

Stéphane Bonnat, the fourth generation of this sweet-toothed family, is the only *chocolatier* in the Alps to roast and grind his own cocoa bean His great-grandfather, who founded Maison Bonnat, invented the delicious Pavé de Voiron, a layer of hazelnut praline sandwiched between two layers of almond praline. On the tour you'll see a *tarare* a rare tool dating back to 188C used to open the cocoa bean and remove its precious flesh.

Spotcheck

B3-C3

Things to do

Paragliding
Route des Savoir-faire
Walk to the Saint-Même
cirque

WIth children

Saint-Hilaire funicular railway
Donkey trekking

Within easy reach

Aiguebelette lake (p.146)
Paladru lake (p.158)
Grésivaudan valley (p.180)

Tourist offices

ADT Chartreuse:
☎ 04 76 88 64 00
Saint-Pierre-de-Chartreuse:
☎ 04 76 88 62 08

Saint-Pierre-de-Chartreuse

25 km (16 miles)
E of Voiron

Musée de la Grande Chartreuse

Follow signs for
La Correrie
☎ 04 76 88 60 45
Open daily 9.30am-noon
and 2-6.30pm, May-
Sept.; 9.30am-6.30pm,
July-Aug.; 10am-noon
and 2-6pm, Apr. and Oct.
Admission charge.

This magnificent forest wilderness has remained almost
unchanged since 1084, when
St Bruno and his six followers
arrived to establish the first
order of Carthusian monks.
The Grande Chartreuse, cradle
of this devout order, is still a
monastery and retreat and is
therefore not open to visitors.
However, a museum housed in
the former convent reveals the
secrets of monastic life, and a
30-minute walking tour in the
surrounding countryside allows
you to share the peace and
serenity of the beautiful setting.

Wood sculpture

Information from the
tourist office.
Third week in July.
Every summer, Saint-Pierre-de-
Chartreuse hosts an international wood-carving tournament.
A dozen sculptors from around
the world compete to transform
a tree trunk into a work of art
in less than five days, watched
by an enthusiastic audience.
The competition takes place
during the Rencontres Brel, a
festival of French song.

Saint-Hugues

3 km (2 miles) S of Saint-
Pierre-de-Chartreuse

Arcabas frescoes

**Ensemble
Départemental d'Art
Sacré Contemporain**
Église de Saint-Hugues
☎ 04 76 88 65 01
Open daily (exc. Tues.);
closed Jan.
*Free admission (ask
about guided tours).*

Housed in the church at
Saint-Hugues, this regional
collection of sacred art features
the work of contemporary
artists. The biblical frescoes of

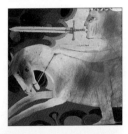

A TASTE OF CHARTREUSE

Map available from Chartreuse tourist offices

The initiative of a group of local farmers, the Route
des Savoir-faire is a tourist trail that criss-crosses
the Chartreuse range, with 23 different stops where
you can discover the best of the region's crafts and
farm produce. Gilles and Claire Belanger (Mohair et
Cimes, Saint-Hugues ☎ 04 76 88 65 04) breed and
raise Angora goats, famous for their long, silky wool
(mohair), and welcome visitors who want to find out
about the animal. Cheese lovers should stop at
Plantimay farm (Ferme de Plantimay, Saint-Joseph-
de-Rivière, 12 km/7 miles east of Voiron ☎ 04 76
55 25 26), to taste Chartreuse Tomme and creamy
Saint-Marcellin that simply melts in the mouth.

Arcabas are like cartoon strips. Painted from 1952 onwards, using a mixture of red clay, honey, candy sugar and charcoal, some of the works are very clear and figurative, while others are more abstract, a riot of forms and colours. Don't miss the magnificent 3x3 m (10x10 ft) *La Résurrection*.

Ferme-Auberge de Brévardière
Haut de Saint-Hugues
☎ 04 76 88 60 49
Open daily, by appt.
This auberge was opened recently by Céline Roux, who prepares traditional farmhouse dishes with great flair, using rabbit, veal and kid goat meat, accompanied by cheese gratins and rhubarb tarts. All the ingredients come fresh from her parents' farm. The restaurant is housed in a former barn, with *essendoles* (p.90) on the roof, larch-wood tables and chairs, and a fine spruce chimney.

Saint-Hilaire
20 km (12 miles)
E of Saint-Hugues
Paragliding school
Prévol Parapente
Le Chalet
☎ 04 76 08 38 71
Open daily, Apr.-Nov.; call for details, out of season.

For a bird's-eye view of the magnificent scenery of the Chartreuse mountains, sign up for a two-and-a-half day course at the Prévol paragliding school (around €215). Participants start in the training centre, then graduate to a tandem flight with an instructor, before taking off for a first solo flight (see p.46 for more on paragliding).

Funicular railway
Upper or lower station
☎ 04 76 08 00 02
Open daily, Apr.-early Dec.; phone ahead for departure times.
Admission charge.

Ideally, walk down to the lowe station and take the train back to the top. From Saint-Hilaire follow the Sentier du Pal de Fe marked footpath (yellow), that begins 50 m/160 ft along the road on the right of the church The walk down takes around 1.5 hours (wear comfortable shoes). The funicular railway was built between 1920-23, an is a remarkable feat of engin-eering. Climbing 740 m/2,400 ft in just 20 minutes, the train passes through the steepest tunnel in the world, 130 m/43 ft long, and offers superb view of the Grésivaudan valley and the Belledonne mountains.

Le Touvet
11 km (7 miles)
NE of Saint-Hilaire
Château
☎ 04 76 08 42 27
Guided tours Sun. and public hols., Easter-1 Nov.; daily (exc. Sat.), July-Aug.
Admission charge.
The magnificent gardens of th former fortified château have been restored to their original classic 18th-C. French style, with boxwood borders, water features and a patchwork of orchards and vegetable garden The château has various reception halls for hire, and

CHARTREUSE REGIONAL NATURE PARK

Established in 1995, the Parc Naturel Régional de Chartreuse is a protected area covering 69,000 ha/ 170,000 acres, with over 700 km/430 miles of signposted trails. You can pick up maps and useful tips at the tourist offices at Saint-Pierre-de-Chartreuse (Place de la Mairie, ☎ 04 76 88 62 08) and Saint-Pierre-d'Entremont (Maison Intercommunale ☎ 04 79 65 81 90).

has been in the same family since 1528, bearing witness to a dynastic history.

Saint-Pierre-d'Entremont (Savoie)

13 km (8 miles) N of Saint-Pierre-de-Chartreuse
Le Cirque de Saint-Même
Signposted on the D45E
Leave your car at the cirque car park (charge on summer weekends and public hols.), and follow the yellow signs of the Sentier des Cascades ('waterfall trail'). The attractive falls (860 m/2,800 ft), which feed the Guiers Vif river, are set in beautiful surroundings, under a rocky cliff. On the way back to the car park, the path follows the left bank of the river. Allow 2.5 hours for a round trip (change in elevation: 170 m/560 ft).

Entremont-le-Vieux (Savoie)

5 km (3 miles) N of Saint-Pierre-d'Entremont
Donkey trekking
Sherpane animal farm

Guiers Vif river, beneath the Cirque de Saint-Même

Les Martenons
☎ 04 79 65 83 73
Open for bookings all year round.
Sherpane's donkeys, mules and hinny (a cross between a female ass and a horse) know their way around the steep paths of the Massif de la Chartreuse. Sophie Robert, your host and guide, runs half-day (€92) and full-day excursions (€153), revealing the secrets of the mountains as well as the correct way to control the animals, which are more co-operative and gentle than you may think.

Entre-Deux-Guiers

12 km (7 miles) W of Saint-Pierre-d'Entremont
The pilgrim's staff
Bernard Boursier
Rue de Verdun
☎ 04 76 66 07 75
Guided tours Thurs. and Fri. 10am and 2.30pm, July-25 Aug.; shop open Mon Fri. 8am-noon and 2-5pm.
Admission charge.
The Boursier family have been soaking, stripping, sanding, bending, straightening and carving chestnut branches to make these sturdy walking sticks for five generations. The tour of the workshop reveals all the stages of this traditional craft, the work of strong and highly experienced hands.

Vienne,
a Roman city

Sprawling across both banks of the River Rhône, the city of Vienne is an open-air museum, with Gallo-Roman, medieval and Renaissance remains. Vienne la Belle was one of Roman Gaul's most significant settlements, with around 30,000 inhabitants – as many as today. The administrative and religious centre of the city is on the left bank of the river, and the warehouses and fine private residences are on the right bank.

Temple of Augustus and Livia
Pl. Charles-de-Gaulle
Not open to the public.
Built around 20 AD, this temple is the twin of the Maison Carré in Nîmes. Over the centuries it has performed various functions including a church, the Temple de la Raison (temple of reason) in the French Revolution and a commercial court. The 19thC. writer Mérimée (author of *Carmen*), who worked for the Commission for Historic Monuments, finally had it placed under a protection order.

Jazz greats and great jazz
Festival Jazz à Vienne
☎ 04 74 85 00 05
End June to mid-July.
Admission charges.
First held in 1981, this jazz festival draws up to 150,000 visitors each year, who pack the Cybèle gardens, the Club de Minuit and the seats of the ancient amphitheatre to hear concerts by some of the finest contemporary jazz musicians. There have been some legendary performances, such as the year Sonny Rollins played for 2 hours 27 minutes non-stop to a spellbound audience.

Tour of Vienne
Information from the tourist office
Tour (approx. 2 hrs) twice weekly in July-Aug.; one per month, out of season
Admission charge.
This guided tour takes in the remnants from the Gallo-Roman, medieval and Renaissance periods, such as

CONTEMPORARY ART

In Rue Chantelouve, behind the municipal theatre, there's a mural painted in 1995 by the 'Cité de la Création', a group of artists from Lyon. Apeing the style of a piece by Étienne Rey (1789-1867), which hangs in the fine arts museum (Musée des Beaux-Arts, Place Miremont ☎ 04 74 85 50 42), the mural incorporates various public figures connected with the region, including the jazz singer Dee Dee Bridgewater and puppetmaster Laurent Mourget, a former resident of Vienne.

Spotcheck
A3

Things to do
Vienne town tour
Visit Ampuis vineyards

With children
Archaeological site and museum
Île du Beurre nature centre

Within easy reach
La Côte-Saint-André (p. 159)
Saint-Marcellin (p. 160)

Tourist offices
Vienne: ☎ 04 74 78 87 87

he Cathédrale Saint-Maurice and the beautiful façades in Rue des Orfèvres (Nos 11 and 9), Rue des Clercs and Rue Marchande. Built in the 5th-17thC., these grand residences reflect the town's

importance as a commercial centre, with its celebrated regional fairs, and thriving printing industry.

Gourmet cuisine
Pyramide restaurant
4, Bd Fernand-Point
☎ 04 74 53 01 96
Closed Tues. and Wed.
Located in the town centre, near the pyramid, this restaurant was opened in 1923 by Fernand Point, a great name in French cuisine. Now owned by Patrick Henriroux, La Pyramide continues to offer some of the finest cooking in the region. Come for weekday lunch under the plane trees in the courtyard garden (set menu €45, incl. wine and coffee).

Saint-Romain-en-Gal (Rhône region)
km (0.6 miles) W of Vienne (right bank of the Rhône)
Magical mosaics

Archaeological museum and site
Gde Rue de la Plaine
☎ 04 74 53 74 00
Open daily (exc. Mon.), 9.30am-6.30pm.
Admission charge; guided tours; children's workshops.
The archaeological museum in Saint-Romain-en-Gal houses an exceptional collection of mosaics. Among the finest are *Le Châtiment de Lycurgue* and *Orphée*. A single mosaic pavement can contain up to 2 million tiny schist, limestone or marble tesserae, or tiles.

Orphée mosaic

Ampuis (Rhône region)
8 km (5 miles) SW of Saint-Romain-en-Gal
Ampuis wines
According to the poet Martial (1stC. AD), the sunbaked Côtes-Rôties vineyards on the hillsides of Ampuis are the oldest in France. Today the area produces red *vins de garde*

(vintage cellar wines), made with Syrah and Viognier (10-20%) grapes, which develop notes of laurel, spice and earth as they mature. Many local vineyards welcome visitors.

Tupin-et-Semons (Rhône region)
2 km (1 mile) S of Ampuis
Île du Beurre nature centre
Centre d'Observation de la Nature de l'Île du Beurre
Car park S of Tupin on the N 86
☎ 04 74 56 62 62
Open Mon.-Fri. 8am-5pm and Sun. pm.
The marshland between the River Rhône and its tributaries is popular with a wide variety of bird species, including grey herons, little egrets and kingfishers. In its centre lies the Île du Beurre, a name derived from *bièvre*, meaning 'beaver'. You're unlikely to see these animals during the day, but you may see their teeth-marks on pieces of wood. The nature centre will lend you binoculars, and also organises a range of events.

Index

This guide was written by Marie-Hélène Chaplain and Annie Crouzet, with the help of Chrystel Arnould, Marie Barbelet, Julie Cot, Sylvie Hano, Claire Labati, Thierry Laurent and Laurent Séminel.

Illustrated maps: Philippe Doro

Cartography: © Idé Infographie (Thomas Grollier)

Translation and adaptation: Y2K Translations (Email: info@y2ktranslations.com)

Additional design and editorial assistance: Christine Bell, Jane Moseley, Michael Summers

We have done our best to ensure the accuracy of the information contained in this guide. However, addresses, telephone numbers, opening times etc. inevitably do change from time to time, so if you find a discrepancy please do let us know. You can contact us at: hachette@orionbooks.co.uk or write to us at Hachette UK, address below.

Hachette UK guides provide independent advice. The authors and compilers do not accept an renumeration for the inclusion of any addresses in these guides.

Please note that we cannot accept any responsibility for any loss, injury or inconvenience sustained by anyone as a result of any information or advice contained in this guide.

First published in the United Kingdom in 2002 by Hachette UK

Distributed in the United States of America by Sterling Publishing Co., Inc.
387 Park Avenue South, New York, NY 10016-8810

A CIP catalogue for this book is available from the British Library

ISBN 1 84202 166 4

Hachette UK, Cassell & Co., The Orion Publishing Group, Wellington House,
125 Strand, London WC2R 0BB

Printed in Slovenia by DELO tiskarna by arrangement with Preŝernova družba, d. d.

ADDRESS BOOK

CONTENTS

Practical information

GENERAL TOURIST INFORMATION

Comité régional du tourisme du Rhône-Alpes *(Rhône-Alpes Regional Tourism Committee)*
104, rte de Paris
69260 Charbonnières-les-Bains
☎ 04 72 59 21 59
www.rhonealpes-tourisme.com

Comité départemental du tourisme de l'Isère
(Isère Regional Tourism Committee)
14, rue de la République
BP 227
38019 Grenoble Cedex
☎ 04 76 54 34 36
www.isere-tourisme.com

Maison Alpes Dauphiné Isère
2, pl. André Malraux
75001 Paris
☎ 01 42 96 08 43
www.isere-tourisme.com

Association touristique départementale de Savoie *(Savoie Regional Tourism Assn.)*
24, bd de la Colonne
73000 Chambéry
☎ 04 79 85 12 45
www.savoie-tourisme.com

Maison de Savoie
31, av. de l'Opéra
75001 Paris
☎ 01 42 61 74 73
www.maisondesavoie.com

Association touristique départementale de Haute-Savoie
(Haute-Savoie Regional Tourism Assn.)
56, rue Sommeiller
BP 348
74012 Annecy Cedex
☎ 04 50 51 32 31
www.hautesavoie-tourisme.com

Fondation pour l'action culturelle internationale en montagne
(Mountain Culture Assn.)
Hôtel du Département
73018 Chambéry Cedex
☎ 04 79 96 74 37

Maison de la montagne
3, rue Raoul-Blanchard
38000 Grenoble
☎ 04 76 42 45 90

TOURIST BOARDS

Groupement promotionnel du Sud Grésivaudan *(South Grésivaudan Tourist Board)*
22, cours Vallier
38160 Saint-Marcellin
☎ 04 76 38 67 20
gpsg@wanadoo.fr

Beaufortin Promotion
73270 Beaufort
☎ 04 79 38 38 62

Office de tourisme du massif des Bauges *(Massif des Bauges Tourist Office)*
73630 Le Chatelard
☎ 04 79 54 84 28

Haute-Maurienne Vanoise Information
District de Haute-Maurienne
73480 Lanslebourg
☎ 04 79 05 91 57

Maison de la Vanoise
Pl. de la Vanoise
73500 Termignon
☎ 04 79 20 51 67

Agence de développement touristique de la Chartreuse
(Chartreuse Tourist Board)
Pl. de la Mairie
38380 St-Pierre-de-Chartreuse
☎ 04 76 88 64 00
www.parc-chartreuse.net

Sud-Dauphiné Tourisme
Rue Breuil, 38710 Mens
☎ 04 76 34 69 99

Agence de développement touristique du Vercors
(Vercors Tourist Board)
Pl. Mure-Ravaud
38250 Villard-de-Lans
☎ 04 76 95 15 99
adt.vercors@espace-vercors.tm.fr

Avant Pays Savoyard Tourisme
73470 Novalaise
☎ 04 79 36 09 29

Fédération Rhône-Alpes de Protection de la Nature *(Environmental Conservation Society)*
32, rue Sainte-Hélène
69002 Lyon
☎ 04 72 77 19 99

Rhône-Alpes Thermal
(Rhône-Alpes Spas)
16, rue Chenal
38580 Allevard-les-Bains
☎ 04 76 45 07 48

ACCOMMODATION RESERVATIONS

Loisirs Accueil Savoie
(Leisure Activities Board)
Maison du tourisme
24, bd de la Colonne
73024 Chambéry Cedex
☎ 04 79 85 01 09

Loisirs Accueil Haute-Savoie
(Leisure Activities Board)
17, av. d'Albigny, 74000 Anne...
☎ 04 50 23 96 00
resa@cdt-hautesavoie.fr

SPORTS ASSOCIATIONS

Ligue Rhône-Alpes de vol libre
(Paragliding and Hang Glid...
Chemillieu, 01300 Nattage
☎ 04 79 44 40 78
www.ligue-rhone-alpes.ffvl

Fédération française d'aérostation
(Ballooning Assn.)
6, rue Galilée, 75116 Paris
☎ 01 47 23 56 20

Fédération française ski alpin *(Alpine Skiing Ass...*
50, rue des Maquisats
BP 2451
74011 Annecy Cedex
☎ 04 50 51 40 34

France Ski de fond
(Cross-Country Skiing)
725, fbg Montmélian
Espace Affaires
73000 Chambéry
☎ 04 79 70 35 04
www.ski-nordic-france.cor

Association française de snowboard
Rte du Parc du Souvenir
06500 Menton
☎ 04 92 41 80 00

Fédération française de canoë-kayak (Raf...
(Canoeing Assn.)
87, quai de la Marne
94340 Joinville-le-Pont
☎ 01 45 11 08 50

Fédération française de voile *(Sailing Assn.)*
55, rue Kleber, 75116 Pari...
☎ 01 44 05 81 00

Fédération française de la montagne et de l'escalade *(Climbing Ass...*
8, quai de la Marne
75019 Paris
☎ 01 40 18 75 50

FME Grenoble (Isère,
avoie, Haute-Savoie)
enoble Climbing Assn.)
, av. Constantine
100 Grenoble
04 76 40 63 26

omité régional de
ndonnée pédestre
Rhône-Alpes
alking Assn.)
aison du tourisme
, rue de la République
027 Grenoble
and ☎ 04 76 54 87 85
w.ffrp.asso.fr

ub Alpin Français
bing Club)
, av. Lumière, 75019 Paris
01 53 72 87 00
.vtt@wanadoo.fr

dération française de
éléologie *(Caving Assn.)*
), rue Saint-Maur
011 Paris
01 43 57 56 54
w.ffspeleo.fr

tenne régionale de
Fédération française
spéléologie
gional Caving Branch)
rue Delandine
002 Lyon
04 72 56 09 63
yon@wanadoo.fr

ndicat national
s accompagnateurs
montagne
ountain Guides Assn.)
av. des Chevaliers-Tireurs
000 Chambéry
04 79 62 18 58

ub Rhône-Alpes
che *(Fishing Club)*
mité régional du tourisme
ône-Alpes
, rte de Paris, 69260
arbonnières-les-Bains
04 72 59 21 59
w.rhonealpes-tourisme.com
w.Adapra.org

dération française
Cyclotourisme
cle Tours Assn.)
ue Jean-Marie Jégo
13 Paris
01 44 16 88 88

re Cheval Vert
aison du tourisme
rse Riding)
rue de la République
227
10 Grenoble Cedex
and ☎ 04 76 42 85 88

Getting there

BY PLANE

AIRLINES

Air France
☎ 0 820 820 820
www.airfrance.fr

British Airways (Lyon, Geneva)
☎ 08457 77 333 77
www.british-airways.com

Buzz (Lyon, Grenoble,
Chambéry)
☎ 0870 240 7070
www.buzzaway.com

easyJet (Geneva)
☎ 0870 600 0000
www.easyjet.com

Go (Lyon)
☎ 0870 607 6543
www.go-fly.com

AIRPORTS

Lyon Saint-Exupéry
☎ 04 72 22 72 21
www.lyon.aeroport.fr

Chambéry Aix-les-Bains
☎ 04 79 54 49 54

Annecy Meythet
☎ 04 50 27 30 06

Grenoble Saint-Geoirs
☎ 04 76 65 48 48

BY TRAIN

The TGV network links the
main towns, while regional
trains serve the smaller towns
☎ 08 36 35 35 35
Info. line: ☎ 08 36 67 68 69
www.sncf.fr

MAIN STATIONS

Lyon Perrache/Lyon Part-Dieu
Savoie: Chambéry, Aix-les-
Bains, Albertville, Bourg-
Saint-Maurice, Modane
Haute-Savoie: Annecy,
La Roche sur Foron,
Annemasse, Thonon, Évian,
Cluses, Saint-Gervais,
Chamonix, Vallorcine
Isère: Grenoble, Voiron,
Vienne, Bourgoin-Jallieu

BY CAR

ROAD MAPS

Michelin Maps no. 74 and 77,
scale 1/200 000
IGN Map for Rhône-Alpes,
scale 1/300 000

CAR HIRE

Avis: ☎ 08 120 05 05 05
www.avis.com
Europcar: ☎ 08 03 35 23 52
www.europcar.com
Hertz: ☎ 01 47 03 49 12
www.hertz.com

USEFUL ADDRESSES

These pages contain over one hundred and eighty accommodation addresses in the Frenc[h] Alps. The list is split into five categories (campsites, youth hostels, walking shelters, gîtes an[d] bed and breakfast). Within each category, the addresses are listed alphabetically by tow[n] name. The number of triangles indicates the price range of each entry and refers to th[e] cost per night per person in the case of youth hostels, gîtes and walking shelters. The pri[ce] indication in the hotel category is based on a double room.

▲ under €30
▲▲ €30-45
▲▲▲ €45-61

▲▲▲▲ €61-92
▲▲▲▲▲ over €92
♥ A dream venue

CAMPSITES

ABONDANCE

Le Pré
☎ 04 50 73 00 93
Open June to end-Sept. and mid-Dec. to end-Apr.
49 sites

AIX-LES-BAINS

Alp'Aix
20, bd du Port-aux-Filles
☎ 04 79 88 97 65
Open Apr. to end Sept.
90 sites

Le Pêcheur
160, av. du Petit-Port
☎ 04 79 54 77 77
Closed Jan.
41 sites

ANNECY

Camping du Belvédère
8, rte du Semnoz
☎ 04 50 45 48 30
Open early Apr. to early Oct.
121 sites

LE BOURGET-DU-LAC

Camping de l'Île aux Cygnes
☎ 04 79 25 01 76;
04 79 26 12 12 (Town Hall)
Open May-Sept.
Harbour and private beach
267 sites

CHAMONIX-MONT-BLANC

La Mer de Glace
200, chem. de la Bagna
(towards Les Praz)
☎ 04 50 53 44 03
Open mid-May to end-Sept.
150 sites

Les Cimes
28, rte des Tissières
(towards Les Bossons)
☎ 04 50 53 19 00 ;
04 50 53 58 93
Open June to end-Sept.
100 sites

CHANAZ

Camping Municipal des Îles
(On the banks of the Savières canal)
☎ 04 79 54 58 51 ;
04 79 54 57 50 (mairie)
Open Mar. to mid-Dec.
120 sites

LA CLUSAZ

Le Plan du Fernuy
Rte des Confins
☎ 04 50 02 44 75
Open June to mid-Sept. and 25 Dec.-Easter
80 sites

DOUSSARD

La Nublière
☎ 04 50 44 33 44
Open 1 May-30 Sept.
459 sites

DUINGT

Le Familial
☎ 04 50 68 69 91
Open Apr. to mid-Oct.
40 sites

LE GRAND-BORNANT

Le Clos du Pin
(On the road to Bouchet valley)
☎ 04 50 02 70 57;
04 50 02 27 61
Open mid-June to mid-Sept. and Dec. to early May
61 sites

MENTHON-SAINT-BERNARD

Le Clos Don Jean
☎ 04 50 60 18 66
Open June to mid-Sept.
90 sites

PRAZ-SUR-ARLY

Chantalouette
☎ 04 50 21 93 59
Closed May and Oct.-Nov.
39 sites

RUMILLY

Le Madrid
☎ 04 50 01 12 57
𝔉 04 50 01 29 49
madrid@winner.fr.
Open July-Aug.
109 sites

SAINT-JEAN-D'AULPS

Le Solerey
☎ 04 50 79 64 69
Open all year
35 sites

SAINT-PIERRE-DE-CURTILLE

Camping Municipal Bel A[ir]
☎ 04 79 54 25 48
(Town Hall)
Open Apr. to Oct.
35 sites

SAMOËNS

Le Giffre
☎ 04 50 34 41 92
Open all year
310 sites

SCIEZ

Le Léman
Bonnatrait
☎ 04 50 72 72 51;
04 50 72 71 28
Open Apr. to end-Oct.
20 sites

SEVRIER

Le Panoramic
22, chem. des Bernets at Cessenaz (2 km from Sevri[er])
☎ 04 50 52 43 09
Open May to end-Sept.
220 sites

Le Verger
Chuguet
☎ 04 50 52 41 33
Open May to mid-Oct.
16 sites

SIXT-FER-À-CHEVAL

Camping Municipal du Fer-à-Cheval
☎ 04 50 34 12 17
Open June to Sept.
103 sites

ALLOIRES

Coeur des Prés
04 50 23 04 66;
50 60 71 87
Open May to mid-Sept.
0 sites

HONON-LES-BAINS

Saint-Disdille
de Saint-Disdille
04 50 71 14 11
Open Apr. to Sept.
5 sites

Lac Noir
av. de Sénevullaz
04 50 26 07 28 ;
50 71 12 48
Open May to end-Sept.
0 sites

EYRIER-DU-LAC

mping de la Plage
rcel Flouret
04 50 60 10 99
Open May-Sept.
sites

ENNE

Flon
du Rhône
04 79 36 82 70
Open mid-June to early Sep.
sites

YOUTH HOSTELS

X-LES-BAINS

menade du Sierroz
04 79 88 32 88
04 79 61 14 05
-les-bains@fuaj.org
Open Feb.-1 Nov., private
okings only
rooms

NECY

te de Semnoz
04 50 45 33 19
04 50 52 77 52
sed Dec. and early Jan.
beds

AMONIX-MONT-BLANC

**, montée Jacques
mat**
04 50 53 14 52
04 50 55 92 34
monix@fuaj. org
Open Dec. to early Sept.
ept 2 weeks in May
beds

LA CLUSAZ

▲
Rte du Col de la Croix-Fry
☎ 04 50 02 41 73
🇫 04 50 02 65 85
la-clusaz@fuaj.org.
Closed out of season,
private bookings only
82 beds

ÉVIAN-LES-BAINS

▲
Av. de Neuvecelle
☎ 04 50 75 35 87
🇫 04 50 75 45 67
jptreil@mjc.hautesavoie.net
150 beds approx.

MORZINE

▲
Chem. de La Coutettaz
☎ 04 50 79 14 86
🇫 04 50 74 44 71
76 beds

GÎTES D'ÉTAPE (HIKING REFUGES)

AUSSOIS

▲ ♥
Fort Marie-Christine
☎ 04 79 20 36 44
Open 20 May-1 Nov.
and 20 Dec.-20 Apr.
10 8-bed dormitories

BELLECOMBE-EN-BAUGES

▲
Le Roc des Boeufs
James Blanc, Le Mont
☎ 04 79 63 34 14
Open all year
3 dormitories, 19 beds

LES HOUCHES

▲
Chalet Tupilak
Emmanuel Ratouis, Coupeau
☎ and 🇫 04 50 54 56 66
7 rooms, 25 beds

LA ROCHE-SUR-FORON

▲
Le Charmagit
Gilles et Marie-Hélène,
Gay-Perret
250, rue de la Vernaz
Amancy *(1.5 km/1 mile from
La Roche)*
☎ and 🇫 04 50 25 87 22
12 rooms, 36 beds

SAMOËNS

▲
Les Moulins
Mireille Chauvaud-Gaboriau
☎ and 🇫 04 50 34 95 69
Open all year
4 rooms, 16 beds

ACCOMMODATION

GÎTES AND B&Bs

ABONDANCE

▲▲
Liliane Berthet
Charmy L'Envers
☎ and 🌐 04 50 73 02 79
4 rooms

AILLON-LE-JEUNE

▲▲
Gîte du Vieux Four
Robert Baulat, Chez Curiaz
☎ 04 79 54 61 47
3 rooms

▲▲
La Grangerie
Bruno Gunther, Les Ginets
☎ 04 79 54 64 71
4 rooms

AIX-LES-BAINS

▲▲
Jean Bogey
16, all. du Chevreul
☎ 04 79 35 16 57
1 room for 3 people

ANNECY

▲▲▲▲
Jean-Paul Michel
1, pl. du Château
☎ and 🌐 04 50 45 72 28
6 rooms

ARÊCHES

▲
Le Solaret
Marie-Thérèse Blanc
Chem. des écolières
1, pl. du Château
☎ and 🌐 04 79 38 14 25
Open all year
2 rooms and 5 studios

▲
La Charmette (gîte)
Joël and Régine Bellaiche
Les Carroz
1, pl. du Château
☎ and 🌐 04 79 38 18 12
2 rooms and 2 dormitories
Half-board

ARGENTIÈRE

▲▲▲▲
La Ferme d'Élisa
394, chem. des Rosières
☎ 04 50 54 00 17
🌐 04 50 54 21 09
Open in season
4 rooms

▲
Auberge La Boerne
Gilbert Mugnier
288, Trélechamps
☎ 04.50 54 05 14
🌐 04 50 54 15 53
Closed mid-Nov. to mid-Dec.
7 rooms, 38 beds

BELLECOMBE-EN-BAUGES

▲▲
Sophie Pricaz
Villard Derrière
☎ 04 79 63 36 33
3 rooms

BESSANS

La Bessannaise
Centre de ski et de
randonnées pédestres
(Skiing and Walking Centre)
☎ 04 79 05 95 15
🌐 04 79 05 84 66
150 beds in rooms of 1 to 3
people; €365 for 10 days
(summer); €311 for 5 days
(winter) full board, with ski hire
and lessons (cross country
skiing, snowshoes, walks)

CHAMONIX-MONT-BLANC

▲▲▲
La Girandole
Pierre and Georgette Gazagnes
46, chem. de la Persévérance
☎ 04 50 53 37 58
🌐 04 50 55 81 77
3 rooms

▲▲
La Crèmerie du Glacier
(gîte)
Jean-Claude Chapouton
333, rte de Rives
Les Bossons
☎ 04 50 55 90 10
Half-board
7 rooms, 24 beds

LA CHAPELLE-D'ABONDANCE

▲▲
Les Carlines
Maryse and Edmond Benand
Sous le Saix
☎ and 🌐 04 50 81 36 36
4 rooms

CHÂTEL

▲▲
La Savoyarde
Françoise and Gilles Cornu
Rte des Fréneits
☎ and 🌐 04 50 73 23 17
Open Apr. to Nov.
6 rooms

LA CLUSAZ

▲▲
Chalet La Sence
Patricia and Dominique Suize
Le Gotty
☎ 04 50 02 42 81
Open June to Oct. and
Dec. to Apr.
3 rooms

LES GROSEILLIERS

▲▲
Annie and Désiré Thovex
La Rochette
☎ and 🌐 04 50 02 63 29
2 rooms

COMBLOUX

▲▲
Marie-Thérèse Balmand
278, chem. du Bois Roulet
☎ 04 50 58 61 69
1 room

▲
Les Fovrents
Ginette and Claudy Crivelli
Chem. des Fovrents
☎ and 🌐 04 50 58.63.89
4 rooms, 19 beds

CONFLANS

▲▲▲
Marie-Claude Hardy
21A, rue Gabriel-Pérouse
☎ 04 79 32 00 66
2 rooms, 8 beds

ÉVIRES

▲
Hélène Duperthuy
☎ 04 50 62 00 72
2 rooms

LE GRAND-BORNAND

▲▲
La Bournerie
Sylvie Vadon, at Chinaillon
☎ and 🌐 04 50 27 00 28
5 rooms

HAUTELUCE

▲
Chalet de Colombe
At Colombe
☎ 06 11 09 09 10;
04 79 38 82 03
Open 1 June-15 Oct.
and early Jan. to end-Mar.
Gîte for 5 people and 8/9
dormitory beds

LES HOUCHES

▲▲▲
La Ferme d'en Haut
Marie-Joëlle Turc
152, rte des Aillouds
Le Crêt
☎ and 🌐 04 50 54 74 87
4 rooms

MEGÈVE

▲▲
**Guy and Gisèle
Maillet-Contoz**
684, rte du Petit Bois
Demi-Quartier
☎ 04 50 21 48 28
1 room

Closed one week at Easter
and one week in Nov.
10 rooms, 35 beds

SAINT-PAUL-SUR-YENNE

▲▲▲▲▲
Château de La Terrossière
Jeannine Conti
☎ and 🖷 04 79 36 81 02
3 rooms

SAMOËNS

▲
Le Couve-Loups
Pierre-Jean Lange
Les Allamands
☎ 04 50 34 13 58
6 rooms, 29 beds

SEVRIER

▲▲▲
Carole Barrucand
Les Charretières
Les Mongets
☎ and 🖷 04 50 52 43 30
6 rooms

THONES

▲▲
Les Matins Clairs
Michèle Bibollet
BP 74
☎ and 🖷 04 50 02 66.60
Open in season and
weekends out of season by
appointment
Half-board
6 rooms, 30 beds

VAULX

▲▲
La Ferme sur les Bois
Marie-Christine Skinazy
Le Biolley
☎ 04 50 60 54 50
annecy.attelage@wanadoo.fr
Open Easter-1 Nov.
4 rooms

VIZILLE

▲▲
Le Clos
Chez Jeanne et Alain
Blanchon
93, rue des Jardins
☎ and 🖷 04 76 68 12 71
Open all year
2 rooms

HOTELS

ABONDANCE

▲▲
Hôtel de l'Abbaye
☎ 04 50 73 02 03
🖷 04 50 81 60 46
20 rooms

---

rme des Granges
nadette and Jean
inet-Marquet
13 Les Granges
04 50 21 40 50
oms

EUSSY

e d'Ivoray *(gîte)*
rard Gudefin
04 50 43 06 32
oms, 30 beds

Presbytère *(gîte)*
04 50 43 02 72 (tourist
ce); 04 50 43 02 19
en all year
oms, 18 beds

ORZINE

▲▲ (p. 104)
s de la Coutettaz
04 50 79 08 26
sed May and Oct. to Nov.
f-board weekly bookings,
oms

PIN

♥
Brimbelles
nique Joly, le Bourg
04 76 06 60 86
sed Dec. to Jan.
eople

ROCHE-SUR-FORON

Haut Broys
via Charmillot
, rue des Quatre-Piquets
04 50 25 84 58;
33 57 97 33
oms

Clarines
ude and Dominique
ssoud
, chem. de l'École
range
and 🖷 04 50 25 10 17

NT-ANTOINE L'ABBAYE

♥
rie-Thérèse and
ri Philibert
Voureys
04 76 36 41 65
en all year
eople

NT-GERVAIS

Mélusine *(gîte)*
phane Lettoli
chem. du Creux
04 50 47 73 94

AIX-LES-BAINS

▲▲▲▲
Astoria
Pl. des Thermes
☎ 04 79 35 12 28
📠 04 79 35 11 05
Closed end-Nov. to mid-Jan.
135 rooms

▲▲▲▲
Le Manoir
37, rue Georges 1ᵉʳ-de-Grèce
☎ 04 79 61 44 00
📠 04 79 35 67 67
90 rooms

▲▲▲
La Pastorale
221, av. du Grand-Port
☎ 04 79 63 40 60
📠 04 79 63 44 26
pastoral@club.internet.fr
Closed Nov. to Apr.
30 rooms

▲▲
Notre-Dame des Eaux
6, bd des Côtes
☎ 04 79 61 13 87
📠 04 79 34 06 96
contact@notredamedeseaux.fr
Closed early Dec. to end-Feb.
70 rooms

ALBERTVILLE

▲▲▲ ♥
Le Roma
Chemin du Pont Albertin
☎ 04 79 37 15 56
Open daily.
146 rooms

ANNECY

▲▲▲▲
Le Palais de l'Isle
13, rue Perrière
☎ 04 50 45 86 87
📠 04 50 51 87 15
26 rooms

▲▲▲
Hôtel du Château
16, rampe du Château
☎ 04 50 45 27 66
📠 04 50 52 75 26
hotelduchateau@multimania.com
Closed mid-Nov. to early Jan.
16 rooms

▲▲▲
Hôtel de Savoie
1 pl. Saint-François-de-Sales
☎ 04 50 45 15 45
📠 04 50 45 11 99
hotel@hoteldesavoie.fr.
20 rooms

▲▲
Super Panorama
7, rte de Semnoz
☎ 04 50 45 34 86
Closed Jan. to mid-Feb.
Closed Mon. and Tues.
5 rooms

ARÊCHES

▲▲
Hôtel Viallet
Rte de Saint-Guérin
☎ 04 79 38 10 47
📠 04 79 38 11 51
Closed out of season
15 rooms

ARGENTIÈRE

▲▲▲▲▲
Les Becs Rouges
47, chem. de Vardes, Montroc
☎ 04 50 54 01 00
📠 04 50 54 00 51
lesbecs@euroscan.com
Closed Nov. to mid-Dec.
24 rooms

▲▲
Les Randonneurs
39, rte du Plagnolet
☎ 04 50 54 02 80
📠 04 50 54 20 82
les.randonneurs@libertysurf.fr
Closed mid-Nov. to mid-Dec.

AUSSOIS

▲▲▲ ♥
Hôtel du Soleil
15, rue de l'Église
☎ 04 79 20 32 42
Closed 20 Apr.-15 June
and 20 Sep.-17 Dec.
22 rooms

AUTRANS

▲▲▲
Hôtel le Vernay
Le Vernay
☎ 04 76 95 31 24
Closed 2 weeks in Spring
from Mar.-early Apr. and 2
weeks end-Sept. to early Oct.
17 rooms

BEAUFORT

▲▲
Le Grand Mont
Pl. de l'Église
☎ 04 79 38 33 36
📠 04 79 38 39 07
Closed end-Apr. to beg. May
and Oct., 13 rooms

▲
Hôtel de la Roche
Av. du Capitaine-Bulle
☎ 04 79 38 33 31
📠 04 79 38 38 60
Closed Sun. pm out of
season, Nov. and 1 week in
Apr., 17 rooms

BOURG-D'OISANS

▲▲
Hôtel Florentin
Rue Thiers
☎ 04 76 80 01 61
📠 04 76 80 05 49

Closed 1 Oct.-15 Jan.
18 rooms

▲▲
L'Oberland
Av. de la Gare
☎ 04 76 80 24 24
📠 04 76 80 14 48
Closed 1 Nov. and 8 days in
May, 30 rooms

BOURG-SAINT-MAURIC

▲▲
L'Autantic
69, rte d'Hauteville
☎ 04 79 07 01 70
📠 04 79 07 51 55
Open all year
23 rooms

LE BOURGET-DU-LAC

▲▲ ♥
La Cerisaie
618, rte des Tournelles
☎ 04 79 25 01 29
📠 04 79 25 26 19
Closed Nov. and Jan.
7 rooms

CHAMBÉRY

▲▲▲
Hôtel des Princes
4, rue de Boigne
☎ 04 79 33 45 36
Open daily
45 rooms

▲▲
City Hôtel
9, rue Denfert-Rochereau
☎ 04 79 85 76 79
📠 04 79 85 86 11
40 rooms

▲▲▲
Hôtel le France
22, fbg Reclus
☎ 04 79 33 51 18
Open all year
48 rooms

CHAMONIX-MONT-BLA

▲▲▲▲▲
La Savoyarde
28, rte des Moussoux
☎ 04 50 53 00 77
📠 04 50 55 86 82
lasavoyarde@wanadoo.fr
14 rooms

▲▲▲▲
Hôtel Gustavia
273, av. Michel-Croz
☎ 04 50 53 00 31
📠 04 50 55 86 39
hotel@hotel-gustavia.com
47 rooms

AA
berge du Manoir
te du Bouchet
☎ 04 50 53 10 77
🖶 04 50 53 36 37
bergedumanoir@aol.com
sed Nov.
rooms

Chaumière
2, rte des Gaillands
☎ 04 50 53 13 25
🖶 04 50 53 70 81
npdebase.chaumiere
anadoo.fr
sed mid-May to mid-June
d Oct.-Nov.

tel du Montenvers
er de Glace)
☎ 04 50 53 87 70
v. juil. et août
en July and Aug.
rooms and 30 dormitory
ds

CHAPELLE-
-VERCORS

♥
tel Bellier
☎ 04 75 48 20 03
sed Tues. pm and Wed.
: July-Aug. By appt. from
v. to Mar.
rooms

ÂTEL

rc-en-Ciel
Petit Châtel
☎ 04 50 73 20 08
🖶 04 50 73 37 06
en in season, winter
d summer
rooms

s Fougères
☎ 04 50 73 21 06
sed mid-Apr. to 1 July
d 1 Sept. to mid-Dec.
f-board in winter

CHATELARD

♥ (p. 140)
alets d'Orgeval
mountain pastures
☎ 04 79 54 80 44
en early June to early Oct.
dormitory beds

CLUSAZ

AAA
auregard
☎ 04 50 32 68 00
🖶 04 50 02 59 00
el-beauregard.fr
sed in Nov.
rooms

AAAA
Les Chalets de la Serraz
Rue du col des Aravis
☎ 04 50 02 48 29
🖶 04 50 02 64 12
Closed mid-Apr. to mid-May
and in Oct., half-board
12 rooms

AAA
Floralp
Les Riffroids
☎ 04 50 02 41 46
🖶 04 50 02 63 94
hotel-floral74.com
Closed out of season
20 rooms

AA
Les Airelles
Pl. de l'Église
☎ 04 50 02 40 51
🖶 04 50 32 35 33
info@clusaz.com
Closed May and Nov.
14 rooms

COMBLOUX

AAAAA
Au Cœur des Prés
☎ 04 50 93 36 55
🖶 04 50 58 69 14
Closed end-Sept. to mid-Dec.
and early Apr. to early June
32 rooms

AAA
Les Granits
1409, rte de Sallanches
☎ 04 50 58 64 46
🖶 04 50 58 61 63
Closed out of season
16 rooms

DUINGT

AAA
Le Clos Marcel
All. de la Plage
☎ 04 50 68 67 47
🖶 04 50 68 61 11
lionel@clos-marcel.com
Open Apr. to Sept.
15 rooms

ÉVIAN-LES-BAINS

AAA
Hôtel de France
59, rue Nationale
☎ 04 50 75 00 36
🖶 04 50 75 32 47
Closed mid-Nov. to mid-Dec.
45 rooms

AAA
Le Bois Joli
La Beunaz
Saint-Paul-en-Chablais
☎ 04 50 73 60 11
🖶 04 50 73 65 28
hboisjoli@aol.com
Closed mid-Oct. to mid-Dec.
29 rooms

ACCOMMODATION

LE GRAND-BORNANT

▲▲▲▲▲
Hôtel Les Cimes
Le Chinaillon
☎ 04 50 27 00 38
📠 04 50 27 08 46
info@hotel-les-cimes.com
Closed mid-May to mid-June,
mid-Sept. to end-Nov.
10 rooms

GRENOBLE

▲▲▲▲▲
Hôtel d'Angleterre
5, pl. Victor Hugo
☎ 04 76 87 37 21
Open all year
62 rooms

▲▲▲▲
Hôtel Mercure
12, bd du Maréchal-Joffre
☎ 04 76 87 88 41
📠 04 76 47 58 52
Open all year

GRUFFY

▲▲▲
Aux Gorges de Chéran
☎ 04 50 52 51 13
📠 04 50 52 57 33
Open mid-Mar. to mid-Nov.
8 rooms

HAUTELUCE

▲▲▲▲
Hôtel Le Calgary
Les Saisies
☎ 04 79 38 98 38
📠 04 79 38 98 00
Closed in May, Oct. and Nov.
40 rooms

LES HOUCHES

▲▲▲▲
Le Montagny
490, le Pont
☎ 04 50 54 57 37
📠 04 50 54 52 97
montagny@wanadoo.fr
Closed early Nov. to mid-Dec.
8 rooms

LANSLEBOURG-VAL-CENIS

▲
La Vieille Poste
Grande Rue
☎ 04 79 05 93 47
📠 04 79 05 86 85
Closed 16 Apr.-11 June
and 26 Oct.-26 Dec.
17 rooms

▲
Le Relais du Col
Col du Mont-Cenis
☎ 04 79 05 90 07
📠 04 79 05 86 61
Closed 15 Apr.-1 June
and 1 Nov.-25 Dec.
9 rooms

LANSLEVILLARD

▲▲
Le Grand Signal
L'Adroit
☎ 04 79 05 91 24
📠 04 79 05 82 47
Closed 15 Apr.-15 June
and 15 Sept. -20 Dec.
18 rooms

MEGÈVE

▲▲▲▲
La Chaumine
36, chem. des Bouleaux
Les Mouilles
☎ 04 50 21 37 05
📠 04 50 21 37 21
Closed mid-Apr. to end-June
and mid-Sept. to mid-Dec.

▲▲▲▲
L'Hostellerie
198, rte de Rochebrune
☎ 04 50 21 23 08
📠 04 50 21 18 56
Closed mid-May to mid-June
and mid-Oct. to mid-Nov.
12 rooms

MENS

▲▲ ♥
Auberge de Mens
Rue du Breuil
☎ 04 76 34 81 00
Open all year
10 rooms

MONTMÉLIAN

▲▲
Hôtel Viboud
1, rue du Docteur-Veyrat
☎ 04 79 84 07 24
📠 04 79 84 44 07
Closed Sun. pm, Mon.,
10 days in July and Jan.
8 rooms

MORZINE

▲▲▲
Hôtel Les Lans
Rte du Téléphérique
d'Avoriaz
☎ 04 50 79 00 90
📠 04 50 79 15 22
Closed end-Mar. to mid-
June, Sept. to mid-Dec.
Half-board
32 rooms including 5 suites

▲▲▲
Hôtel Les Prodains
Les Prodains
☎ 04 50 79 25 26
📠 04 50 75 76 17
hotellesprodains@aol.com
Closed end-Apr. to end-June,
early Sept. to early Dec.
15 rooms

PRAZ-SUR-ARLY

▲▲▲
Darbelo
☎ 04 50 21 90 27
📠 04 50 21 80 77
Darbelo@aol.com
Open mid-Dec. to mid-Apr.
and June to Sept.

SAINT-GERVAIS

▲▲
Hôtel Chalet Rémy
Le Bettex
☎ 04 50 93 11 85
📠 04 50 93 14 45
In season, half-board
19 rooms

SAMOËNS

▲▲▲▲
La Renardière
Le Quart
☎ 04 50 34 45 62
📠 04 50 34 10 70
contact@renardiere.com
35 rooms

▲▲▲
Le Moulin de Bathieu
Chalet-hôtel, Vercland
☎ 04 50 34 48 07
📠 04 50 34 43 25
Moulin.du.Bathieu@wanadoo
Closed May and mid-Nov. t
mid-Dec.
6 rooms including 1 suite

SCIEZ

▲▲▲▲▲
Château de Coudrée
Bonnatrait
☎ 04 50 72 62 33
📠 04 50 72 57 28
chcoudree@aol.com
20 rooms

SERVOZ

▲▲
L'Alpe
Chem. du Rucher
☎ 04 50 47 22 66
📠 04 50 91 40 66
Closed May and Oct.
6 rooms

SIXT-FER-À-CHEVAL

▲▲▲
Le Petit Tétras
Salvagny
☎ 04 50 34 42 51
📠 04 50 34 12 02
ptitetra@club-internet. fr
Closed 1 Apr.-1 June
30 rooms

TALLOIRES

▲▲▲▲
Villa des Fleurs
☎ 04 50 60.71.14
lavilladesfleurs@wanadoo.fr

sed mid-Nov. to mid-Dec.
ooms

de Chère
arvines
4 50 60 19 15
4 50 60 28 29
sed winter
ooms

Tranquille
4 50 60 70 43
4 50 60 73 03
tranquille@wanadoo.fr
n June to Sep.
ooms

NON-LES-BAINS

azur
v. du Général-Leclerc
4 50 71 37 25
4 50 71 01 24
l-alpazur@mailme.net
n Feb. to Nov.
ooms

ORENS-GLIÈRES

Chaumière Savoyarde
4 50 22 40 39
4 50 22 81 84
sed end-Sept. to early

ooms

erge des Glières
eau des Glières
4 50 22 45 62
4 50 22 82 37
master@auberge-des-
es.com
sed mid-Apr. to early May
mid-Oct. to mid-Dec.
ooms

AGE

el les Mésanges
acher
4 76 89 70 69
n 1 May-15 Oct., Feb.
ool hols. and weekends
ar.
ooms

ACCOMMODATION

The following pages contain the addresses of over 80 restaurants in which to enjoy regional cuisine and specialities. The entries are listed alphabetically by location. The number of diamonds indicates the average price of a meal.

◆ Under €15
◆◆ €15-30
◆◆◆ €30-45
◆◆◆◆ €45-76
◆◆◆◆◆ over €76
♥ a dream venue

AIX-LES-BAINS

◆◆◆
Lille
Pl. Édouard-Herriot
☎ 04 79 63 40 00
Open end-Apr. to end-Sept.

◆◆
Les Églantiers
20, bd Berthollet
☎ 04 79 88 04 38

◆◆
Le Dauphinois
14, av. de Tresserve
☎ 04 79 61 22 56
Closed Sun. evening and Mon.
Closed mid-Dec. to end-Jan.

◆◆
Les Platanes
Au Petit-Port
☎ 04 79 61 40 54
Closed Nov. to Apr.
Jazz nights and piano-bar

◆
Auberge du Sire
La Féclaz
☎ 04 79 25 80 33
Open all year

ALBY-SUR-CHÉRAN

◆◆
L'Arcadie
Pl. du Trophée
☎ 04 50 68 15 78
Closed Wed., Sun. and in Feb.

ALLEVARD

◆◆
La Tour du Treuil
2, rue de la Tour-du-Treuil
☎ 04 76 97 58 91
Closed Mon., Sun. evening and Jan.

AMPUIS

◆◆
Le Côte-Rôtie
Pl. de l'Église
☎ 04 74 56 12 05
Closed Sun. evening, Mon. and mid-Aug. to mid-Sept.

ANNECY

◆◆◆
L'Atelier Gourmand
2, rue Saint-Maurice
☎ 04 50 51 19 71
🖷 04 50 51 36 48
Closed Sun. and Mon.

◆◆
Le Clos des Sens
13, rue Jean-Mermoz
Annecy-le-Vieux
☎ 04 50 23 07 90
Closed Sun. evening, Mon. and Tues. lunchtime.

APREMONT

◆◆
Tour d'Apremont
Golf d'Apremont
☎ 03 44 25 61 11
🖷 03 44 25 11 72
Closed Mon. and evenings

ARÈCHES

◆◆
Auberge du Poncellamont
☎ 04 79 38 10 23
Closed mid-Apr. to end-May and Oct. to mid-Dec.

AUSSOIS

◆◆
Fort Marie-Christine
☎ 04 79 20 36 44
🖷 04 79 20 38 64
Open end-May to 1 Nov. and 25 Dec.-20 Apr.

BEAUFORT-SUR-DORON

◆
Chalet d'Alpage de Plan Mya
Françoise and Yvon Bochet
L'Etraz, Villard-sur-Doron
☎ 04 79 38 30 15
Open for lunch, end-June early Sept.

◆
Chez Isidore
Av. de la gare
☎ 03 84 25 12 83
🖷 03 84 25 18 54
Closed Mon. evening exc.15 June-15 Sept.; Tues. and Wed. evening by appt.

◆◆
La Pierra Menta
Col du Pré
☎ 04 79 38 70 74
Open end-May to end-Oct.

BONNEVAL-SUR-ARC

◆◆
Auberge Le Pré Catin
☎ 04 79 05 95 07
Open in season except Mon.

BOURDEAU

◆◆ ♥ (p. 137)
Auberge Lamartine
Rte du Tunnel
☎ 04 79 25 01 03
Closed 3 weeks in Jan.
Closed Sun. evening and Mon. and Tues. lunchtime

LE BOURGET-DU-LAC

◆◆◆◆
Le Bateau Ivre
504, rte Nationale,
☎ 04 79 25 00 23
Open early May to early No
Closed Mon. and Tues. lunchtime

BOURG-SAINT-MAURIC

◆◆
Le Bois de Lune
Montvenix
(on the road to Hauteville-Gondon)
☎ 04 79 07 17 92
Open for lunch and dinner summer, evenings only in winter

CHAMBÉRY

◆◆
L'Essentiel
183, pl. de la gare
☎ 04 79 96 97 27
🖷 04 79 96 17 78
Closed Sat. and Sun.

◆◆
Le Tonneau
2, rue Saint-Antoine
☎ 04 79 33 78 26
🖷 04 79 85 49 69
Closed Sun. evening and M

◆
Le Cardinal
5, pl. Métropole
☎ 04 79 85 53 40
Closed Sun. and Mon.

◆
Café Chabert
41, rue Basse-du-Château
☎ 04 79 33 20 35
Closed Sun.

CHAMONIX-MONT-BLA

◆◆◆ ♥
Auberge du Bois Prin
69, chem. de l'Hermine
☎ 04 50 53 33 51
Closed Mon. lunchtime an

. evening. Closed Nov.
2 weeks in spring (Apr.-
).

(p. 127)
son Carrier
te du Bouchet
4 50 53 00 03
ed Mon. exc. July-Aug.
ed 2 weeks in June and
Nov. to mid-Dec.

(p. 128)
3 842'
ess by cable-car from
uille du Midi
4 50 55 82 23
ed Nov. and evenings

. 128) ◆
Montenvers
de Glace
4 50 53 87 70
n for lunch out of season
for lunch and dinner June
ept. Closed mid-Oct. to
Dec

ANAZ

erge de Portout
out
4 79 54 26 01
n Feb. to Nov., daily July
Aug., closed Thurs. and
ings out of season

erge de Savières
4 79 54.56.16
n mid-Mar. to mid-Dec.

CHAPELLE-
BONDANCE

♥ (p. 102)
taurant
Cornettes
4 50 73.50 24
ed mid-Oct. to mid-Dec

ÂTEL

◆
Grive Gourmande
4 50 73 20 10
ed out of season

CLUSAZ

urson
e l'Église
4 50 02 49 80
4 50 32 33 95

Chalet du Lac
des Confins
4 50 02 53 26
n daily in season,
kend and public hols.
of season

LA COMPÔTE

◆ ♥ (p. 140)
Café-Restaurant Châtelain
☎ 04 79 54 82 53.
Closed evenings and Sat. all
year. Closed Sun. out of
season

CONDRIEU

◆◆◆
Beau Rivage
Rue du Beau-Rivage
☎ 04 74 56 82 82
Open all year

CONFLANS

◆◆
Le Ligismond
17, pl. de Conflans
☎ 04 79 37 71 29
Closed Sun. evening. Closed
Mon. July-Aug. Closed Wed.
exc. summer

LA CÔTE-SAINT-ANDRÉ

◆◆◆
Hôtel de France
Pl. Saint-André
☎ 04 74 20 25 99
🅵 04 74 20 35 30
Closed Sun. evening and
Mon. exc. public hols.

ÉVIAN-LES-BAINS

◆◆◆◆
Le Café Royal
Rive sud du lac
☎ 04 50 26 85 00
Closed Dec. and Jan.

◆◆
La Bernolande
1, pl. du Port
☎ 04 50 70 72 60
Closed Wed., Thurs. and
Nov. hols.

◆◆
L'Échelle
Bernex *(10 km/6 miles
from Évian)*
☎ 04 50 73 60 42
Closed mid-Oct to mid-Dec

FEISSONS-SUR-ISÈRE

◆◆◆ ♥ (p. 149)
Château de Feisson
Les Côtes
☎ 04 79 22 59 59
Open daily except Sun.
evening and Mon.

LE GRAND-BORNANT

◆◆◆
La Ferme de Lormay
Lormay
☎ 04 50 02 24 29
Closed lunchtime,
exc. weekends

RESTAURANTS

◆ ♥ (p. 123)
Ferme-Auberge
La Cheminée
Col des Annes
☎ 04 50 27 03 87
Open summer

GRENOBLE

◆
Le Mal Assis
9, rue Bayard
☎ 04 76 54 75 93
Closed Sun., Mon. and
15 July-15 Aug.

◆◆
À Ma Table
92, cours Jean-Jaurès
☎ 04 76 96 77 04
𝕱 04 76 96 77 04
Closed Sat. lunchtime, Sun.,
Mon. and Aug.

◆◆◆◆
Auberge Napoléon
7, rue Montorge
☎ 04 76 87 53 64
𝕱 04 76 87 80 76
auberge-napoleon.fr
Closed Sun., Mon., Tues. and
Wed. lunchtime; closed 29
July-19 Aug.

HAUTELUCE

◆ ♥ (p. 143)
Chalet de Colombe
☎ 06 11 09 09 10
Open daily, June to Aug.;
weekends, Sept. to Oct.

JARSY

◆
L'Arcalod
☎ 04 79 54 81 53
Closed mid-Nov. to 25 Dec.
Closed evenings out of
season

MEGÈVE

◆◆◆◆◆
La Ferme de Mon Père
367, rte du Crêt
☎ 04 50 21 01 01
Open Dec. to Mar.

◆◆◆
Les Fermes de Marie
Chem. de Riante-Colline
☎ 04 50 93 03 10

◆◆◆
Flocons de Sel
75, rue Saint-François-
de-Sales
☎ 04 50 21 49 99
Closed May; closed Tues.
and Wed. lunchtime in
season and Tues. and Wed.
all day out of season.

◆◆
L'Hostellerie
198, rte de Rochebrune
☎ 04 50 21 23 08
Closed Sun. evening and
Mon. out of season

◆ (p. 124)
Ferme-Auberge
du Calvaire
Chem. du Calvaire
☎ 04 50 21 13 58
Open mid-June to mid-Sept.
and 25 Dec to mid-Apr.
Closed Tues.

MORZINE

◆◆◆ ♥ (p. 105)
La Chamade
La Crusaz
☎ 04 50 79 13 91
𝕱 04 50 79 27 48
Closed 3 weeks May-June
and closed Nov.-Dec.

◆
Les Mines d'Or
Vallée de la Manche,
☎ 04 50 79 03 60
Open end-May to 1 Nov.

OZ-EN-OISANS

◆
Auberge de Martine
Passoud
L'Enversin
☎ 04 76 80 73 18
Open May to early Dec.

LE PETIT-BORNANT-
LES-GLIÈRES

◆
Chez Constance
Plateau des Glières
☎ 04 50 22 45 61
Open all year, lunch & dinner

PINSOT

◆◆
Ferme-Auberge du Gleyzin
Le Gleyzin
☎ and 𝕱 04 76 97 53 64
Closed Wed., Thurs., and Fri.
and Sun. evening, exc.
school hols.

LE REPOSOIR

◆
La Chartreuse
Pralong (opp. the church)
☎ 04 50 98 17 11
Closed Wed. and Sun. and
Tues. evening; open daily
July-Aug.

◆
La Colombière
Col de la Colombière
☎ 04 50 90 94 27;
06 60 83 07 40
Open June to mid-Oct.;
closed Mon. evening

RUMILLY

◆
Les Fagots
3, rue de l'Industrie
☎ 04 50 64 58 77
Closed Sun. and Aug.

◆
La Boîte à Sel
27, rue du Pont-Neuf
☎ 04 50 01 02 52
Closed Sun. evening, Mor
and in Aug.

SAINT-ANTOINE-L'ABBΑ

◆◆
Auberge de l'Abbaye
Rue Haute
☎ 04 76 36 42 83
𝕱 04 76 36 46 13
Closed Mon. evening and Tu
out of season; closed Jan.

SAINT-GERMAIN-
LA-CHAMBOTTE

◆◆ (p. 136)
Restaurant-Brasserie
La Chambotte
☎ 04 79 63 11 76
Open daily from Easter-1 N

SAINT-GERVAIS

◆◆
La Maison Blanche
64, rue du Vieux-Pont
☎ 04 50 47 75 81
Closed lunchtime in winter

◆
Auberge de la
Grand-Montaz
32, rte du Fayet
☎ 04 50 93 12 29
Open mid-June-Sept., dai
exc. Mon. evening.

SAINT-GINGOLPH

◆
Relais France-Suisse
Rte Nationale
☎ 04 50 76 70 58
Closed Tues. evening, win
closed 25 Dec.-mid-Jan.

SAINT-JEAN D'AULPS

◆
Chez Zizet
Alpage du Graydon
☎ 04 50 79 68 62
Open June-Sept.

SAINT-PIERRE-
DE-CHARTREUSE

◆ ♥
Ferme Auberge
de Brévardière
At the top of Saint-Hugues
☎ 04 76 88 60 49
Open daily by appt., exc.
Tues. lunchtime

MOËNS

◆
Fandioleuse
Cour
☎ 04 50 34 98 28
en from Christmas to
ter; closed Wed. in Jan.
Sept.; closed in Mar. and
; open daily. in July and

Tornalta
e du Parc
04 50 34 98 68
en daily.

VRIER

◆
erge de Létraz
, rte d'Albertville
04 50 52 40 36
sed Sun. evening and
.

LLOIRES

◆◆ (p. 117)
erge du Père Bise
du Port
04 50 60 72 01
sed Dec.-Jan.; closed
s. and Wed. out of
son

◆
bbaye de Talloires
m. des Moines
04 50 60 77 33
sed Sun. and Mon. out of
son; closed end-Dec. to
-Feb.

ONON-LES-BAINS

◆ ♥
Prieuré
Grande-Rue
04 50 71 31 89
sed Sun. evening and
.; closed Tues. out of
son

erge d'Anthy
ny-sur-Léman
4 50 70 35 00
sed Mon. evening and
s. exc. summer

Cygnes
de Sechex à Margencel
n)
4 50 72 63 10.
sed Dec.-Jan.; closed
s. out of season

◆
Le Victoria
5, pl. des Arts
☎ 04 50 71 02 82
Closed 25 Dec.-1 Jan.

URIAGE-LES-BAINS

◆◆◆◆
Grand Hôtel-Restaurant
Les terrasses
☎ 04 76 89 10 80
Closed Tues., Wed. and
Thurs. lunchtime; closed Sun.
and Mon. exc. July and Aug.;
closed Jan., last week in Aug.
and first week in Sept.

VEYRIER-DU-LAC

◆◆◆◆◆
Auberge de l'Éridan
13, vieille rte des Pensières
☎ 04 50 60 24 00
Open May to Nov.

◆◆
Restaurant L'Amandier
91, rte d'Annecy
Chavoires
☎ 04 50 60 01 22
☎ 04 50 60 03 25
Open daily from mid-June to
mid-Sept.

VIENNE

◆◆◆◆ ♥ (p. 183)
La Pyramide
14, bd Fernand-Point
☎ 04 74 53 01 96
Closed Tues. and Wed.

◆◆
Le Cloître
2, rue des Cloîtres
☎ 04 74 31 93 57
Closed Sat., Sun. and public
hols.

VOIRON

◆◆◆
**Restaurant de Mer,
Philippe Serratrice**
3, av. des Frères-Tardy
☎ 04 76 05 29 88
☎ 04 76 05 45 62
Closed Sun evening, Mon.,
Tues. evening and 20 July-
6 Sept.

RESTAURANTS

HACHETTE TRAVEL GUIDES

VACANCES

Alsace-Vosges	1 84202 167 2
The Ardèche	1 84202 161 3
The Basque Country	1 84202 159 1
Brittany	1 84202 007 2
Catalonia	1 84202 099 4
Corsica	1 84202 100 1
The Dordogne & Périgord	1 84202 098 6
The French Alps	1 84202 166 4
Languedoc-Roussillon	1 84202 008 0
Normandy	1 84202 097 8
Poitou-Charentes	1 84202 009 9
Provence & the Côte d'Azur	1 84202 006 4
Pyrenees & Gascony	1 84202 015 3
South West France	1 84202 014 5

A GREAT WEEKEND IN …

Focusing on the limited amount of time available on a weekend break, these guides suggest the most entertaining and interesting ways of getting to know the city in just a few days.

Amsterdam	1 84202 145 1
Barcelona	1 84202 170 2
Berlin	1 84202 061 7
Brussels	1 84202 017 X
Dublin	1 84202 096 X
Florence	1 84202 010 2
Lisbon	1 84202 011 0
London	1 84202 013 7
Madrid	1 84202 095 1
Naples	1 84202 016 1
New York	1 84202 004 8
Paris	1 84202 001 3
Prague	1 84202 000 5
Rome	1 84202 169 9
Venice	1 84202 018 8
Vienna	1 84202 026 9

Forthcoming titles:
Budapest
Seville

ROUTARD

The ultimate food, drink and accommodation guides for the independent traveller.

Andalucia & Southern Spain	1 84202 028 5
Athens & the Greek Islands	1 84202 023 4
Belgium	1 84202 022 6
California, Nevada & Arizona	1 84202 025 0
Canada	1 84202 031 5
Cuba	1 84202 062 5
Ireland	1 84202 024 2
North Brittany	1 84202 020 X
Paris	1 84202 027 7
Provence & the Côte d'Azur	1 84202 019 6
Rome & Southern Italy	1 84202 021 8
Thailand	1 84202 029 3